MOTOR CITY MUSCLE

Mike Mueller

MBI Publishing Company

First published in 1997 by MBI Publishing Company, 729 Prospect Avenue, PO Box 1, Osceola, WI 54020-0001 USA

MBI Publishing Company books are also available at discounts in bulk quantity for industrial or sales-promotional use. For details write to Special Sales Manager at Motorbooks International Wholesalers & Distributors, 729 Prospect Avenue, PO Box 1, Osceola, WI 54020-0001 USA.

Library of Congress Cataloging-in-Publication Data
Mueller, Mike.
    Motor city muscle : the high-powered history of the American muscle car / Mike Mueller.
      p. cm.
    Includes index.
    ISBN 0-7603-0196-4 (hardbound : alk. paper)
    1. Muscle cars. 2. United States—Social life and customs. I. Title.
    TL23.M74   1997
    629.222—dc21   97-10100

On the front cover: Pontiac's GTO Judge was originally intended to offer high performance at a budget price *a la* Plymouth's Road Runner. In reality, though, it was a rather pricey package. This 1969 Judge is powered by the standard 335-horsepower Ram Air III 400 V-8 and belongs to Timothy Dunlap of Delphos, Ohio.

On the frontispiece: Four-barrel, four-on-the-floor, dual exhausts. Any other questions?

On the title page: The GSX was Buick's top gun in the musclecar battle and one of the great sleepers of the era. Both the red '71 in the foreground and '70 posing behind it reside in the garage of Glenn Dempsey of Fort Atkinson, Wisconsin.

On the back cover: Two different answers to the high-performance question. The 1966 SS 396 Chevelle was the first mass-produced, midsize Chevrolet musclecar. This one is owned by Bob and Christa Gatchel of Clermont, Florida. At the opposite end of the size spectrum was Plymouth's outrageous, mile-long 1970 Superbird. Dale Powell of Safety Harbor, Florida, owns the beaked brawler shown here. Restored gas station site courtesy of Robbie Robinson, Mascott, Florida.

Edited by Zack Miller

Designed by Katie Finney

Printed in Hong Kong

Contents

ACKNOWLEDGMENTS

It was many years before I was able to finally stop grieving over the musclecar's death in the early '70s—even though I was just a bit too young to have really experienced the breed in its heyday. My driving days—make that legal driving days—didn't begin until 1976, a bleak time indeed for performance automobiles. Nonetheless, used car lots were still crowded then with high-powered reminders of what had awed this sometimes-humble author as a child.

One particular dealership on Green Street in my hometown of Champaign, Illinois, always seemed an especially tempting tease for us disco-era teens. Boss 302s, Z/28 Camaros, Charger R/Ts. These and many more legends continually appeared on that lot with prices smeared in soap on the windshields—prices I choked on then, yet would snap up by the handful if found today. Even if I had known then what we all know now, I would've still had to stand by helplessly as these later-to-be-legendary muscle machines rolled off to their fates. Such was my fate at the time to grow up with barely two pennies to rub together.

Now that I'm older, not the least bit wiser, and in possession of at least three pennies, I find myself constantly writing about all those cars, which have long-since been transformed from sheetmetal into gold. Photographing them has also grown into a passion, explaining possibly how I got corralled by Motorbooks International to once again bring the great American musclecar back to life, an almost monumental task that never would've missed deadline after deadline without the help of so many valued friends. And my family.

Doling out thanks begins with my brother Dave, of Flatville, Illinois, who shares my interests in automobiles and is probably most responsible for inspiring me to make a career out of a love for internal-combustion contraptions. His helping hand during photo shoots and assistance in locating feature subjects are greatly appreciated. Same goes for almost everyone else in my clan back in Illinois who were repeatedly recruited for duty on my own private chain gang: little brothers Jim and Ken Mueller, parents Jim and Nancy Mueller, and last but deservedly least, brother-in-law Frank Young. It was Frank's idea to invite me into his Champaign home last year—little did he, my sister Kathy, or their kids, Jason and Michelle, know I would stay for a month while photographing more than 50 musclecars in the Midwest. Guys, next year get a bigger refrigerator. And by the way, did you ever find that ham sandwich I lost under the bed?

As for all the others who weren't obligated by blood to support my efforts, there's long-time friend Ray Quinlan in Champaign and newfound cohort Bill Tower of Plant City, Florida. Neither of these Corvette-crazies has yet to let me down, no matter how demanding my calls, and both have no qualms about traveling along on occasion. Could it be the free lunches?

My good friends at Bill Jacobsen's Silver Dollar Classic Cars, in Odessa, Florida, are also deserving of a round or two on the house. Bill has always allowed me free rein among his fabulous car collection, which was photographed with the able assistance of Silver Dollar's detail demon, Cindy Helmholtz. Many thanks as well go to Silver Dollar's talented restoration crew, Joe Johnson, Dave Caksackkar, and the two Richie Brandls, big and little.

A good pile of priceless help came from my former co-workers at Dobbs Publishing here in Lakeland, Florida.

Outrageous, high-flying musclecars like Plymouth's Superbird certainly look out of place today. But in 1970, shenanigans like these special aerodynamic treatments were all accepted as part of the high-speed game.

Whether it was digging up old photos, scouring through yellowed copies of *Hot Rod* or *Car Life*, or hunting down answers to question after question, the Dobbs guys were always there to lend a hand. Editorial chief Paul Zazarine once again opened his photo archives for this effort, as did *Mopar Muscle* editor Greg Rager, who even let me pester him at home. *Musclecar Review* editor Tom Shaw was right there at the other end of the phone every time as well. DPG headman Donald Farr, too. Let me not forget Jerry Pitt, who kept his cool at his Dobbs directorial post as I overturned his office while rummaging through the Roger Huntington Archives.

Historical photographic support came from many different sources: Brandt Rosenbusch and Eugene Harris at Chrysler Historical, Helen Early at the Oldsmobile History Center, Jim Matison of Pontiac Historical Services, Marty Schorr and Larry Gustin at Buick News Relations, Skip Norman of Gold Dust Classics (800-421-DUST) in Ashland, Virginia, and fellow authors Terry Boyce, Bob Ackerson and John Conde.

Greg Rager supplied various pieces of musclecar memorabilia, as did Larry Weiner, of Motorsports Racing Apparel (619-630-6259) in Vista, California. Weiner's reproductions of the Grand-Spaulding Dodge T-shirts you'll see in the introduction are just one of many nostalgic items offered.

Various car clubs responded quickly to requests for aid in finding suitable photo subjects for this book. In this group was Mark Stevens at the Buick GS Club of America in Valdosta, Georgia; Judy Badgley of the Hurst/Olds Club of America in New Hudson, Michigan; Mark Meekins of the National Chevelle Owners Association in Greensboro, North Carolina; and Wayne Bushey of the National Nostalgic Nova Club in York, Pennsylvania. If you own any of these models, these organizations are definitely for you.

New muscle was also included within these covers. And such shoots would've never been possible without the delivery into my eager mitts of various modern performance machines. Mustangs came courtesy of Louis Reed at Hill Ford in Champaign, Illinois, and Barbara Kinnamon and Anne Booker of Ford's public affairs office in Atlanta, Georgia. Gary McCaskill, of Warden-Martin Pontiac in Champaign, helped dig up a '96 WS6 Firebird, and a '96 Camaro SS was loaned out by Michael Hawkins of Sullivan Chevrolet, also in Champaign. Jim Sawyer, John Clor, and Dan Reid at Ford's Special Vehicle Team public relations office were actually willing to put me in the seat of not just one, but four SVT Cobras over the last few years. And more than one hot Chevy was made available thanks to Mark Leddy, Chevrolet Communications chief in Woodbridge, New Jersey.

Of course, I can't forget all the vintage musclecar owners, they being the real stars of this show. If it wasn't for their willingness, cooperation, patience, and friendship during photo shoot after photo shoot, not one page of this epic would've been possible. Space considerations here preclude giving all these folks their true due, but all of you should know that I will never forget your kind assistance, as well as your wonderful company. And those who went well beyond the call of duty—including big-time Chevy man Dick Hubbard who somehow managed not to shoot me (at least not yet) for dinging his glorious ZL1 Camaro—you know who you are. Gratitude is not a big enough word.

In general order of appearance, the proud owners of all the fine muscle machines portrayed by my Hasselblad on the following pages are: 1970 Plymouth Superbird, Dave and Becky Dillingham, Champaign, Illinois; 1969 Pontiac Trans Am, Patrick Ferrante, Ft. Lauderdale, Florida; 1968 427 Corvette, Guy Landis, Kutztown, Pennsylvania; 1964 Pontiac GTO and 1965 Plymouth Satellite 426, Bill and Barbara Jacobsen, Silver Dollar Classic Cars, Odessa, Florida; 1966 Pontiac GTO, Thomas Smith, Tallula, Illinois; 1968 Pontiac GTO, Terry and Sheron James, Athens, Illinois; 1969 Pontiac GTO Judge, Timothy Dunlap, Delphos, Ohio; 1964 Oldsmobile 4-4-2, Allen Myers, Holt, Michigan; 1965 Buick Gran Sport, Al and Kathy Jones, Plano, Illinois; 1965 Chevrolet Malibu SS 396, Floyd Garrett, Sevierville, Tennessee; 1965 Mercury Cyclone, Blevis Hensley, Harrison,

Ohio; 1967 Dodge Charger 426 hemi, Mike Spencer, Canton, Illinois; 1969 Dodge Charger, Brent and Sherri Evans, Cisne, Illinois; 1967 Chevrolet Camaro Z/28s (two), Paul McGuire, Melbourne, Florida; 1966 Chevrolet SS 396 Chevelle, Bob and Christa Gatchel, Clermont, Florida; 1969 Chevrolet Camaro ZL1, Dick Hubbard, Monticello, Indiana; 1969 Chevrolet Chevelle COPO 427, Fred Knoop, Atherton, California; 1967 Ford Fairlane 427, Dick Spain, Decatur, Illinois; 1968-1/2 Ford Torino GT 428 Cobra Jet, Jerry and Sharlene Titus, Arcola, Illinois; 1969 Ford Fairlane Cobra, Neil and Denise Montgomery, Arthur, Illinois; 1966 and 1967 Oldsmobile 4-4-2 W-30s (two), Roger Brink, Palm Harbor, Florida; 1970 and 1971 Oldsmobile 4-4-2 W-30s (two), Todd Nelson, Land O' Lakes, Florida; 1970 Dodge Super Bee 440 Six Pack, Steve Lehner, Springfield, Illinois; 1970 (white) and 1971 (red) Buick Stage 1 GSXs (pair), Glenn Dempsey, Fort Atkinson, Wisconsin; 1968 Chevrolet Impala SS 427, Eric Ball, Roswell, Georgia; 1962 Pontiac Super Duty Grand Prix, Allan and Louise Gartzman, Skokie, Illinois; 1965 Pontiac 2+2, Allan Peranio, Coral Springs, Florida; 1966 Ford Galaxie 7-Litre, Dale Nichols, Orlando, Florida; 1969 Ford Galaxie XL GT, Bill and Barbara Jacobsen, Silver Dollar Classic Cars, Odessa, Florida; 1964-1/2 Ford Mustang "Hi-Po" convertible, Jim and Lynda Fannin, Bloomington, Illinois; 1967 Ford Mustang GTA, Bernie and Zona Gail Doty, Strasburg, Illinois; 1968-1/2 Ford Mustang 428 Cobra Jet, Dick Spain, Decatur, Illinois; 1969 Ford Mustang Mach 1 428 Cobra Jet, Dennis and Kate Crow, Oakwood, Illinois; 1967 Plymouth Barracuda Formula S 383, Mike and Betty Ganson, Greene, Iowa; 1969 Plymouth 440 'Cuda, Tom and Chris Wenstadt, Cadillac, Michigan; 1967 Dodge Dart GTS 383, Allen and Connie Schroer, New Knoxville, Ohio; 1969 Dodge Dart Swinger 340, Keith Rohm, Wapakoneta, Ohio; 1966 Chevrolet Nova SS L79, Roger Quin, Washington, Illinois; 1969 Chevrolet Nova SS 396, Dan Bennett and Jim Beckerle, Festus, Missouri; 1967 Chevrolet Camaro SS 396 L78, Dick Hubbard, Monticello, Indiana; 1968 Pontiac Firebird 400 coupe (blue) and 1968 Pontiac Firebird 400 Grand Marque convertible (metalic green), Chris Philip, Pinellas Park, Florida; 1969 AMC "Big Bad" Javelin, Bruce Rambler, Palmyra, Pennsylvania; 1967 Buick GS-340, Glenn Dempsey, Fort Atkinson, Wisconsin; 1969 Plymouth Road Runner, George Weisser, Morton, Illinois; 1970 Oldsmobile Rallye 350, Steve Doty, Shelbyville, Illinois; 1964 Ford Thunderbolt and 1965 Ford A/FX Mustang, David Gieger, Elkhart, Indiana; 1966 Ford Fairlane 427, Jerry and Carol Buczkowski, South Bend, Indiana; 1969 Chevrolet Camaro COPO 427, Mick Price, Atwood, Illinois; 1969 Chevrolet Camaro Z/28, Jack Hunter, Boca Raton, Florida; 1970 Ford Boss 302 Mustang, Bernie and Zona Gail Doty, Strasburg, Illinois; 1970 Mercury Cougar Eliminator, Dale Nichols, Orlando, Florida; 1970 Plymouth AAR 'Cuda, Gary Dunkirk, Taylorville, Illinois; 1970 Dodge Challenger T/A Six Pack, Robert Yappell, Princeton, Florida; 1969 Dodge Charger 500 and 1969 Ford Talladega, Dan Andrews, Lakeland, Florida; 1969 Mercury Cyclone Spoiler IIs (two), Randy Lewis, Toledo, Ohio; 1969 Dodge Charger Daytona, 1970 Plymouth Superbird and 1970 Shelby GT 500, Bill and Barbara Jacobsen, Silver Dollar Classic Cars, Odessa, Florida; 1965 Shelby GT 350-R, Harris Conner, Chamblee, Georgia; 1966 Shelby GT 350H, Jim and Lynda Fannin, Bloomington, Illinois; 1969 Yenko Camaro 427 and 1969 Yenko Chevelle 427, Mick Price, Atwood, Illinois; 1967 Nickey Camaro 427, Felix and Barbara Lopez, Chicago, Illinois; 1968 Dana Camaro 427, Milton Robson, Gainesville, Georgia; 1971 Baldwin-Motion 454 Camaro, Jon Bischol, Omaha, Nebraska, 1968-1/2 Ford Mustang 428 Cobra Jet, Chris and Deborah Teeling, Enfield, Connecticut; 1970 Ford Torino Cobra Tasca Special, Steve Novak, Decatur, Illinois; 1969 Hurst/Olds, Bill Fricker, Englewood, Ohio; 1973 and 1974 Hurst/Olds coupes (two), James and Robyn Pedigo, Jamestown, Indiana; 1969 AMC Hurst SC/Rambler, Ed & Joyce Miller, Anna, Ohio; 1970 Chevrolet SS 454 LS6, Dr. Samuel TerBeck, Knoxville, Illinois; 1970 Oldsmobile 4-4-2 W-30, Gary Gernhardt, Sidney, Illinois; 1970 Buick GSX Stage 1, William Sprosty, Rawson, Ohio; 1970 Ford Torino Cobra, Wayne Myers, Toledo, Ohio; 1970 Ford Boss 429 Mustang, Barry Larkins, Daytona Beach, Florida; 1970 Mercury Cyclone Spoiler, Paul Melchert, Tinley Park, Illinois; 1970 Chevrolet Camaro Z/28, Kevin Emberton, Edmonton, Kentucky; 1970 Dodge Challenger R/T, Matthew Rohm, Wapakoneta, Ohio; 1970 Plymouth Hemi 'Cuda, Neil Wedeking, Marble Rock, Iowa; 1970 Dodge Coronet R/T, Shawn Werts, Urbana, Illinois; 1970 AMC Rebel Machine, Bruce Rambler, Palmyra, Pennsylvania; 1971 Ford Boss 351 Mustang, Steve and Stacy Collins, Jacksonville, Florida; 1971 Plymouth GTX 440+6, Steve and Janice Wright, Decatur, Illinois; 1972 Ford Mustang Mach 1, Len And Sandy Sabato, Champaign, Illinois; 1973 Buick Gran Sport Stage 1, Fernando Alvare, Wesley Chapel, Florida; 1974 Pontiac Trans Am 455 Super Duty, Paul Markey, Pinellas Park, Florida; 1985 Chevrolet Monte Carlo SS, Brian Weisser, East Peoria, Illinois; 1969 Pontiac Firebird 400 convertible and 1995 Pontiac SLP Firehawk Firebird convertible, Chris Philip, Pinellas Park, Florida; 1996 Pontiac WS6 Trans Am, Eric Kivisto, Gibson City, Illinois.

If I've forgotten anyone here—and I know I probably have—please forgive me. The names of all the men and women I contacted while chasing down leads, doing research, begging for photographs, or just looking for help actually number well into the hundreds. All of your efforts are no less appreciated—I know what you did for this project even if the readers here don't. A hearty thanks to everyone.
—Mike Mueller

Introduction

WHO PUT THE MUSCLE IN MUSCLECAR?
Defining the Breed's Era and Aura

From its humble origins now a century behind us, the automobile, however wondrous, has always in its essence simply represented a single-purpose, straightforward solution to a problem that has plagued man since the beginning of time: how to get from point A to B with as little fuss or muss as possible? The concept is commonly known as practical transportation, which in the minds of the vast majority of drivers stands as the only fair description for their cars. As it did yesterday and hopefully will again tomorrow, a car starts, it goes, and it gets you there; usually in one piece, sometimes with the family and/or luggage along for the ride. Convenient, definitely. Comfortable, maybe. Conducive to upward mobility, without a doubt. But what about competitive?

Picture this: A primordial life form, thoroughly satisfied with itself, emerges from the ooze to squirm its way out of its watery incubator onto dry land, only to find a fellow form already there triumphantly learning to breathe oxygen, thus gaining the upper hand—if it had had one. Additional evolution follows, as do limbs and the ability to stand erect. Next thing you know, fire is discovered, along with practical tools like, say, the wheel. But even as the first stone roller is being chipped out, another finer one is finding form a few caves down, this new-and-improved model able to do its work quicker and with less sweat. Natural selection, after all, waits for no one, a lesson not missed by our fittest ancestors whether they were searching for food or an easier, shorter route to the Far East by sea. Eons before we discovered a need for political correctness, our forepersons had recognized the need for speed.

And wouldn't you know it? That need has played a prominent part in the automotive history stage show since the first sparks started igniting combustion internally.

Charles Brady King may have beaten Henry Ford onto the streets of Detroit in 1896 with the Motor City's first horseless carriage, but it is old Henry who commonly gets credit as the man who best helped put America on wheels. Like King, who had taken part in this country's earliest organized auto race in November 1895, Ford was fully aware of the automobile's competitive potential, as well as what a high-powered reputation could do to help secure a manufacturer's place in the market. Almost a decade before he was mastering mass production on the way to putting a polite, purely practical Model T in every garage, Henry Ford was in 1902 tinkering with his rude, crude, and massively engined "999" racing machine. With legendary speed merchant Barney Oldfield at the tiller, the 999 racer brought Ford early fame and respect.

Race on Sunday, sell on Monday. Although this adage wouldn't make the automotive lexicon for another half century, its basic meaning wasn't lost on America's pioneering automakers. Henry Ford was not alone. Sanctioned competition represented the road to prominence for many dozens of car companies between the turn of the century and World War I. From there, speed contests at places like Bonneville, Pikes Peak, and Daytona continued to help promote sales back in the showroom, and still do today. Simply put, speed sells. Always has, always will. Practicality may represent the automobile's prime purpose, but a little performance (or a lot) has never failed to attract its fair share of prospective buyers.

Mercer and Stutz were, just prior to World War I, among the first in this country to almost exclusively rely on performance as a main selling point. Two decades later, the Great Depression be damned, Indiana's

By 1963, almost everyone was singing the musclecar's praises as high-performance and hot rodding briefly overshadowed young love as America's top rock music topic. Among the best remembered hot car tunes of the early '60s were *409* from the Beach Boys and Jan and Dean's two epics, *The Little Old Lady from Pasadena* and *Dead Man's Curve*.

Opposite: Only one car has run non-stop from its birth in the '60s supercar era up through today: Pontiac's Trans Am. In 1994, Pontiac marked 25 consecutive years of muscle-bound T/A ponycars with a special 25th anniversary model.

Early roots of the musclecar craze can be traced back to 1955 when Chevrolet first offered triple-digit speed to the common man at a common man's price. They didn't call Chevy's first overhead-valve V-8 "The Hot One" for nothing. Keys to the high-winding 265-cubic-inch small-block's success were its short stroke and individual, lightweight, ball-stud rocker arms. *Chevrolet Motor Division*

Auburn-Cord-Duesenberg triumvirate would combine both power and prestige into a lavish, luxurious package the likes of which American car buyers had never seen before—and haven't since. These examples, however, like essentially all prewar performance offerings, were only available to the fortunate few.

Money then became less of an issue after World War II when rampant competitive pressures led automakers to try anything and everything to turn buyers' heads. Speed still sold, only now it started selling like it never had before. Real power began finding its way into the hands of more and more people once General Motors introduced its thoroughly modern overhead-valve V-8s in 1949, kicking off a horsepower race that helped set the '50s rockin' 'n rollin'. In 1955, Chevrolet amazed everyone by putting its own new OHV V-8 between low-priced fenders, and for the first time, uncommon performance was readily available to the common man. In fully loaded, "Power Pack" form, Chevy's "Hot One" could run with anything on the market, including cars that cost half again as much or more.

Yet, the Hot One aside, the decade's top performers were still quite pricey, and almost without exception only came in limited numbers. All this began changing, seemingly overnight, once the '50s faded away into the '60s, a time when any man, woman, or child (from 16 to 116) could've strolled into almost any showroom and rolled out behind the wheel of a car built with basically one intention: to go like hell.

We all know the names, most having long since become the stuff of legends. GTO. SS 396. Boss Mustang. Road Runner. The list goes on and on, made up of a wide array of '60s and '70s automobiles; many colorful (both literally and figuratively), some not, all hot to trot. While rapid acceleration was far and away the number one priority here, some of these cars could actually handle a little, and many even stopped relatively well. "Relatively" is the key term to the entire equation, for what qualified as state-of-the-art one year paled in comparison to what Detroit wrought 12 months later. Or what we take for granted today. As it's always prone to do, progress continued marching on during the '60s and '70s, especially so far as performance was concerned.

Back then, these purpose-built performers were known as "supercars," an apt, certainly simple description for machines that, although they weren't quite faster than a speeding bullet, were still capable of making your heart leap into your throat in a single bound. Today we call them "musclecars," a moniker that was being used occasionally by 1970, but didn't really come into vogue until after these strong-running vehicles retired from the scene and began gaining collector value. Like the dinosaurs before them, musclecars came into this world, briefly made a lot of noise, fell victims to a changing environment, then ended up in museums. Unlike those bleached stacks of bones, however, the American musclecar has managed to rise from the dead to once again roam the streets of this continent looking for prey. But that is a tale for other pages. First generation first.

By most definitions, the original musclecar era officially began in 1964 with the arrival of a ground-breaking machine from Pontiac Motor Division that, as *Car and Driver's* David E. Davis, Jr., later wrote in 1975, "appeared on the American scene like a Methodist minister leaving a massage parlor." No, the GTO obviously wasn't the first American car to offer obscene amounts of horsepower. It was the way Pontiac packaged its latest brand of performance that had the congregation swooning.

Before GTO, big cubes in big cars wearing big price tags represented the only way for American buyers to meet their need for speed. Although PMD people still believed bigger was better, they were also apparently convinced that less could be more. Their idea was so simple:

Muscle Definition

What is a musclecar? By every definition, a musclecar is a performance model, a high-performance model to be more exact. So then why do most definitions only begin defining in 1964? Wasn't Detroit building high-performance automobiles in the '50s? Certainly. And all those factory super stockers of the early '60s were obviously no slouches as well when it came to flexing muscles. But none of these high-priced, often high-strung, always low-production vehicles were meant for the masses; nor, in many cases, for the street. High performance, to that point, was very limited in scope.

Not so after 1964 once the new breed of midsized, big-engined, relatively mass-produced "supercars" arrived. While it is fair today to retroactively refer to all high-powered machines—'50s, '60s or otherwise—as musclecars, it is only right to begin talking muscle with the cars that first drew public attention to American-style performance in a big way. As John Stuart Mill might have seen it, those supercars of the mid-'60s were the first automobiles to offer the great-est amount of performance to the greatest number of performance buyers. At least from a utilitarian perspective, they deserve the title as America's first musclecars.

That established, what then specifically set off a supercar from the rest of the mild-mannered crowd? How high did performance have to reach in the '60s and '70s to qualify as muscle-bound? What was a musclecar and what wasn't? Clearly, a '71 Mach 1 Mustang fitted with a big, bad 429 Super Cobra Jet V-8 qualified. But did the same car—looking just as big and bad with spoilers, Magnum 500s, and black stripes—make the grade if its scooped hood hid not an SCJ, but the base Mach 1 V-8 that year, Ford's 302 Windsor small-block with its two-barrel carburetor?

In Mopar terms, all Road Runners, GTXs, and R/Ts were musclecars, but all Chargers, Barracudas, and Challengers weren't, even though they, too, often looked and acted the part. Like in the latter group's case, the same could be said for most of Ford's Mustang GTs. And Chevrolet's Corvette certainly should be considered a musclecar, but is generally not welcomed into the club since America's sports car has an exclusive niche all to its own. As it is, fiberglass fans prefer it that way.

With the Corvette's technical exclusion explained, it becomes possible to point out that Pontiac's Trans Am stands as the only muscle machine born in the '60s supercar era—1969, to be exact—to run continuously up to today. Chevrolet's Z/28 Camaro, created two years before, temporarily faded from the scene after 1974, then returned midyear in 1977 to restart its equally long legacy, still present and accounted for in 1997 and still one of Detroit's most potent.

Drawing a strict line between what was and wasn't a supercar back in the '60s isn't easy today, and basically did-n't matter back then, especially to Detroit's automakers, who—believe it or not—were no dummies. They knew hot looks actually did a better job of selling cars than hot performance. Some automotive writers in the '60s and '70s did try to claim a supercar was only a supercar if it came equipped with so many horses—just how many, however, was typically a matter of opinion. And, as they always will, opinions then varied.

Some modern-day magazine moguls have also tried to retroactively define the breed by quantification using such measuring sticks as horsepower-to-weight ratios and such. Two stumbling blocks exist for this overly ambitious endeav-or. Again, who decides where the cut-off numbers begin? Additionally, how can you hope to create an exact formula relying on inexact advertised output figures, many of which were grossly overstated in the early '60s, some convenient-ly understated in the late '60s and early '70s?

Perhaps it is best to simply have each of you decide for yourself. Musclecars came in all forms and fashions. We all have our favorites, fast, faster, or fastest. All things rarely being equal, who's really to say which ones belong in the fra-ternity and which don't?

Why not just let the tires do all the talking?

While nearly all Corvettes could easily qualify as musclecars—and technically should—the fiberglass two-seat breed is generally left out of the fraternity, a fact not disappointing in the least to most Vette people since the car already enjoys its essentially exclusive status as "America's sports car." Carroll Shelby's killer Cobras are "slighted" on these pages for similar reasons.

Two men and their baby: Ford General Manager Lee Iacocca and product planning chief Donald Frey stand next to the affordable, sporty car that in 1964 truly proved that a youth market did exist and was ripe for the picking. The front plate on this Mustang refers to Iacocca's goal to best Detroit's sales record for a first-year model. He wanted to sell at least 417,000 new ponycars by that model's first birthday, April 17, 1965. He did. *Ford Motor Company*

take a lightweight midsized bodyshell, stuff it full of big-car engine, throw in a bit of heavy-duty hardware and a stick on the floor, then top it all off with a price more readily within reach of the younger, speed-hungry set. Or those young at heart.

As luck would have it, a youthful trend was just starting to make its presence known in the marketplace when the GTO arrived. Actually, luck had nothing to do with it; anyone with enough fingers and toes could've figured it out. Start with 1946, add 16 years, and what did you have? Try an ever-growing army of eager, newly legalized drivers, sons and daughters of the hundreds of thousands of lonely soldiers who returned home after World War II ended.

The "baby boom" these veterans created promised a flood of teenagers and young adults for the '60s, all ripe for the picking in the eyes of marketing moguls. By 1970, 52 out of 100 Americans were 30 years of age or younger, a fact the business world had already noticed. As Ford Motorsports Director Jacque Passino then explained in a *Motor Trend* guest editorial, "while the kids don't spend all of the money in this country, they are the

ones everybody is playing to." Continued Passino, "the mini-skirt wasn't invented because the little old lady from Pasadena wanted one. But she's probably wearing one today, because it's all she can get. Some large chain department stores don't even stock clothes for the over-30 set anymore."

Probably the first mass market genius in Detroit to fully recognize the baby boomer was Ford's Lee Iacocca, father of the fabled Mustang. Sporty and truly affordable, the first "pony car" ended up being just the ticket to catch the eye of this new breed. In 1964, some 400,000 of them came running to jump on this equally new bandwagon. Yet as wildly popular as the Mustang was, bucket seats and a floor shifter alone didn't quite do it for everyone.

Many of the boomers then just coming of age had as kids watched while the teens of the '50s had scared their parents to death, as many naysayers saw it, hot rodding their way to hell. As much as everyone from priests to politicians predicted otherwise, the fire-breathing hot rod, along with the paganistic rock 'n roll music that blared from its radio, did not help bring about the fall of civilization as we know it. At least not yet. On the contrary, hot rodding inspired an entirely new industry, the aftermarket performance parts business, which, as the '60s wound down, was raking in more than $1 billion in annual sales. The impetus behind this windfall? "It's the much talked about youth market that has pushed sales to such heights," pointed out Passino. "The kids are out there in legion."

"Statistics show that today's kids like cars," he continued in 1970. "Economists estimate that teenagers and those just out of their teens spend $3.5 billion annually on automobiles and automotive items. Automobiles are no different from clothes. The kids of today want an 'in' look in the things they wear. They also want the 'in' thing with regard to cars. This had led to the demand for the so-called muscle cars and has helped to create the tremendous growth pattern in the accessory business."

Increased interest in performance also came about by way of an increased interest in official competition. What began as unsanctioned, unsafe street corner showdowns in the '50s quickly became professional drag racing, which by the end of the decade was up and running, as well as attracting the interest of Detroit's movers and shakers, who recognized yet another quick way to promote their products. By 1960, factory-built super stockers were becoming more prominent, themselves leading to the rapid development of competition parts programs. This in turn fostered additional engineering work aimed at increasing everyday performance. All the while, horsepower hounds were watching, waiting for what would come next from Detroit—hopefully something in the form of a socially acceptable, street-going hot rod.

The early-'60s super stocks themselves—Max Wedge Mopars, Super Duty Pontiacs, lightweight Ford Galaxies, and such—were high-priced, low-tolerance, gnarly beasts never meant for civilized duty. Easily the closest thing then to a really cool, hot daily driver was Chevrolet's Super Sport Impala, introduced in 1961 along with the fabled 409 V-8, a potent combination that had everyone saving their pennies and dimes and singing its praises.

Chuck Berry could crow about all the Cadillacs he wanted, that was '50s stuff. On June 4, 1962, Capitol Records released a single cut by five West Coast surfers titled, appropriately enough, *Surfin' Safari*. Three months later, disc jockeys decided to try out the flip side of that 45, and quickly discovered another bitchin' hit for the Beach Boys, a song that reportedly helped cast their Capitol contract in stone. Written by Gary Usher and Beach Boy Brian Wilson, *409* not only supplied Chevrolet with some really fine publicity, the 1-minute,

**For the man who wouldn't mind riding a tiger
if someone'd only put wheels on it—Pontiac GTO**

58-second classic also emerged as the first truly big, nationally popular rock 'n roll car tune.

In rapid succession beginning in 1961, the Beach Boys helped turn American teenagers on to the Southern California surfing craze, then really got their blood pumping with sounds of engines revving and tires squealing. Although most teens already knew what girls were for, that didn't stop the Wilson brothers and friends from also supplying more than one refresher course.

Suddenly it seemed nothing else in the early '60s mattered, not the Sputnik-inspired Space Race, Kennedy's Bay of Pigs, Southern civil rights struggles, nor the asterisk next to Roger Maris' 61 home runs. And certainly not a little-known military involvement just then gaining momentum in an even lesser-known Southeast Asian jungle. As far as beach-blanket-bingo-playing young Americans were concerned, it was females, fast cars, more females, and fun, fun, fun—at least until daddy took the T-bird away.

By 1963, hot rod hits had become all the rage on the airwaves, with the Beach Boys and Capitol Records leading the way. *Shutdown* was released in April, followed by *Little Deuce Coupe* in August; the former telling the tale of a fuel-injected Sting Ray besting a 413 Mopar, the latter bragging of a '32 flathead Ford rod—"you don't know

While real performance came only as a high-priced option for the typically mild Mustang in 1964, hot horsepower was the GTO's main selling point from the outset. Thus, it was quickly recognized as Detroit's first true musclecar. This early Pontiac ad helped usher in this new breed, as well as its soon-to-be-recognized reputation as "the Tiger."

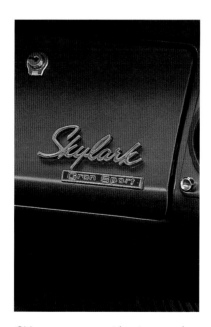

GM copycats were quick to jump on the GTO bandwagon, with Buick's new entry in the mid-sized musclecar sweepstakes coming in 1965. Although not anywhere near as proliferous, nor as revered, as Chevy's SS moniker, the GS nameplate did adorn many formidable performance machines in the '60s and '70s.

The more things change, the more they stay the same. As they still are today, T-shirts represented the cheapest, easiest way to show your high-powered allegiance in the '60s—in this case to Mr. Norm's Grand-Spaulding Dodge, Chicago's legendary home to Mopar muscle for more than 10 years. These shirts, along with many other pieces of Mr. Norm paraphernalia and various musclecar era nostalgia items, are being reproduced today by Motorsports Racing Apparel in Vista, California.

what I got." Another popular early car crooner, Capitol's Dick Dale—called by *Life* magazine "a thumping teenage idol who is part evangelist, part Pied Piper"—also made *Billboard's* Top 100 in October with *The Scavenger*.

Beach Boy clones, Jan and Dean, spun out *Drag City* for Liberty records in December, then really got rolling the next year with *Dead Man's Curve* and *Little Old Lady From Pasadena*. Released in March 1964, *Dead Man's Curve* made it to No. 8 on the charts. Three months later, *Little Old Lady* debuted in her shiny red super stock Dodge and roared all the way to No. 3.

From there, the list of car songs and car singers ran rampant, though most barely made it off the line. Groups like the Chevelles, Eliminators, Burning Slicks, and Four-Speeds—the latter led by *409* pensman Gary Usher—did tunes like *Boss Barracuda*, *Hot Rod Surfin'*, *Stick Shift*, and *Let's Go To The Drag Strip*. On the more popular side of the vinyl, the Ripchords hit the charts running in December 1963 with *Hey Little Cobra*, which eventually reached No. 4. Soon making No. 4 as well was a song released by Ronny & The Daytonas in August

1964. As *409* had done in 1962, this hit, *G.T.O.*, served as a tribute to one of the hottest factory cars then on the street. Young people ate it up, both the song and the car.

Clearly, the pump had been primed by the time Pontiac shocked the troops in 1964 with its GTO, soon known more affectionately both by its promotions-hyped nickname, "Tiger," and its street-slang tag, "the Goat." Everything was in place—the young, thrill-hungry population, the hip music, the good vibrations—and everything was cool, except for the economy, which had heated up considerably. Dances like the Watusi and the Frug were cool. The Beatles' hair was cool. Perhaps most importantly, cars were cool; and the hotter the performance, the cooler the car. It just might have been the best time ever to be young. It certainly was a great time to be building automobiles.

Like Iacocca, Pontiac General Manager Elliot "Pete" Estes had eyes, he could see the market was ready for a mass-production musclecar, an exciting machine aimed directly at the hot-blooded, younger buyer. Estes was so sure of this, he gave his wholehearted support to a supposedly taboo project that ivory tower execs at General Motors would've surely pooh-poohed had they not missed the chance. Upper office protests, however, were quickly hushed once GTOs began screaming off showroom floors at a rapid rate—revenues talk, posturing walks. No doubt about it, Pontiac's 1964 recipe for success was every bit as historic as Ford's.

Performance cars had been present in the '50s. Chevy's Corvette. Chrysler's 300. Plymouth's Fury. But suddenly in the '60s they started showing up in grand numbers. Picking up on Pontiac's lead, Oldsmobile transformed its F-85 into the famed "4-4-2"—"four-barrel, four-on-the-floor, dual exhausts." It initially featured more machismo than muscle, nonetheless, Mercury's Cyclone also debuted midyear in 1964 to help kick off another proud performance legacy. In 1965, Buick's Skylark became the Gran Sport, and Chevrolet shoehorned its new Mk IV big-block V-8 between Chevelle fenders, creating the SS 396. Chrysler Corporation got its act rolling in 1966 with its 426 "street hemi," the perfect power option for Dodge's sleek, new Charger. At that same time, American Motors was busy preparing a complete image makeover based on its own new brand of muscle, the two-seat AMX, introduced for 1968.

By then, musclecars were available in all sizes, from full-sized boulevard brutes like Chevrolet's SS 427 Impala, to polite pony cars like Pontiac's Firebird 400. And they were seemingly everywhere; parading up Woodward Avenue north of Detroit, screaming down U.S. 30 Dragstrip near Chicago, cruising around Ventura Boulevard in L.A. They were sitting, uncommonly

patient, waiting to be sold on lots at Tasca Ford in East Providence, Rhode Island; Royal Pontiac in Royal Oak, Michigan; Chicago's Grand-Spaulding Dodge; and Dana Chevrolet in South Gate, California.

For 25 cents in 1968, any Dodge musclecar fan, of driving age or not, could've joined the "Scat Pack," with initial membership bringing two lapel badges, a pair of decals, and a catalog offering even more paraphernalia, including commemorative clothing, of course. That same year, Mattel Toys introduced "Hot Wheels," the "fastest metal cars in the world." Sixteen different mini-replicas were originally offered, six modeled after popular performance cars. Snatched up by millions of kids for less than a dollar apiece then, some of these minute, metal-flake, muscletoys today bring hundreds from grown-up kids, both serious (really serious) collectors and those bent on celebrating their simpler days. Even hotter are the cars those Mattel toys copied. Real-life musclecars like Hemi 'Cudas, SS 454 Chevelles, and 427 Fords can sometimes trade for upwards of $50,000 on the collector market; some have even gone into the six-digit realm during peak exploitative investing periods.

To think the GTO basically started it all, and did so in very rapid fashion.

What made Pontiac's pioneering performance car so appealing in 1964? "The message was straight-line speed," continued David E. Davis in his 1975 *Car and Driver* retro tribute. "And it felt like losing your virginity, going into combat and tasting your first beer all in about seven seconds." As for the historic aspect, the '64 GTO was, in Davis' always far-from-humble opinion, "the first Muscle Car. . . a violent, virile catalyst-car that set the pace and tone for five or six years of intense horsepower promotion out of Detroit City, the hallmark of a period that seemed like the culmi-

nation of all the dreams of all the enthusiasts on all the back roads in this country, but a period that in reality was nothing more than that—the period at the end of one short paragraph of automotive history."

Short indeed. A victim of both itself, as well as changing attitudes, the musclecar quickly skyrocketed in popularity, reaching its zenith in 1970, then even more quickly raced to its demise. By 1972, it was essentially all over but the shouting for everyone save GM's speed merchants, who somehow managed to keep a few embers burning up through 1974. It would take the better part of 10 years before the sparks started flying again.

Why the quick death? For starters, the American musclecar then represented—and in most respects still does today—an obvious paradox. We are instructed by law to drive responsibly and respectfully when getting from point A to B, all the while keeping safely within established speed parameters. Why, then, would we need a car capable of doubling posted highway limits with ease? As socially responsible statistics apparently tell us, speed not only sells, it also kills. Hitting triple digits or roaring from rest to 60 miles per hour in 6 or 7 seconds on public thoroughfares serves very few purposes other than to occasionally supply more tragic statistics to help support this claim.

First used as part of a high-profile Impala performance package in 1961, Chevrolet's Super Sport image was eventually applied to almost every model offered in the '60s and '70s, from compact Chevy II, to mid-sized Chevelle, to utilitarian El Camino, to upscale Monte Carlo. Station wagons and now trucks have even been so honored. Is it any wonder then that Chevy's "SS" lettering represents the best remembered badge from the musclecar era?

Musclecar fans young and old demonstrated their loyalty to Dodge power by joining the Scat Pack club. Decals, stickers, and T-shirts hopefully enticed the youngest of this club to grow up and buy one of the Scat Pack's four-wheeled members, perhaps a Charger R/T or Dart GTS. Also appearing here in the upper righthand corner is a decal depicting Plymouth's promotional performance team, the Rapid Transit System.

Few musclecar buyers knew the men behind the machines in the '60s. But most men behind the wheels of musclecars then knew Hurst's Golden Shifter Girl, Linda Vaughn, shown here during a 1969 promotion at Daytona. Vaughn's ample attributes, not the least of which was her smile, helped solidify her role as an ambassador of sorts for American high-performance. *Roger Huntington Archives, courtesy Dobbs Publishing*

While Linda Vaughn was promoting Olds performance indirectly by way of the Hurst company, the division's factory muscle offerings were officially overseen in a long-running ad campaign by one "Dr. Oldsmobile" and his "zany assistants." Included on the good doctor's staff was Elephant Engine Ernie, Hy Spy, Esses Fernhill, Shifty Sidney, and Wind Tunnel Waldo. *Oldsmobile Division, General Motors Corporation*

Of course the issue here wasn't about need, it was about want. Freedom of choice is supposed to be one of our unalienable rights as Americans, no? Yes. Or at least yes to certain degrees. As the fates allowed, those degrees were less strict when the musclecar was born. Cliché aside, the early '60s was a more innocent age, especially so for the young American male who seemingly dreamed only of flexing his hormones in a hot car with his best girl alongside. All in all, it was a less complicated moment in history, a time when men were men, women weren't, and fewer rules ruled, so much so that next to no one worried about the implications of the unlimited sale of raw horsepower.

No one was there to say we couldn't drive fast cars when the first GTO hit the streets in 1964. And almost no one apparently was concerned that cars like this red-hot Pontiac tended to use fossil fuels by the brontosaurus load, then spit out the by-products to the distinct detriment of the breathable air supply. Only Southern Californians knew how bad smog could get, right? As for gasoline supplies, who cared how much we used when the barrel appeared bottomless and a gallon dipped out only cost a quarter, as it had for years?

The times, however, were soon a-changin'. One year after the GTO's birth, Washington was abuzz with activi-

ty that would almost immediately affect the way we all looked at the cars we drove.

An intense issue in California since 1959, protecting the atmosphere reached national importance in 1965 when the Clean Air Act of 1963 was amended. Automotive emissions controls, up to that point, had been a West Coast thing, starting somewhat meekly in 1961 with California clean air crusaders' specifications that all cars sold new in their state use the newborn positive crankcase ventilation system. Previously, all engines simply vented their crankcase vapors directly into the atmosphere via a road draft tube or such. What the PCV valve did was reroute those gases back into the intake to be reburned. In 1963, all American cars started using PCV valves.

Two years later, California problem-solvers began concentrating on the real root of the air pollution problem: exhaust contaminates. Mandated "smog equipment" for exhaust systems on California cars were already in place when the Clean Air Act was amended in 1965. Among the immediate national repercussions was a Congressional requirement that all automobiles sold in America use similar systems by 1968.

Although few in the fast lane truly took note at the time, this 1965 edict, even then, represented the proverbial handwriting on the wall. Federally mandated smog controls did arrive in 1968 to start cramping the musclecar's style, albeit slowly at first. This chokehold notwithstanding, American horsepower continued running

strong for another two years. But then additional, even tighter controls helped strangle the life out of the beast. With the further mandated use of lower octane unleaded fuels looming right around the corner, automakers in 1971 were forced to make major compression concessions within their engines, effectively all but nailing the lid on the musclecar's coffin.

Additional factors also contributed to the musclecar's untimely death. Along with the Clean Air Act, Congress in 1965 kicked off an especially vigorous investigative campaign focusing on what Detroit was doing to make its cars as safe as possible. Hearings conducted that summer by Senator Abraham Ribicoff, among other things, thrust East Coast lawyer Ralph Nader into the public consciousness, then led to a new wave of tough automotive safety legislation—as well as a change in the average American's attitude toward everyday driving. Nader's legendary literary assault on the auto-making industry, *Unsafe At Any Speed*, was published a few months later.

"For over half a century, the automobile has brought death, injury, and the most inestimable sorrow and deprivation to millions of people," began Nader's grim prose. "With Medea-like intensity, this mass trauma began rising sharply four years ago reflecting new and unexpected ravages by the motor vehicle. A 1959 Department of Commerce report projected that 51,000 persons would be killed by automobiles in 1975. That figure will probably be reached in 1965, a decade ahead of schedule." If American car buyers previously hadn't been aware of just how safe or unsafe their cars were, they were by the fall of that year.

But many of us didn't need to be quoted accident rates in order to change the way we looked at performance cars. As early as the summer of 1964, *Motor Trend* magazine had warned speed-conscious readers of a possible future stumbling block. Stating already that "the idea that horsepower is dangerous is deeply ingrained in the thinking of official America," a prophetic *MT* report explained that insurance industry executives were then considering tacking additional surcharges, some as high as 25 percent, atop premiums for cars with heavy-duty horsepower-to-weight ratios. By 1967, an unmarried, under-25-year-old male could expect to pay as much as $700 a year to insure his GTO—and this with a clean

driving record. Even if the musclecar had somehow survived into the '70s, most average young men would've never been able to afford them.

Of course, insurance officials basically couldn't have cared less about automotive safety; the fearful stack of statistics Nader and fellow crusaders relied on only helped them reap even greater windfalls. On the other side of the coin, Detroit people tried to typically argue that most of these statistics were misleading; considering the volume of miles traveled, 50,000 highway fatalities a year was "within reason." Others claimed the cars themselves were not guilty of killing, drivers were; improving highway safety shouldn't overly concentrate on building totally safe cars, it should focus on training safer drivers.

While playing spin doctor with death tolls bordered on detestable, the latter arguments did have their merits. Nonetheless, this logic basically fell on deaf ears as Washington's stance gained momentum. In his January 1966 State of the Union address, President Lyndon Johnson effectively squelched Detroit's defense when he claimed our dangerous streets and highways represented this country's second largest problem, topped only by his own personal headache, the Vietnam War.

By midyear 1966, more than 300,000 young American soldiers would be in Southeast Asia fighting that war; a half million by the end of 1967. Like the '60s themselves, U.S. military involvement in Vietnam began innocently enough with 3,500 ready-for-action Marines landing at Da Nang in March 1965 to join the 20,000 or so "advisors" already in the country, reportedly to help stem Communist aggression. Over the following six weeks, we sent 80,000 more troops, essentially all initially going with heads held high, many leaving their beloved musclecars safely behind in garages awaiting their expected return. A few of these once-proud machines are still silently waiting, rusting away. Of the 2.8 million men and women who served in the Vietnam War from its clandestine beginnings following the end of World War II to its merciful close in 1975, more than 55,000 made the ultimate sacrifice.

Southeast Asia, however, wasn't the only place where Americans clashed in the '60s. As if President Kennedy's assassination in November 1963 hadn't been enough of a wake-up call announcing an end to simpler

Almost every automaker has relied on the Gran Turismo image at one time or another. Probably most confident of the GT badge was Ford. Mustang GTs were leaders of the Dearborn performance pack from 1965 to '68. Shown here is the prominent prow of a '68 Torino GT. Behind those two red letters is a 428 Cobra Jet big-block V-8.

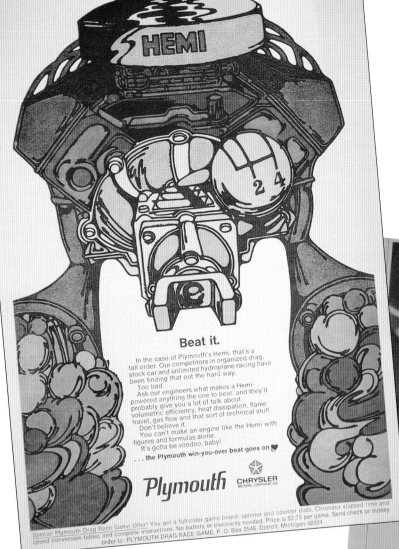

Most young men not yet of driving age in 1968 remember the little bombs introduced that year by Mattel Toys. Still running strong in today's youth market, "Hot Wheels" miniatures have long since become collectors items, with asking prices for some early models running well into the hundreds of dollars. One of the more popular Hot Wheels sets featured "the Snake" and "the Mongoose," which in 1970 mimicked drag racers Don Prudhomme and Tom McEwen's real-life funny cars.

Psychedelic handiwork was hip in the '60s and early '70s, appearing on everything from kid's lunch boxes, to album covers, to clothing, to the walls of pop art museums—and on the pages of car magazines. Chrysler Corporation was especially hip to the hippie movement, as demonstrated by various far-out ad campaigns and the seemingly endless groovy shades of paint applied to Dodge and Plymouth musclecars.

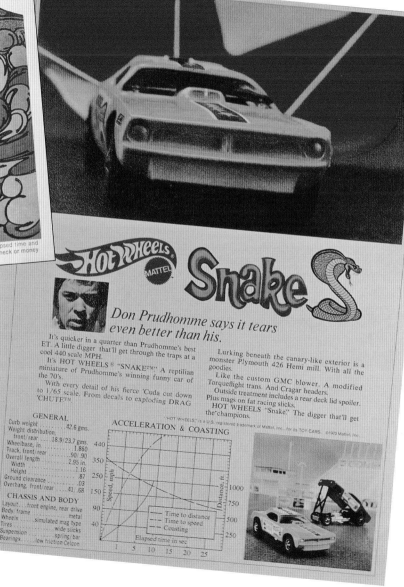

Horsepower wasn't Plymouth's only strong suit in 1969; flower power was also a selling point that year. The Barracuda's "Mod Top" option added a then-trendy floral pattern to the car's vinyl roof and interior. Incorporating a matching floral mini-skirt into the mix was purely up to you. *Chrysler Historical Archives*

days, innocence back on the home front was quickly traded for social awareness and civil unrest as hippie squared off against "Big Brother" over various issues, not the least of which involved that detested, protested war in Vietnam. Bob Dylan didn't quite get it right. The less complicated times that welcomed the musclecar's birth in 1964 didn't just change, they were obliterated. By 1968, "revolution was in the air," as was a cloud of smoke—and what was being burned wasn't tobacco. Long hair was in, undergarments were out. Psychedelic and hallucinogenic joined the lexicon—the Beatles' hit *Lucy in the Sky with Diamonds* reportedly portrayed a trip, but that journey didn't involve an automobile.

Popular music went from bubble gum to acid rock. While females typically remained a hot topic for lyricists, hot cars were apparently no longer worth singing about. No self-respecting, groovin' teen in 1969 would've been caught dead with a Beach Boys album. Hell, the Wilson brothers themselves even left their short-haired, wholesome harmony approach—as well as their surf boards, hot rods, and bleach-blonde beach babies—behind, only to fail miserably in the drug-heavy pop culture of the early '70s.

As the '60s closed, the younger set's attentions turned to free love, free speech, and free concerts, the latter coming once hoards of rock fans overwhelmed the establish-

ment's bourgeois gates and fences at landmark events like the Atlanta Pop Festival. "The Man" was the perceived enemy, while Mother Nature was the one to embrace. Peace was the priority; all we needed was love. So how could a hedonistic, hydrocarbon-huffing, who-cares-about-little-animals kind of personal indulgence like the musclecar prosper at a time supposedly ruled by the passive, pot-smoking, flowers-in-their-hair, "we generation?"

First, consider that "flourished" was a relative term. Down a bit from its peak in 1966, Pontiac's GTO still attracted 87,684 customers in 1968. The following year, Chevrolet sold 86,307 SS 396 Chevelles and Plymouth moved 84,420 Road Runners. These were easily Detroit's three most popular musclecars; from there the list of rivals, although reasonably long, dropped off considerably as far as the population beneath each banner was concerned. As for total automobiles delivered, performance and otherwise, that figure reached 8.8 million in 1968, 8.2 in 1969. At best, performance models never exceeded 10 percent of the total market in any given year. Boiling it all down, the musclecar existed in a very tight niche—it wasn't an automobile made for everyone, only those who were made for it.

Second, just maybe the "counter-culture" era wasn't nearly as encompassing as casual history tends to make

Stricter emissions standards, growing safety concerns and sky-rocketing insurance costs all worked together to bring an abrupt end to the musclecar's reign in the early '70s. Turning heads had always been an easy task for American performance cars, but by 1971 the trick had become not to draw attention—from the dreaded insurance man.

Plymouth CHRYSLER MOTORS CORPORATION

The standard insurance rating is standard.

New 383 and 340 cubic inch Road Runners receive the blessing of a standard insurance rating.

Who from?

From the companies that issue the majority of automobile insurance in this country, that's who.

Now that's pretty important considering the Road Runner is still the car you've come to know and love.

This year's version comes with (among other things) fat tires, high-flow cylinder heads, 4-barrel carburetion and heavy-duty brakes and suspension.

And a wider rear track and shorter wheelbase.

And, as you can see, a super slick new body.

Go see it and the other R.T.S. Plymouths ('Cuda, Duster 340 and GTX) at your Plymouth Dealer's.

Beep-Beep.

The Rapid Transit System. Coming through.

out. Sure, all that flower power stuff appeared especially pervasive in places like Berkeley and "the Village." But for most average young people living in the real world across the country, the hippie phenomenon was less of a socio-political movement and more of a fashion statement, much as its punk, rap, and grunge successors have been in more recent years.

Automakers of the '60s and '70s even embraced the hippie fad, most prominently in their advertising. Artwork, especially Chrysler Corporation's, was wildly psychedelic and even insinuated drug-induced fantasies. Groovy, long-legged female models were photographed sans bras with hip-hugging bell-bottoms painted on pert, ripe-apple butts—like speed, sex also always sells. The cars themselves were the Boss, the Heavy Chevy, and the Judge, as in "here come da'. . . ." Striping glowed in the dark. Bright, fluorescent paint choices were Grabber Blue, Hugger Orange, and Go Mango. AMC opted for the "Easy Rider" route, using a red, white, and blue theme—the "American way"—for its muscle-cars in 1969 and 1970. Plymouth even went so far as to offer a flowered "Mod Top" vinyl roof option for its '69 Barracuda.

By 1970, some of the musclecar's appeal did appear to be aimed at the peace-loving hair-hat crowd. But beneath those Peter Max exteriors remained a chauvinist pig of an automobile, a maniacally macho machine that, even though *Purple Haze* may have been the accompaniment of choice playing on that 8-track beneath the dash, was still best suited for a crew-cut-wearing driver with gasoline, not LSD, running in his veins. For those who always loved them, high-powered, high-profile musclecars were still cool in the early '70s, even if threatening the well-being of small children, fouling the air, and depleting the world's oil supplies wasn't.

As if federal actions to reduce exhaust emissions and insurance agents' exploitation of growing safety concerns hadn't been enough to run the American musclecar into extinction, a newfound need to make our cars more fuel efficient became a major priority in the '70s with the arrival of an "energy crisis" fueled by the Arab oil embargo of October 1973. Hit hard where it hurts most—in their wallets—American car buyers quickly came to grips with this new need; so quickly that the fuel-hungry musclecar all but vanished overnight with nary a whimper, as did the demand for such "gas hogs." By 1974, buying a gallon of gasoline was no longer child's play, with the average price at the pump almost doubling to more than 53 cents—and that was just the beginning. At the same time, it was the very last straw for the musclecar.

Automakers at that point had already proven themselves more than willing to dress their offerings up in cape and leotards even if the supercar punch wasn't there. As it turns out, fast looks sell almost as easily as real speed, even more so when real speed is no longer available. As the '70s progressed, true performance machines were unceremoniously replaced by "tape-stripe" impostors—no, Ford fans, those "Starsky and Hutch" Torinos of 1976 weren't musclecars. Not even close.

Arguably, the last truly hot musclecar—perhaps coincidentally, perhaps not—was also a Pontiac. In 1974, the 455 Super Duty Trans Am was still running every bit as strong as most of its muscle-bound predecessors from the "pre-smog-motor" days. But it, too, bit the dust, effectively ending the first-generation musclecar era exactly 10 years after it had begun.

Those years still rank among the fastest in American automotive history.

Arguably, Detroit's last great musclecars were Pontiac's Super Duty Firebirds of 1973 and '74. Even limited by Federal emissions restrictions, the 455 SD V-8 was still one tough customer, a powerplant able to beat many free-breathing performance mills of the "pre-smog motor" era.

Chapter One

PONTIAC PRIMES THE PUMP

The Musclecar Age Begins with the GTO

From an automotive perspective, the times really began a-changin' in '64. This was the year of the pony car, Ford's wildly popular, mass-marketed Mustang, the sporty compact that rearranged the way John and Jane Q. Public looked at practical transportation. And, of course, it was also the year of the "Tiger," Pontiac's GTO, the muscled-up macho-mobile that allowed most average Joes a new look at high performance. Before the GTO, Joe generally was stuck on the outside peering in at high-priced, heavyweight haulers or purpose-built, race-ready machines, neither of which he could afford, nor afford to drive. Although musclecars like the GTO were by no means cheap, the new brand of performance they offered came both at easier-to-reach prices and in forms better suited for socially acceptable everyday use.

A pivotal year for gearheads? Without a doubt.

Then again, 1964 was a pivotal year for many, much more important things; a time for a changing of the guard in various arenas, all adding up to a new way every American looked at their life and their lifestyle.

The year began with Surgeon General Luther Terry in January releasing his office's report on cigarette use, which claimed that smoking "contributes substantially to mortality from certain specific diseases and to the overall death rate." Warning labels aside, a pack of Lucky Strikes rolled up in a T-shirt sleeve remained a popular fashion statement.

Eleven months later, incumbent Lyndon Johnson defeated conservative Republican candidate Barry Goldwater for the presidency, along the way promising us a future in the "Great Society." A Great Society for

all Americans. On July 2, Johnson had signed the Civil Rights Act; a few weeks later, a federal court in Atlanta upheld a Congressional ruling that barred racial discrimination in public accommodations, in doing so ordering a local motel to admit blacks. Admitting was one thing, accepting was another. In August, the bodies of three murdered civil rights workers were found buried on a Mississippi farm, their case as well as their names all but forgotten until retold in the 1988 movie, *Mississippi Burning*. Far more memorable was the name of Reverend Martin Luther King, Jr., who in October garnered the Nobel Peace Prize, then donated its $54,600 value to the civil rights movement.

Two days before those three graves were uncovered in Mississippi, a trio of North Vietnamese patrol boats half way around the world had attacked the U.S. destroyer *Maddox*, reportedly in international waters, in the Gulf of Tonkin. On August 5, American planes retaliated, bombing North Vietnamese installations. Two days later, Congress passed the Gulf of Tonkin Resolution, fully opening the door for the White House to use "all necessary measures" to squelch hostile action in Vietnam. LBJ then had no way of knowing such measures would eventually cost more than 50,000 American lives, as well as his commander-in-chief post—immediately following the bloody Tet offensive in South Vietnam early in 1968, our battle-weary 36th president announced he would not seek another term that fall.

The GTO received reams of free publicity from this legendary *Car and Driver* cover story depicting a mythical showdown between Pontiac's musclecar and the Ferrari from which its name was "borrowed." The performance blurb at the top was equally mythical.

Opposite: Most drivers probably saw more of the opposite end of the '64 GTO 33 years ago, but this impressive facade became well recognized nonetheless. It quickly lead the way for many more musclecar mimics to follow.

Pontiac General Manager Pete Estes, at left, celebrates a new division production record in June 1964 as a GTO convertible rolls off the line. The GTO that year also set a Pontiac first-year model sales standard. *Paul Zazarine collection*

Remembered more today for his drug-trafficking entanglements and stainless-steel sports car venture, John DeLorean in his heyday stood tall as one of Pontiac's prime movers and shakers. In July 1965, he stepped into the division's general manager post after Pete Estes moved over to Chevrolet. *Paul Zazarine collection*

Opposite: By 1966, the GTO was Detroit's most popular musclecar by a wide margin. Pontiac sold 96,646 "Goats" that year, a total that not only represented a high for the GTO, but for all performance machines. Ever.

On the homefront in 1964, the typical (median) family earned $6,848 a year. The typical loaf of bread cost 19 cents; the typical pound of coffee, 59. Thirty cents more would've put a six-pack of Old Milwaukee in your Frigidaire. And a pair of "Jeepers" canvas high-top basketball shoes were regularly priced at $2.99, while Levi's "Sta-Prest" pants were $6.98.

A gallon of gloriously leaded regular down at the corner Sinclair station cost no more than a quarter, and sometimes less than 20 cents in neighborhoods stricken by ever-present "gas wars." New car prices varied from the Ford Falcon's $1,985 bottom line-up to $6,630 for a Cadillac Eldorado Biarritz convertible.

Pontiac's first GTO started out at about a grand more than the compact Falcon, $500 more than the Mustang. Now, $500 was no small chunk of change in 1964, but you had to consider the chasm spanned by that price difference. Buying a pony car for less than $2,400 that year meant putting yourself in a bucket seat to the left of a floor shifter controlling a three-speed transmission mated to a yeoman six-cylinder powerplant—pure practicality painted to look like a sporty plaything. It required every bit of that $500 and more to create a really hot V-8 Mustang, then able only to stay within eye-shot of a Goat. "If you began adding options to the Mustang so that it was comparably equipped," explained Eric Dahlquist in a 1973 *Motor Trend* retrospective review, "the GTO seemed the best bargain to come along since the Auburn Speedster."

Average Joe apparently agreed. Wholeheartedly. Initially hesitant to jump onto the supercar bandwagon, PMD Sales Manager Frank Bridge had pegged 1964 GTO sales at about 5,000. By the time the tire smoke cleared, Pontiac had sold 32,450 Goats, and could have easily let loose that many more had production been able to keep up. In a record sales year for the entire division, the '64 GTO instantly became Pontiac's best-selling first-edition model of all time.

With the shackles cast off, 1965 GTO sales did double 1964's, eventually surpassing 75,000. Another 96,946 followed in 1966, firmly demonstrating what performance buyers already knew—the GTO was America's number one supercar. Although the Chevelle SS did finally take over the top yearly performance sales spot for good in 1969—86,307 to 72,287—Pontiac's powerful progenitor remained the big bully to beat on the street. As *Motor Trend* explained, the "GTO is the leader of the supercars. It trails Chevy's SS 396 in sales, but it is the others who are trying harder. In image, performance and class, the 'Tiger' is the car to equal."

All told, the GTO was the best-selling performance machine of the entire musclecar era. Counting the rebodied

Count the tigers!

Listen to the Colpix recording "GeeTO Tiger" by the Tigers (a great new group of swingers!), and count the number of times the word *tiger* is sung in the record. (Complete rules are listed below.)

And win one in the HURST-GeeTO Tiger Contest!

Win the original GeeTO Tiger—a wild '65 GTO with special Hurst-gold paint and unique tiger-appointed interior. It's set up to go. Features Pontiac's big-gun 360-hp mill with 3 deuce carbs, transistorized ignition and 4-speed close ratio box with a gold-plated Hurst shifter. All riding on a full set of gold anodized Hurst custom wheels. Wild!

(To see a "live one" stop by your local Pontiac dealer's. He's got his own version of this one-of-a-kind Hurst hustler.)

6 more prizes from Hurst!
To runner-up winners Hurst is giving away: two sets of Hurst custom wheels. Two Competition Plus 4-speed shifters. And two Synchro/Loc 3-speed shifters.

100! Prizes! 100!
Still more. Like auto-stereos. Record albums from Colpix Recordings. And subscriptions to *Hot Rod*, *Motor Trend*, *Car Craft*, *Rod & Custom*, and *Teen*. The editors of these magazines are honorary judges and will assist George Hurst in selecting the winners. Their decision is final.

One more time!
All you have to do is: 1) Listen to the record "GeeTO Tiger" by the Tigers. 2) Put down on a sheet of paper the number of times the word *tiger* is sung in the record. 3) On the same sheet write, in 25 words or less, "Why I would like to own the original GeeTO Tiger"—the car that inspired the song. 4) Send

your entries to:
Hurst Performance Products
P. O. Box X509, Dept. "HR"
Glenside, Pa.

That's all you have to do. But do it quick. Entries must be postmarked no later than July 31, 1965 and become the property of Hurst Performance Products. Contest not valid where prohibited by state or local law.

HURST

1973 variety and downsized Ventura-based 1974 version, Pontiac sold 514,793 Goats—subtracting those last 350-powered models brought total big-block production to 507,735. Even though Chevrolet did build 577,600 SS Chevelles between 1964 and 1973, more than one-sixth of that total consisted of the lower-performance small-block V-8 and frugal six-cylinder models built in 1964 and the 350-equipped cars of 1971-1973. No matter how you looked at it, the GTO was Detroit's most popular musclecar.

And to think GM people never wanted to build it. At least those at the top didn't, and they mattered. From Chairman Frederic Donner on down, the prevailing attitude among GM's executive elite in the early '60s was anti-performance. So much so that Donner's office in January 1963 issued a memo to all division heads to cease and desist in various racing activities—highly successful, high-powered programs that executives had determined to have grown well out of hand.

Pontiac's Super Duty Catalinas had been winning at National Hot Rod Association drag strips since 1960, and in 1961 had begun dominating NASCAR ovals as well. Chevrolet engineers had been busy, too. The fearsome Z11 409 lightweight drag package emerged midyear in 1962, the first of Zora Arkus-Duntov's stripped-down, race-ready Grand Sport Corvettes hit the

test track that December, and the legendary Mk IV "Mystery Motor" stood ready, willing, and able to take Daytona by storm in January 1963.

Donner's memo, however, brought all these projects to a screeching halt—the Super Duty Pontiacs and Z 11 Chevys were history, while the five Grand Sports (of 125 originally planned) Duntov built somehow were squirreled off into supposedly private racers' hands. The beastly 427-cubic inch Mystery Motor did manage to run NASCAR's Daytona 500 in February, then was quickly whisked away into obscurity, at least for the moment—it would return in more civilized 396-cubic-inch form for the street in 1965. As for the track, GM divisions were officially out of racing beginning in 1963.

GM's anti-racing stance actually dated back to 1957, a time when all of Detroit's automakers were—repeated public denials aside—in up to their eyebrows at the track; Chevrolet, to the tune of a $750,000 bet; Ford, a reported $2.5 million. A horsepower race had reached alarming proportions as these two longtime low-priced rivals battled along with Chrysler to see which factory could gain the most publicity through a race-winning reputation. Remember, speed sells. In more ways than one.

Then, just when things were really speeding up, the black flag was dropped. At a meeting in May of the Automobile Manufacturers Association, AMA chairman Harlow "Red" Curtice proposed that the group's membership sever their race track ties. All agreed, and on June 6 the infamous AMA "ban" on factory racing was approved. From then on, not only would member companies "not participate or engage in any public contest, competitive event or test of a passenger cars involving or suggesting racing or speed," they would also not advertise "the actual or comparative capabilities of passenger cars for speed, or the specific engine size, torque, horsepower or ability to accelerate or perform in any context that suggests speed."

In actuality, the AMA's factory racing ban was nothing more than ink, a paper tiger most members only paid lip service to, each in their own thinly veiled fashion. Not so Ford. Even though the AMA had no policing ability—no way to enforce the ban, nor punish violators—Dearborn's conservative general manager, Robert McNamara, began following the resolution to the letter, leading his company out of the performance arena. Meanwhile, Chevrolet and Pontiac kept running stronger than ever at the track and on the street, although with far less flag waving than before the AMA ban.

Was it just coincidence that the man behind the ban, AMA chairman Red Curtice, was also GM's president? And was it only luck that the AMA ban came along to help slow Ford in its tracks just as the Blue Oval was preparing to best the Bow-Tie on the yearly sales charts for the first time in two decades?

Anyone with eyes could've seen what was going on. Most, however, looked the other way as Chevrolet, Pontiac, and, to a lesser degree, Oldsmobile parts books in the late-'50s began filling up with a wide array of heavy-duty, high-performance pieces reportedly intended for special use in police cars, taxi fleets, or marine applications. The fact that these components also amazingly worked well in a race car was apparently yet another lucky break, both for the purportedly private racer and GM's image-conscious promotions people.

Bystanders, innocent or otherwise, in 1958 also couldn't have missed the prominent presence of Pontiac chief Semon E. "Bunkie" Knudsen at Daytona, there in the winner's circle celebrating a NASCAR victory by a Pontiac pilot. GM's answer to the obvious question? The wealthy Knudsen was not directly representing his company, per se, he was quenching his own personal thirst for speed by financing supposedly private Pontiac racing efforts out of his own deep pockets. The parts and people may have been Pontiac's, but the dollars were Bunkie's. Right. In any case, whatever Knudsen may have shelled out came back to him in waves by way of corporate bonuses as Pontiac victories at the track quickly began translating into fast sales on the showroom floor.

Although Pontiac's Tri-Power performance option dated back to 1957, it didn't gain true fame until it became the GTO's top power choice in 1964. Those three Rochester two-barrels remained a main attraction beneath a GTO hood up through 1966 (shown here). Multiple carbs were deleted from GM options lists—save for the Corvette—by upper office order in 1967.

The fifth-edition GTO got a fresh, shapelier body and a new, dent-resistant Endura nose. That innovative plastic bumper also helped convince *Motor Trend* editors that the restyled GTO was the "Car of the Year" for 1968.

A tie-in to the times, both in image and make-up, the GTO Judge was initially intended as a bare-bones budget bomb. In reality, it ended up being a higher-priced spoof of sorts of the high-profile late-'60s performance genre. The name came from television's popular "Laugh-In" comedy show. Approximately the first 2,000 '69 Judges were all painted Carousel Red. Any GTO shade was made available after February 1969.

Knudsen, then 43, had come on board at Pontiac in June 1956 as GM's youngest-ever general manager, and his mission had been to revive that division's tired, aging image. "You can sell a young man's car to an old man," claimed his prime motto, "but you'll never sell an old man's car to a young man." In short order, Bunkie transformed Pontiac from your grandpa's car company to a builder of true excitement.

With the division's first modern overhead-valve V-8, introduced in 1955, already in hand, Knudsen began waking things up immediately. In September 1956, he lured Chief Engineer Elliot Estes away from Oldsmobile and rescued a young engineer named John Z. DeLorean from what was left of once-great Packard. Not long afterward, he began cavorting with Daytona Beach speed merchant Smokey Yunick, who then found himself on the payroll of his fourth competition-conscious automaker in five years, following Ford, Chevy, and Hudson. Once the right people were in place, performance quickly became Pontiac's main selling point.

In 1957, Pontiac introduced "Tri-Power," its fabled triple-carburetor option, which was basically stolen away, along with Estes, from Oldsmobile. New that year as well was the limited-edition Bonneville, the first of various PMD models to shamelessly borrow a heady, high-

speed image for its name. Standard Bonneville power came from a fuel-injected V-8, another hot first for the division. Even hotter race-ready equipment continued coming, despite the AMA ban, as fast-thinking Pontiac men like Bill Klinger and Malcolm "Mac" McKellar kept working as if nothing had changed.

It was Klinger and McKellar—the latter noted most for his series of high-performance camshaft designs—who were the main minds behind Pontiac's Super Duty parts program, which was organized in clandestine fashion in 1959. The formidable 389 Super Duty V-8 appeared in 1960; its enlarged, more intimidating 421 brother emerged the following year. Both were basically unbeatable on the NASCAR circuit in 1961 and 1962, a fact not missed by many not-so-innocent bystanders.

Among these was another young mover and shaker in Detroit, Lee Iacocca, who in November 1960 had taken over as Ford Division general manager after Robert McNamara had moved up to president. Under McNamara's direction in the post-AMA ban days, Ford had become very much like Pontiac had been before Bunkie: practicality was present in droves, excitement was sorely lacking. As Iacocca later explained in his autobiography, McNamara "was a good businessman, but he had the mentality of a consumerist. He believed strongly in the idea of a utilitarian car, whose purpose was simply to meet people's basic needs." The Falcon was the feather in McNamara's cap, while the Mustang was Iacocca's baby—both cars set first-year industry sales records, but for obviously different reasons.

Iacocca disagreed with McNamara's support of the AMA ban, as well as the man himself. According to the new general manager, his predecessor "was the quintessential bean counter." Continued Iacocca, "at their best, bean counters [have] impressive analytical skills, [but] by their very nature, tend to be defensive, conservative and pessimistic. On the other side are the guys in sales and marketing—aggressive, speculative and optimistic. In any company, you need both sides, because natural tension between the two creates its own system of checks and balances. If the bean counters are too weak, the company will spend itself into bankruptcy. But if they're too strong, the company won't meet the market or stay competitive."

Ford's efforts to stay competitive had begun before Iacocca's ascension. On April 27, 1959, Dearborn sent a message to GM officials detailing Ford's plans to offer high-performance options. Also mentioned was a possible revamping of the AMA agreement. No reply came, leaving Ford to try the same tack Pontiac and Chevrolet had already embarked upon. Under the guise of "law enforcement parts development," Ford engineers assembled their 360-horse 352 Interceptor Special V-8, the first in a long line of muscle-bound FE-series big-blocks. By 1960, it became clear the gloves were just about to come off—in 1961, Ford would introduce a 401-horsepower, 390-cubic inch, triple-carb FE, followed by an even larger 405-horse, 406-cube version in 1962. The AMA factory racing ban was supposedly still in effect as the '60s began, but was obviously carrying less weight by the day.

Hot Rod's Ray Brock took a poke at analyzing the situation late in 1960. "Just a year ago, Ford introduced an optional 360-horsepower engine in an attempt to regain some of the performance prestige lost during the years 1958 and '59," he wrote. "Now, probably 98 percent of new car buyers would not consider ordering their car with a high-performance engine. But the interesting fact is that a large number of the 98 percent are influenced by the way the brand they are considering has been performing at major stock car races or on the local drag strip. A 1957 AMA edict banned all factory participation and will continue to do so. If the outcome of these races is going to influence overall sales, then it is wise for the factory to give that 2 percent interested in performance something to work with."

Iacocca and crew couldn't have said it any better. But then Henry Ford II did. In a 300-word press release

sent out in June 1962, Dearborn's main man—who, by the way, also had just been re-elected AMA president—spoke of how Ford had initially adhered "to the spirit and letter of the [AMA's] recommendations." However, continued the release, "as time passed, some car divisions interpreted the resolution more and more freely, with the result that increasing emphasis was placed on speed, horsepower and racing. As a result, Ford Motor Company feels that the resolution has come to have neither purpose nor effect. Accordingly, we have notified [the AMA] that we feel we can better establish our own standards of conduct with respect to the manner in which the performance of our vehicles is to be promoted and advertised."

Chrysler issued a similar statement soon afterward claiming, among other things, that the 1957 AMA ban was "inoperative." GM execs equivocated, saying they would continue endorsing the resolution as "sufficient time has not been available to evaluate the full implications" of Ford's decision. Others needed no more than a New York minute.

"Henry Ford II has dropped the green flag on what could be a new era in stock car racing," read a September 1962 *Car Life* report. While GM people were busy mincing something usually found out standing in a field, *Car Life's* editors were lauding Henry Ford II for his bullish honesty. He deserved "a healthy round of applause for being the first industry leader to face the facts as they really are. He has admitted candidly that such things as 406 cubic-inch engines and triple carburetion aren't in keeping with the intent of the [AMA] resolution."

From there, that resolution was all but dead, at least for Detroit's "Big Three." Interestingly, as late as the spring of 1967, press reports were still mentioning the

After a complete restyle left many GTO followers cool to the latest Goat in 1973, Pontiac performed a total transformation the following year, downsizing the once-proud musclecar progenitor as a Ventura-based offering for 1974. This was the last GTO. *Pontiac Historic Services*

Oldsmobile's response to the GTO was its mid-sized 4-4-2, introduced midyear in 1964. Still Greek to many musclecar fans even today, the 4-4-2 reference stood for the original car's "four-barrel carburetion, four-on-the-floor, and dual exhausts."

While most early musclecars were typified by a big engine in a not-so-big body, the 4-4-2 had to wait for its fair share of large-displacement power. Standard underhood fair in 1964 was this 330-cubic-inch Rocket V-8, rated at 310 horsepower. The chrome treatments appearing here are non-stock, owner-installed touches.

AMA ban, this time in reference to Kenosha, Wisconsin's, American Motors, which at the time remained in accordance with the 10-year-old edict in yeoman, if not puritanical, fashion. But not for long. Like Ford had earlier, AMC was then preparing to trade a dull, boring image for one of fast furiousness, using racing wins and high-performance teases as selling tools right alongside proven practicality.

At Ford, Iacocca's plan to pull his company out of its late-'50s doldrums quickly formulated into the "Total Performance" campaign, a promotional program that involved an unprecedented multi-million-dollar factory supported racing effort that soon spread its influence around the world. By 1966, Ford-powered race cars had seemingly won it all; on NASCAR superspeedways and NHRA drag strips, at Indy, across the Atlantic at Le Mans. But what did Total Performance mean back here on Mainstreet U.S.A?

Iacocca's answer to the press came on April 19, 1963:

"To many, performance is thought of as top speed and acceleration. It is that, for sure, but it is also much more. Performance is roadability. Roadability is what allowed Dan Gurney to win [NASCAR's] Riverside 500, a race in which the average speed was only 90 miles per hour. Performance also is braking power—not just the brute ability to lock the wheels, but the smooth, balanced division of stopping power to each wheel. It is steering, the precision with which the driver's command is passed on to the wheels. It is suspension that soaks up bumps without wheel bounce; traction that keeps going in mire; seats scientifically contoured to resist weariness. Total performance literally is hundreds of things that let you control an automobile more safely and cover ground more swiftly.

"When Ford built the world's first low-priced V-8 in 1932 critics said it was dangerous and extravagant; that the 'average man' didn't need such power and would abuse it. Today, there still are critics who say performance above a certain level should be forbidden. This is not sound logic. Even the lowest powered [American] cars can top 80 miles per hour—and that is speed enough to be dangerous if you misuse it.

"Performance has been integral in the long history of the Ford Motor Company. Today, Americans are driving cars that [handle] better, [are] easier to control and—in many cases, capable of speeds greater than the racing cars of only a few years ago. We at Ford believe in performance, because the search for performance—Total Performance—made the automobile the wonderfully efficient, pleasurable machine it is today—and will make it better tomorrow."

Iacocca's words aside, Ford's definition of performance remained tough to understand for most daily drivers in the early '60s as Dearborn's high-powered products looked strong at the track, yet paled considerably on the street. Discounting the occasional 427 Galaxie and a small collection of racing-inspired specialty machines, Blue-Oval musclecars didn't really start rolling until 1968, when, coincidentally, Semon Knudsen became Ford Motor Company president after resigning as GM's executive vice president.

Bunkie had left Pontiac in November 1961, moving over to Chevrolet to continue pumping a performance image there while on the way up GM's corporate ladder. In his place as PMD general manager went Pete Estes, while John DeLorean moved up into the chief engineer's chair. Bill Collins, who played a major part in the Super Duty program, was DeLorean's main man in engineering.

Yet another prime player in Pontiac's performance scheme at the time was Jim Wangers, part-time drag racer, full-time advertising man for PMD's ad agency, MacManus, John and Adams. Having joined the firm in June 1958, Wangers' early responsibilities included writing sales promotions. But he also promoted Pontiac's rapidly rising performance image from behind the wheel, driving "Hot Chief," a Super Duty Catalina, to both the Super Stock and Top Stock Eliminator titles at the NHRA Nationals in Detroit on Labor Day 1960. And like Iacocca at Ford, Wangers was well aware of who would be buying these potent Pontiacs in the decade ahead.

As Eric Dahlquist later concluded—with no concessions to the father of the Mustang—in a 1973 *Motor Trend* review, "Jim Wangers is maybe the most savvy marketing man who ever drove down Detroit's Woodward Avenue. When he discovered a strike richer than the Comstock lode—the Youth Market—he came to wield as much product influence as some general managers." By 1963, Wangers had become, in Dahlquist's words, "convinced that the time was ripe for a special, new kind of automobile, a hybrid that melded European sports car flair with big, gut-pulling American V-8 engines." And he wasn't going to stop until he had convinced Pontiac insiders of the same thing.

This new kind of automobile may have required a big American V-8, but what it didn't need was a big American body. Discounting a Rambler here or a Crosley there, nearly all American cars of the '50s only came in one size—full—meaning that all previous performance cars also only came in one size—large. Individual automakers (Big Three automakers, that is) didn't start offering multiple model lines—an arrangement taken for granted for 30-some years now—until 1959, when Chevrolet kicked off the American compact era with its "pancake-six" Corvair.

Ford followed suit with McNamara's Falcon in 1960, as did Chrysler Corporation with the Valiant. In 1962, Dearborn expanded its line-up once more, this time trying an intermediate route with its downsized Fairlane, a model running midway between its full-size Galaxie and the compact Falcon.

GM's "senior compacts," Buick's Special and Oldsmobile's F-85, appeared in 1961. Included in the senior compact deal was a little more size, a lot more prestige, and a bit more engine than the air-cooled Corvair—a small V-8, cast of aluminum no less, was standard.

More closely related to the economical, Spartan Chevy II, which debuted in 1962, Pontiac's new small car for 1961, the Tempest, was a budget buggy powered by a standard "slant-four" engine—created, curiously, by simply sawing Pontiac's 389 V-8 in half. Additional Tempest innovations included independent rear suspension incorporating a transaxle tied to the slant four by a deflected "rope driveshaft," the latter used to reduce vibration. All this engineering wonderment packed into such a small, practical package helped earn Pontiac its second "Car of the Year" award from *Motor Trend*, the first having honored the all-new Wide Tracks in 1959.

In 1963, Pontiac fitted the upscale Tempest, the LeMans, with an optional 326 V-8, a refreshing 260-horse shot in the arm that nonetheless fell well short of transforming the big compact into a true performance machine. On the other hand, the dozen or so '63 Tempests built with 421 Super Duty V-8s for factory-experimental (FX) drag racing competition were veritable rockets on wheels. But of course these totally uncivilized beasts were meant only for professional racers, never for the street.

Super Duty shenanigans such as these were shot down anyway once GM kill-joys' cease and desist memo came down from the 14th floor early in 1963. Considering their public claim of the previous year that their divisions were still abiding by the anti-racing ban, how could GM executives have stood by while Pontiac and Chevrolet openly courted racing glory?

"Ever since the AMA adopted—I think you can term it a recommendation—back in 1957, we have had

Buick in 1965 combined loads of class and prestige with a beefed chassis and Wildcat power, then wrapped it all up in its tidy Skylark bodyshell to produce the Gran Sport, a "gentleman's bomb" as most saw it.

Buick's GS initially relied on the division's antiquated "nailhead" V-8 for standard power, in this case the 325-horsepower, 401-cubic-inch "Wildcat 445" big-block. A thoroughly modern 400-cubic-inch big-block V-8 would appear in 1967.

a policy on our books, and we haven't had any change in it," explained Chairman Frederic Donner at a press conference held February 16, 1963. Fine. So what about the Grand Sport Corvettes, Super Duty Pontiacs, and Mystery Motor Chevys? "Very often you run into interpretations of policies that to an outsider might look like violations," continued Donner. "That distance between interpretation and violation is a very delicate one."

Not so delicate was what Donner's words smelled like. Obviously, GM people had chosen to see no evil until external pressures forced their hands. To many, Donner's response to his company's escalating performance practices may have appeared as a reply to ever-

present, yet calm automotive safety concerns. Perhaps closer to reality were GM concerns involving possible anti-trust action then simmering in Washington. Stopping Pontiac and Chevrolet in their tracks was a convenient way to sidestep any additional unwanted attention as GM attempted to "keep its nose clean" while tiptoeing around what some federal lawmakers claimed were monopolistic business practices. Not at all willing to play shell games with Donner was crusading Senator Robert Kennedy, who—inspired by the arrogance of both the man and his mega-corporation—later minced no words at all while heatedly taking GM's chairman to task during the Ribicoff auto safety hearings in 1965.

Whether it was political posturing or not, GM's anti-racing stance stood reasonably firm in 1963. And along with banning factory involvement at the track, Donner's office also instituted a maximum displacement limit for all GM models—discounting Chevrolet's Corvette—below the full-sized ranks. V-8s could be used, but they could not exceed a size amounting to one cubic inch per 10 pounds of curb weight—a 3,400-pound car could be equipped only with an engine measuring less than 340 cubic inches. Simplified, the limit was generally reported at 330 cubic inches, which, appropriately enough, was the size of Oldsmobile's new small V-8 for

1964. Between that engine and Pontiac's 326 was Chevrolet's 327-cubic inch small-block, also newly introduced that year.

This 330-cubic inch restriction applied to compacts as well as GM's new intermediate A-body line-up. Previously relying on unit-body construction, the "B-O-P" triumvirate—Buick's Special/Skylark, Oldsmobile's F-85/Cutlass, and Pontiac's Tempest/LeMans—all were reborn in 1964 on the longer, full-framed A-body chassis. Yet another A-body, Chevrolet's midsized Chevelle, was introduced that year.

So was the GTO.

GM paperwork may have limited how much engine could go into those new A-bodies, but it failed to keep a lid on Jim Wangers' enthusiasm. What were 63 little cubic inches, anyway? As was apparent to DeLorean's engineering crew already, Pontiac's 389 V-8 used the same motor mounts and was the same size externally as its 326-cubic inch little brother—in Wangers' speed-sensitive opinion, dropping the bigger, badder big-block beneath a LeMans hood would be a piece of cake. DeLorean and Bill Collins had toyed with a 389-powered Tempest in 1963, but predictably found the unit-body/rear-transaxle layout to be an uncooperative patient as far as a potent performance infusion was concerned. This was not the case concerning the 1964 A-body platform with its rigid, perimeter-rail frame, conventional transmission location, and solid rear axle.

Recognizing this obvious opportunity, Wangers put his idea on paper late in 1963. As he explained in a 1991 *Automobile Quarterly* (volume 29, number 2) account, "I wrote a memo to DeLorean suggesting the creation of a new Super LeMans for 1964 to help make the market forget quickly about the unfortunate slant four, rope driveshaft era. The cast iron 326 was already scheduled as the available V-8 option, so why not set up a super high-performance version with the larger displacement 389-cubic-inch V-8? What an image builder! [It] could provide Pontiac with a one-of-a-kind high-performance specialty car that no one else could offer."

According to Pontiac's high-performance hype-master, DeLorean wrote "Has Wangers got something here?" across the top of the memo, and sent it to Collins. "How soon do you want to drive it, John?," came Collins' reply. A prototype was at that moment almost completed. So much for the groundwork.

Making the 389 LeMans a production reality was another story. GM executives weren't about to look the other way this time. They didn't have to. With Pete Estes's approval and support, DeLorean managed to sneak the car through corporate entanglements before anyone could say no. Some tried. Sales Manager Frank Bridge hated the idea, and reportedly said so in loud

tones. Estes, on the other hand, was all in favor. As Wangers put it, Pete told Bridge, "you certainly ought to be able to get rid of 5,000 of those. The really big job is gonna be mine in handling the corporation." Without Estes's influence at the top, the project undoubtedly would've never gotten past the proposal stage.

The key to the whole plot involved how the car was packaged. A new model needed committee approval from an upper level to reach production. Such a stumbling block would've never been breached. Instead, Estes' group created a special options package, which required nothing in the way of corporate approval. Official release of the package came October 1, 1963.

Conveniently buried at the bottom of the 1964 LeMans order sheet, option code W62 included a 389 V-8 wearing high-compression 421 heads, dual exhausts, a Hurst-shifted manual trans, beefy suspension, and U.S. Royal Tiger Paw redline treads. Subtle exterior identification was accomplished by adding twin dummy hood scoops, typical badging, and a blacked-out grille. Fed by a single four-barrel carburetor in standard form, that 389 produced 325 horsepower. Adding Pontiac's trademark Tri-Power upped the output ante to 348 horses.

Once into the dealer network, the W62 option wasn't going to be withdrawn, no matter how much the guys on the 14th floor wailed. As it was, their complaints were soon drowned out by the sounds of Tiger Paws clawing at pavement all across the country. And with their hands forced by the obvious presence on the streets of a GM intermediate with an engine larger than 330 cubic inches, upper office decision-makers had no choice but to

CONTINUED ON PAGE 39

The ever-present Bunkie Knudsen—then Chevrolet general manager—introduces the all-new A-body Chevelle, in top Super Sport trim, to the press in August 1963. Having already played a major role in turning Pontiac into a hot car company, Knudsen later quit General Motors in 1968 to join archrival Ford, where he once again began working his high-performance magic.

Performance 101

The concept of putting a lotta power in not-a-lotta car actually predated the GTO by three decades. Buick in the '30s had begun offering the big Roadmaster straight-eight in the lighter Special body, calling this hot package the Century. Then GM engineers introduced their first modern overhead-valve V-8 in 1949. This new engine was exciting enough as a Cadillac powerplant; beneath the hood of a much lighter, more agile Oldsmobile, it was downright thrilling. Thanks to its industry leading power-to-weight ratio, the Olds Rocket 88 represented—in many opinions— Detroit's first musclecar.

It's mostly a matter of semantics. That is, determining which car truly was Detroit's first musclecar. Granted, Pontiac's GTO does stand as a milestone; it was initially unique in its specific approach to the youth market, and it was the muscle-bound machine that helped bulldoze the way for an entirely new age. But there was a bigger picture—American performance history didn't just begin in 1964. And Pontiac certainly wasn't the first to stuff a bigger, more powerful engine into a smaller, lighter car.

Buick designers just before World War II may well deserve credit for first realizing that abiding by physical laws was better than trying to beat them. In 1936, the gentlemen from Flint introduced their Century, which used the big, heavy Roadmaster's powerful straight-eight engine in a platform based on the less-hefty Special's shorter wheelbase. This simple combination quickly placed the Buick Century among this country's cars to beat, both on the street and at the track. And it remained as such well into the '50s.

Then along came GM's modern, trend-setting overhead-valve V-8s in 1949. Of high-winding, short-stroke design, the new 160-horsepower 331-cubic inch V-8 qualified Cadillac as Detroit's most powerful offering. At the same time, Oldsmobile put a smaller 303-cube version to work hauling around a lot less tonnage. With a power-to-weight-ratio that probably ranked as Detroit's best, the 135-horsepower Rocket 88 instantly transformed Oldsmobile into the leader of the postwar performance pack—and an early dominator on the newborn NASCAR stock car racing circuit.

In the '50s, a stock car was very much a stock car, or at least it could then be compared far more closely to what you could buy off the showroom floor. Thus, when those "Fabulous Hudson Hornets" with "Twin-H Power" started winning NASCAR races by the bunch in 1951, witnesses knew streetside Hudsons were no slouches, regardless of how many your grandma had driven. Armed with two less cylinders than their V-8 rivals, Hudson's Hornets were indeed among the hottest cars around up until the "stepdown" model was discontinued after 1954.

In 1955, Chrysler picked up where Hudson had left off as the brutish 300 letter-series models began kicking tail on NASCAR tracks like nothing ever seen before. Chrysler's C-300 took its name from its power source, the 300-horsepower 331 Firepower "hemi" V-8—"hemi" for hemispherical combustion chambers. Introduced in 1951, the innovative Firepower V-8 was always among Detroit's strongest engines in the '50s. When it was included as part of Chrysler's luxurious letter-series package in 1955, the hemi helped redefine American-style performance.

While many "old-timers" point to the Olds Rocket 88 as being Detroit's first musclecar, the Chrysler 300 does qualify—discounting independent oddities like the Muntz Jet—as the first American car engineered and marketed as a pure performance machine. Again, remember, the single-faceted Corvette, introduced in 1953, was classed by itself as a sports car. As it was, the comfortable, status-laden C-300 was every bit as quick in 1955 as a cramped, somewhat crude V-8 Corvette, even with the big luxury cruiser's obvious weight handicap.

That handicap was never a factor as the letter legacy continued on in proud, powerful fashion; the 300B made the scene in 1956, followed by the 300C, 300D, and so on, all offering loads of luxury with an equal amount of prestigious performance.

Chrysler Corporation broadened its performance image in 1956, following up in the 300's tire tracks with two other limited-edition, high-powered products, DeSoto's Adventurer and Plymouth's Fury, and a NASCAR-inspired options group, Dodge's dominating D-500. While the Adventurer would soon fade along with the division that built it, and the Fury would lose its exclusive appeal after 1958, the D-500 remained a hot option up though 1961.

While Chrysler divisions were warming things up, Chevrolet engineers were busy dropping Corvette V-8s into passenger cars, first with twin four-barrel carburetors in 1956, then with Ramjet fuel injection the following year. Studebaker supercharged its Golden Hawk in 1957, as did Ford its Thunderbird before the AMA racing ban brought such shenanigans to a halt—at least in Dearborn terms.

Chevrolet and corporate cousins Oldsmobile and Pontiac, a division reborn in 1956 under new management, continued pumping up performance projects even after the AMA edict was inked. Both Olds and Pontiac added triple carbs in 1957, and the latter also tried fuel injection that year. Chevrolet introduced "three deuces" in 1958 atop its new 348-cubic inch V-8, the forerunner of the famed 409, itself unveiled along with the first of Chevy's popular Super Sport models in 1961.

By then, automakers had become entangled in the factory super stock battles. If musclecars of the '60s could be considered sumo wrestlers, an early-'60s super stocker was Godzilla—and poor Tokyo wasn't the target. Aimed primarily at good ol' American drag strips, all super stocks were ultra-high-compression, fuel- (and often oil-) gulping, open-exhaust-belching, bare-bones beasts built only to race.

PMD's outrageous 421 Super Duty, born late in 1961, was soon joined in 1962 by Mopar's 413 Max Wedge, and later on by Chevy's Z11 409, which actually displaced 427 cubic inches. In 1963, Mopar forces upped the super stock ante with an even larger, more-brutal 426 Max Wedge. Then Chrysler blew everyone away the next year with the 426 race hemi, a totally uncivilized animal that literally did change all the rules. NASCAR officials banned the race hemi in 1965, claiming it wasn't a stock production engine. No problem. The 426 street hemi appeared as a regular production option in 1966 to make everything legal.

By then, the supercar had taken over as the youth market stepped up in droves, all ready for a less exotic, far less expensive brand of performance that worked as well running to the store as it did rampaging down a quarter-mile. The factory super stocker quickly faded from the scene. In its place came the mass-marketed machine known and loved today as "the musclecar."

Whether you believe the musclecar was born in 1964, 1949, 1955, or whenever, you can't leave this page behind without be treated to a treatise that, in *Motor Trend's* December 1967 issue, tried to define the then latest new breed of American automobile. And explain its arrival. All in a bit more than 25-words-or-less.

Slip this long-winded, somewhat groovy ode to the supercar on for size:

"There's no one energized soul among the entire Enthusiasm Generation who deserves all the credit for this whole supercar bag. These mechanical muscles just happen to represent the final, universal coupe-de-grace cop-out on conventional civilization that began the moment some hairy-faced, stogie-smoking rebel turned his back on Austria some 75 years ago and went home and started writing about everybody's Id. From that moment on, you couldn't fight it. One by one the insouciant rascals of the new lands said they were tired of all the dumb things that were going on and that it was about time to get about this business of living. So, they became educated early and asserted themselves and did some dumb things, but eventually, some found their goal—their faculty of feeling. And your supercar, m'boy, is an expression of that faculty. Too many followers still do dumb things, like scorn education and drive like a latent something-or-other, but most of the others know what it all means. . . namely, that the whole world is up tight with several kinds of strife and dehumanizing technocracies, and about the best thing we can all use right now is a good, old fashioned emotional enema. So, what the centerfold syndrome doesn't satisfy, the supercar does. Back in '63 the same kind of receptive nerve ends at Pontiac detected that somewhere out there in torque-thrilled jollyland were scads of potential synapses tingling for activity, yet lying idle on the brink of deterioration with the rest of the walking, talking residue of the Industrial Revolution. Sure, Pontiac was planted deep in the middle of the Great Midwest, but they were capable of those same, honest, God-given sensations of touch and sound and sight and smell, as the rest of us. There are two differences. They knew what to do and were in a position to do it. Voila! The 1964 GTO! Covered with hair, just like that first rebel, and stuffed with the quivering thews of 375 [sic] long-armed, Detroit-type horses, it was nearly everything the churning viscera could want. . . movements and sensations and sweet, audible, bellowing strength. The monkey was gone from the back of spirited youth, and within a year or two, every manufacturer had a version of good ol' Catharsis-Eight. For the few without reason, it is transient, blind relief. . . but those with reason, for whom the supercar is intended, have recovered a substantial part of that adventure and feeling to which all of us are entitled as long as we are human."

Can you dig it?

Still others believe this machine was the first true musclecar. In 1955, Chrysler combined luxury and prestige with its hot 331 hemi V-8, creating the C-300, a car named for its industry-leading horsepower figure, 300 of course. Although obviously much bigger and heavier, this beautiful brute could still run right along with Chevrolet's sporty Corvette. Chrysler Historical Archives

CONTINUED FROM PAGE 35

adjust the rules, making 400 cubes the new top limit for the corporation's lesser model lines beginning in 1965. Later, in 1970, even that limit would disappear as Pontiac, Oldsmobile, and Buick began arming their mid-sized musclecars with the massive 455-cubic-inch big-block, Chevy its 454 Mk IV V-8.

As for Pontiac's first musclecar in 1964, DeLorean (and perhaps Collins) is credited for once more borrowing on someone else's high-flying image when it came time to find a name. First came Bonneville in 1957, then LeMans in 1961, Grand Prix in 1962. This time, it was "Gran Turismo Omologato," Enzo Ferrari's fabled label for his legendary 1962 red racer. In Yankee terms, Ferrari's words meant Grand Touring Homologated, the last word referring to the process by which a production car becomes legal to race in sanctioned competition.

As Wangers recalled in 1996, "John [DeLorean] basically came up with the idea. At the time, GTO was a really fresh, new image in the U.S. marketplace, thanks to Ferrari. We rationalized that Ferrari did not have a lock on the name—it was a generic term belonging, if to anyone, to the FIA [Federation Internationale de l'Automobile, racing's international governing body]. It was an FIA classification term. No way anybody could claim absolute ownership of it. Ferrari didn't qualify anyway, they didn't build enough cars to claim title to it."

Yet no one in the sports car world cared that Enzo had failed to meet homologation standards with his 250 GTO; he didn't build the FIA-required 100 production examples in a given 12-month span. A legend was still a legend. And in many opinions, Pontiac's GTO represented an outrageous affront to Ferrari's legend.

"These thefts were bad enough," began a March 1964 *Road & Track* tirade, in reference to the LeMans and Grand Prix. "Now, however, Pontiac has gone even further, lifting the exact designation of a highly successful GT racing car. There is an unforgivable dishonesty in such a practice as this and the insult should be sufficient to prevent any intelligent person from regarding it with anything except derision."

After using two pages to calm down a bit, *Road & Track's* reviewers did manage to temporarily overlook that insult, claiming the '64 GTO was "quiet, smooth docile, relatively inexpensive and definitely a touring car, not a racing car." But then they just had to get in one last parting shot. "We think that if the name-calling committee had chosen something more fitting the car, there would be no argument, because it is a good machine. But a real GTO? Not in our humble opinion."

David E. Davis' staff at *Car and Driver* didn't quite take it so hard, beginning an early GTO review by pointing out that the "purist crowd is so offended by the pirating of a Ferrari name that they can do little but stamp their collective foot and utter lady-like oaths about the inequity of it all." Continued the *CD* report, "what they overlooked in their hysterical spleen-venting is that the Pontiac GTO, suitably equipped with catalog options, is one of the best high speed touring cars in the world."

Then came the cover story to end all cover stories, an epic creation (in more ways than one) that helped hammer both Pontiac's GTO and *Car and Driver* magazine into the car crowd's collective consciousness.

Once again it was Jim Wangers' idea.

The subtle fashion by which the GTO was initially threaded through GM red tape also helped contribute to a definite drought early on as far as good promotional ink was concerned. Suitable test vehicles for the press were just not readily available late in 1963. For a December 1963 *Hot Rod* review, Ray Brock relied on a fully loaded, 325-horsepower, automatic-transmission, highway-axled convertible, not exactly a combination you'd call top performance. Although he was enthusiastic about the car, Brock's test results were predictably tame. Wangers was predictably pissed.

Describing Brock's *Hot Rod* review as "an insult to all Pontiac's hard work," "the most involved and aggressive press agent in all of Detroit," as Davis called him, then set out to do the car justice. First, he had DeLorean supply him with two specially prepared GTO coupes. He then took them to Ace Wilson's Royal Pontiac in Royal Oak, Michigan. Wilson's dealership had, since 1959, been home to much Pontiac performance development, as well as many successful drag racing projects. There, Wangers' two GTOs were given the "Bobcat" treatment, consisting of all the hottest PMD parts available and a few well-rehearsed tweaks. No, these Royal Bobcat GTOs weren't "factory stock," not even close. But that didn't stop Wangers from making them available for a *Car and Driver* road test.

And it certainly didn't stop Davis from testing them. Or putting one of them on his cover, albeit by way of artist's rendition. Along with a Ferrari GTO. In a side-by-side shootout. Beneath a banner reading "Tempest GTO: 0-100 in 11.8 sec."

In Wangers' always-racing mind, the GTO vs. GTO matchup was a natural. "We felt it was a neat idea," he

Ford men, at first slow to react to the GTO's challenge, chose instead to keep running with the big, rarely seen 427 Galaxies and spritely Mustangs, the latter armed with the 271-horsepower "High Performance" 289 in top form. Fairlanes had been using the "Hi-Po" 289 since 1963, a fact quickly lost on horsepower hounds who recognized in 1964 that there was no substitute for cubic inches—and GM had many more to offer.

Opposite: Only 200 '65 Malibu SS 396s—known today by their RPO code, Z16—were built, with one additional convertible reportedly going to a company official. Excluding that Sierra Tan ragtop, Z16 exterior shades were Regal Red, Tuxedo Black, or Crocus Yellow. All were fully loaded promotional machines featuring as standard equipment a 375-horsepower 396 big-block, a Muncie four-speed, big Impala brakes, and a rigid convertible frame with a beefed suspension and rear sway bar. The mag-style wheelcovers were also standard.

Mercury's first mid-sized musclecar arrived, almost in secret, well into the 1964 model year. Initially, the Cyclone offered much more performance imagery than real performance. Standard features included simulated chrome-wheel wheelcovers. But beneath the hood was a mundane 210-horsepower 289. This '65 Cyclone is one of 12,347 built.

A sporty interior was a standard Cyclone feature from the beginning. In this '65 Cyclone's case, optional gauges atop the dash join the typical tach. Buckets and a floor shifter were part of the deal.

remembers, "even though we knew we didn't belong on the same track. But if we could just stay with the Ferrari. . . ."

Davis loved the idea, basically because he was at the time hot for a way to vault his newly renamed magazine—it had just been reborn from its *Sports Car Illustrated* roots—into the American mainstream. "I didn't know then that they were rethinking their entire image," added Wangers. "They had recognized they'd better jump on the Detroit bandwagon and quit that sports car kick." Wangers' idea looked like just the ticket, if only they could get their hands on the Ferrari side of the showdown.

A privately held 250 GTO could not be found, and Luigi Chinetti, head of Ferrari's North American dealer works, wasn't quite so keen on the idea. The Italian-American road test comparison was, according to Wangers, "a lose-lose situation for Ferrari." A Prancing Horse would gain nothing by trampling a Goat. "Chinetti saw it that way," Jim continued, "he wasn't about to make a GTO available to us." Instead, *Car and Driver's* crew simply created a mythical matchup, using the definitely real high-banks of Daytona International Speedway as a stage for their fantasy play.

"We sailed around Daytona like crazy people, had the times of our lives and shared a growing gut feeling that we were really on to something," Davis later wrote in 1975. "The staff bought the GTO's act with a unanimity rare in our experience. And we said so."

Written mostly by Davis, *Car and Driver's* famous March 1964 cover story did point out the obvious, that such a comparison was very much akin to pairing apples with oranges. If the two GTOs had indeed met, the Pontiac would've been no match on a European-style road course. Then again, the Ferrari wouldn't have stood a chance on a Yankee drag strip, not after the Royal Bobcat machine screamed through the quarter-mile in an unbelievable 13.1 seconds, topping out at 115 miles per hour. Sixty miles per hour from rest took only 4.6 shocking ticks, with the aforementioned 100 miles per hour plateau incredibly reached after another 7.2 seconds. "Ferrari never built enough GTOs to earn the name anyway," came *Car and Driver's* classic conclusion. "Just to be on the safe side though, Pontiac built a faster one."

Exactly how much faster was a product of both Wangers' loose definition of factory stock and Davis' feigned dedication to proper and exacting statistical analysis. "You've got to remember," recalled Wangers with a chuckle, "all timing was done with hand-held stopwatches; there was not a whole lot of accuracy involved. But since the numbers went in our favor I wasn't about to complain. The magazine's [0-100 in 11.8 seconds] cover blurb? That car wouldn't have done that

rolling off the top of the Empire State Building." Ten years later, Davis remained unrepentant in every way, but humorously recalled that blurb, "which the magazine's technical department still hasn't lived down."

Car and Driver readers in 1964 couldn't get to their corner mailboxes fast enough after seeing that cover. "I am at a loss for words to describe the utter scorn I have for this piece of very bad, very dishonest journalism," wrote Henry E. Payne III from Charleston, West Virginia. Typing in two-part harmony, John and Al Hatch announced from New Jersey that they'd "finally been exposed to the most asinine article to ever appear in any sports car magazine, bar none! Is this a sports car magazine or a Detroit propaganda bulletin?" Added Texan Courtland Bell, "I would like to protest such irresponsible journalism as your magazine put forth concerning the Pontiac Tempest. You boys should really try to do better if you expect to stay in the business."

Davis' magazine did stay in business; better than ever, in fact. Pumped-up Pontiac propaganda or not, that controversial cover story, according to its author, "accomplished just what we had been trying to do for months: to get the attention of the audience and clearly establish us as a contender in the automotive publishing

Chrysler was never a weakling when it came to muscle, but fell well short of its GM rivals as far as a go-fast image was concerned. Thus, cars like this '65 Satellite with its potent 426 wedge big-block were easily overlooked in Detroit's early musclecar race.

Not to be confused with its totally uncivilized 426 Max Wedge and 426 race hemi cousins, Plymouth's 1965 426 street wedge represented a more socially acceptable way to flex Mopar muscle. Output was 365 horses for this more practical big-block.

biz. *Car and Driver* was finally on its way—and the GTO did it."

On the flip side, that cover story also helped do it for the GTO. "It was absolutely magnificent publicity for us," concluded Wangers. "It was one of the most significant pieces of merchandising we did." A bit overwritten, perhaps, but Davis' account of the thrilling new GTO's feel supplied the bold ink Wangers had sought. "People read his words then went into a Pontiac dealership and felt it for themselves. The car burned rubber forever, because of those massively inferior tires, and the carburetors howled thanks to those low-restriction breathers. It *was* a thrill."

Pontiac's first supercar was, of course, nowhere near as formidable in mild-mannered stock form as *Car and Driver* made out. Yet, although the original GTO wasn't more powerful than a locomotive, it was a 15-flat performer in the quarter-mile, it was able to do the time-honored 0–60 trek in a click less than seven seconds, and it could look awfully cool while doing it. It could also

carry the family comfortably along when it wasn't. It may not have been a Ferrari killer in real life, but this new American automobile was unlike anything a Yankee horsepower hound had ever seen.

"The real difference between the GTO and everything else of its type at the time was muscle," read Davis' 1975 recount. "Back in 1964, Ford was pumping millions of dollars into a vast promotion called 'Total Performance,' and all the racing entrepreneurs in the country were benefiting hugely from massive transfusions of Ford money. But Ford couldn't make it happen on the street. Not so, GTO. The basic GTO with the basic hot set-up just let you climb inside and then asked you, 'How far, how soon, daddy?' [NASCAR driver] Fred Lorenzen might run like hell in his Holman-Moody Ford, but somehow the [Fords] you could buy never made your eyes bug out. Pontiac, on the other hand, put it right out there on the street; and the seekers of truth along Woodward Avenue and Ventura Boulevard understood."

The storm may have soon calmed following *Car and Driver's* theatrics in early 1964, but the GTO's presence continued growing in prominence, thanks both to its own individual performances as well as even more high-profile promotional ploys. One of Pontiac's earliest advertisements claimed the '64 GTO was "for the man who wouldn't mind riding a tiger if someone'd only put wheels on it." Let U.S. Royal put "Tiger Paws" on the road and Esso a "Tiger in Your Tank"—it was Pontiac that put you behind the wheel of "the Tiger."

That summer, *G.T.O.*, by Ronny and the Daytonas, rode Billboard's chart at number three for 17 weeks, selling 1.25 million copies along the way. Others in the

"California sound" crowd, including the Beach Boys and Jan and Dean, tried to jump onto the Tiger bandwagon with similar singles of their own, but missed the boat—the former after asking too much money for the chance to cut a GTO single before the Daytonas.

The Tiger image took full flight in 1965, appearing prominently in dealer gimmicks, print ads, and over the airwaves; the latter by way of *GeeTO Tiger*, a Pontiac-created promotional tune sung by—who'd a-thunk it?—The Tigers.

It may not have played all that long on the radio, but this little propaganda ditty did play a major role in a special promotion sponsored by the ever-present Hurst Performance Products company, in conjunction with the Petersen Publishing people, they of *Hot Rod* and *Motor Trend* fame. All an eager listener had to do was count the number of times "tiger" was used in *GeeTO Tiger*, write that figure down on a piece of paper along with 25 words or less explaining "why I would like to own the original GeeTO Tiger," and send it in to Hurst before July 31, 1965. Hurst Products' main man, George Hurst, and various Petersen editors then served as judges, picking 19-year-old Alex Lampone from the Milwaukee area as the grand prize winner. Lampone's prize was the original GeeTO Tiger, a customized '65 GTO wearing non-stock Hurst Gold paint and gold-anodized Hurst wheels.

Clearly, the GTO craze was really cooking after no more than a year on the road. Soon there were GTO shoes from Thom McAn and GTO cologne from Max Factor. There were various GTO trinkets and baubles and a club exclusively formed in 1965 for GTO lovers. For $3, these devotees could join "The Royal Bobcat Racing Team." Members received an I.D. card, jacket patch, decals, promotional publications, and the highly desired Royal Pontiac license plate frame. By 1969, some 55,000 of these frames had gone out to Royal Bobcat Racing Team loyalists of all ages.

Pontiac advertising relied heavily on the Tiger image up through 1966. Then, GM executive James Roche reportedly demanded an end to the campaign after apparently seeing a seductive Barbara Feldon selling Pontiacs while stretched out on a tiger-skin rug. And that was that. Nonetheless, even with the Tiger theme dead and buried, the GTO, now known as "The Great One," continued as one of the best publicized cars—if not *the* best—ever to roll out of Detroit. Thanks, in a big way, to Jim Wangers.

And The Great One continued making big automotive news, emerging in 1968 with a sexy, restyled body crowned with an innovative "Endura" front bumper. Molded in matching body colors, this new nose was both exceptionally attractive and wonderfully functional, its energy-absorbing plastic construction making it dent resistant. Claiming the Endura bumper promised "to revolutionize auto styling and design," *Motor Trend* responded to Pontiac's latest breakthrough by honoring the '68 GTO with its "Car of The Year" award.

Then along came the Judge in 1969. Originally born from a plan to create a bare-bones, all-business GTO to compete with the new breed of no-frills four-wheeled thrills introduced by Plymouth's Road Runner in 1968, the Judge ended up being somewhat of a supercar spoof, a winged-and-decaled image-grabber that was part television-inspired nonsense, all serious stoplight challenger. Standard power came from a 366-horse Ram Air III 400 V-8, with the mean and nasty 370-horsepower Ram Air IV 400—itself also new equipment for 1969—available on the options list. Again, as he had in 1964, DeLorean did the name-calling honors, picking up on the "here come da' judge" gag line then popularized by the television comedy hit "Laugh-In."

The hottest GTO? Without a doubt, the Ram Air IV variety qualified during its short stay on the scene in 1969 and 1970. The low-compression 455 HO GTO that followed in 1971 was no slouch, but it was the beginning of the end. The last LeMans-based GTO appeared totally restyled in 1973 with very little muscle beneath those two NACA-type ducts on its hood. Then came the little 350-powered Ventura GTO, an intriguing machine that many critics at the time welcomed warmly, yet still indicated that it was finally all over for the Goat—and for musclecars as a whole.

Only a 10-year run? It certainly seemed longer than that, especially considering all that went on during those years. And not just in Pontiac terms.

Once Estes, DeLorean, and the boys got things rolling in 1964, there was no stopping the American musclecar. Following Pontiac's lead, General Motors got the jump on the competition as Oldsmobile unleashed a tiger of its own in 1964, followed by Buick and Chevrolet in 1965.

Oldsmobile's first supercar began life, like the GTO, as an options package for its A-body intermediate, the F85. Introduced midyear, the "police apprehender pursuit package," option code B09, helped point the way to "where the actions is," at least according to Olds admen. Those ads also thankfully explained what that name meant—translated, "4-4-2" referred to the car's "four-barrel carburetion, four-on-the-floor, and dual exhausts." While many curbside kibitzers never did get it, and those defining numbers didn't always exactly apply—three-speed manuals and automatic transmissions were soon included in the mix—the 4-4-2 label quickly became one of the more revered musclecar monikers of the '60s. And continued so into the '70s, eventually ending up as one of the longest-running nameplates born in Detroit's supercar era.

"Pontiac had been tremendously successful with the GTO," said former Olds public relations man Jim Williams later in an interview with automotive writer Jan Norbye. "And the 4-4-2 was a way to attract people to [a similar] Oldsmobile product for those who were inclined to buy an Oldsmobile but would otherwise have gone to Pontiac."

According to Williams, Olds Chief Engineer John Beltz "wanted a street machine—not a hot rod." Thus, overall balance, instead of brute force, became the priority. Power came from a pumped-up 310-horsepower version of Oldsmobile's new 330-cubic inch Rocket V-8, certainly a high-level performer, but not out of this world by anyone's standards. *Car Life* reported acceleration numbers for the '64 4-4-2 as 7.4 seconds for 0–60, 15.6 for the quarter-mile.

While more muscle would come soon enough, the real key to the first 4-4-2's hot image was its chassis. Typically, all parts were "heavy-duty," including a hefty anti-sway bar up front. But not-so-typical was the car's standard rear anti-sway bar, a feature that had appeared earlier on American Motors's Rebel in 1957 and Chevrolet's Corvette beginning in 1960. As they always do, Oldsmobile's rear stabilizer helped keep the tail in line and greatly reduced body lean, which in turn helped keep more rubber on the road for increased sureness in the corners. "Although the car still basically understeers," commented *Car Life's* review, "it is within much more manageable bounds."

A quieter, more civilized kind of performer than its corporate cousin from Pontiac, Oldsmobile's 4-4-2 was also the product of a kinder, gentler promotional effort. "Olds never put the kind of push behind the 4-4-2 that Pontiac gave the GTO," Williams explained. That fact, combined with its midyear status, greatly inhibited first-year sales—only 2,999 '64 4-4-2 hardtop, coupes, and convertibles were built.

One year later, now with a 345-horsepower, 400-cubic inch big-block V-8 under its hood, the 4-4-2 legacy really started rolling as 25,003 buyers jumped on the bandwagon. Oldsmobile's first "W-machine," a truly hot 4-4-2-equipped with the W-30 ram-air big-block option, debuted—albeit in very rare, race-ready fashion—in 1966, helping put Olds into the "car-to-catch" category. By 1970, the 455-cubic inch W-30 4-4-2 was running right up with Detroit's best supercars.

That group included Buick's Stage 1 Gran Sport, introduced first in 400-cubic inch V-8 form in 1969, then also boosted up to 455 cubic inches the following year. The 455 Stage 1 represented the ultimate development in the Gran Sport bloodline, which itself had been born early in 1965. Obviously inspired by Pontiac and Oldsmobile's high-powered creations, the engineering crew in Flint dropped the big "Wildcat 445" V-8 from the full-sized

line into the mid-sized Skylark. A bit antiquated—the Wildcat 445 V-8 was of Buick's "nailhead" engine family, which dated back to the division's first modern overhead-valve V-8 in 1953—this big-block bully nonetheless churned out 325 horses and 445 foot pound of torque, thus its name. The first Gran Sport's V-8 displaced 401 cubic inches—one more than GM allowed in intermediate ranks, but who was counting?

Certainly not Buick General Manager Edward Rollert, who called the '65 Skylark GS "a completely engineered performance car designed to appeal to sports car enthusiasts." Simply saying "Zow!," Buick ads called the GS a "Superbird," a reference that would take flight again in much more dramatic fashion five years later splashed across Plymouth rear quarters.

Being from Flint, where "better cars" were built, Buick's gentlemanly GS, in the opinion of *Car Life's* editors, came "off stronger, more distinctive [than high-powered rivals from Chrysler, Olds, and Pontiac] and with something its owners can appreciate"—that being the Gran Sport package's asking price, only $200.53. For that two-hundred bucks, a Skylark buyer got the 401 V-8, a beefier convertible frame and those ever-present heavy-duty chassis upgrades—15,780 anteed up in 1965. Peak production year for the Gran Sport was 1968, when 26,345 were sold, more than half of those being the newly introduced GS 350 small-block variety.

Chevrolet entered the fray in full force early in 1965, more than a year after the always-in-motion Bunkie Knudsen, by then Chevy's general manager, introduced his division's all-new A-body to the press in August 1963. Debuting in top-flight Super Sport trim, the Chevelle was met with endless raves. "Impressed by its clean and handsome styling," read an August 30 *Time* report, "Detroit's normally undemonstrative auto reporters broke into spontaneous applause."

Impressive, certainly. Yet the Chevelle SS, with its 283-cubic inch small-block V-8, was still a lukewarm performer out of the blocks in 1964, and remained not much more so even after the enlarged 327 was made a midyear option. Full-fledged supercar status didn't come until February 1965, when Bunkie again took to the limelight, this time to announce the arrival of Chevrolet's hot, new 396-cubic inch Mk IV big-block V-8. A direct descendant of the NASCAR Mystery Motor that ran the 1963 Daytona 500, the 396 V-8 was introduced in three forms for three cars: the Corvette, the full-sized Caprice, and Chevy's equally new musclecar, the Malibu SS 396.

Planned as high-profile promotional ploy, the first SS 396 was a fully loaded showboat equipped with ample power (375 horses), a state-of-the-art chassis (big Impala brakes, rigid convertible frame, and standard rear stabilizer

In 1966, Dodge finally unveiled the image to go along with all that Mopar muscle: the eye-catching Charger with its flowing fastback body and four-bucket interior. Big news along with the Charger's arrival that year was the debut of the 426 street hemi. This '67 Charger is one of only 117 built with the 425-horsepower hemi. The small decklid lip spoiler was standard along with the hemi.

Although not all renditions qualified as musclecars, Dodge's Chargers of 1968 to '70 still represented perhaps one of the most exciting performance images of the musclecar era. Charger R/Ts with the hemi or 440 V-8 stood as the leaders of the pack. This '69 model is powered by the less-revered, yet still-strong 383 big-block.

Those greater numbers would come in 1966, although at a cost of much of the Z16's standard punch. The 375-horsepower 396, fake mags, mega-stereo, and bucket/console interior were all made options, with a tamer 325-horse Mk IV V-8 becoming the base big-block. Gone was the convertible frame, full-sized brakes, and rear stabilizer, all deep-sixed to help heighten the car's appeal by lowering its base sticker. In 1965, the Z16 Chevelle cost about $4,100; the following year, a more mass-marketed SS 396 began at about $2,800. At that price, the public came running. Sales hit 72,272 in 1966, and remained above 60,000 up through 1970, the year Chevrolet rolled out its SS 454 to join its proven SS 396 sales leader. King of the SS 454s, and undoubtedly one of the meanest musclecars ever to set rubber to the road, was the 450-horse LS-6 Chevelle, a one-hit wonder that came and went in 1970, just in time to make its memorable mark before the curtain began to fall on factory performance.

As mentioned, Ford Motor Company's early approach to the supercar market was more talk than walk. By 1966, Ford owned the world's race tracks, but streetside rivals to GM's new breed of mid-sized muscle were few and far between.

Dearborn's intermediate, the Fairlane, had been treated to Ford's optional 271-horsepower 289 small-block V-8 beginning in 1963, and this reasonably exciting package carried over into 1964 and 65. The "Hi-Po" Fairlane, however, was rarely seen and by no means possessed the image punch, nor performance potential needed to allow it to compete fairly in the GTO class. Even harder to come by, yet definitely dominating, were the formidable 427 Fairlanes of 1966 and 1967, limited-production, competition-conscious cars never meant for the masses. The less-exotic Fairlane GT, introduced in 1966 with Ford's 390 FE-series big-block and loads of sporty appeal, was a nice try, but these attractive, popular machines still didn't carry a stick big enough to whip up on comparable mid-sized competitors.

Mercury's initial approach was at least a bit more image-conscious. Midyear in 1964, the Cyclone appeared as the top performance offering in the Comet line. Racing-flag emblems, rather clever wheel covers that simulated chrome wheels, bucket seats, and a dash-mounted tachometer were all included as part of the Cyclone's standard appeal. Not included was suitable power. The 271-horsepower Hi-Po small-block was

bar), and lots of pizzazz (simulated mag wheel covers, bucket seats and console, and a Multiplex stereo system). No ifs, ands, or buts, this package—listed all together under option code Z16—was a high-flying crowd-pleaser. Wrote *Mechanix Illustrated*'s Tom McCahill, "there's nothing in this world, Charlie, like slipping down the turnpike being belted in the back by 375 horsepower and in the ear by 4-speaker Bach-power!"

Chevrolet built only 200 Z16 coupes (plus one mysterious convertible) in 1965, with many of those going to celebrities, press people, and various executives as part of a plan to obtain as much public exposure as possible. Along with being exceptionally hard to find, Chevy's first SS 396 was also a hard bargain. Regular production option (RPO) Z16 was priced at $1,501.05. Add that to a '65 Malibu Super Sport's $2,600 base price and we can only wonder how many drivers would've seen the U.S.A. in a Z16 Chevrolet had the car been built in greater numbers.

reportedly a rare option, but standard power came from a mundane 210-horse 289. A nice dose of obligatory chrome dress-up couldn't disguise the plain fact that the original Cyclone V-8 would never rank as a bully on the beach. Later Cyclones, however, would kick more than their fair share of sand in rivals' faces.

Sure, the big, brawny 427 Galaxies were nothing to sneeze at, and Hi-Po Mustangs were fast fun machines. But in Ford terms, a suitable supercar representative didn't make the scene until April 1968, when the 428 Cobra Jet V-8 debuted. A simple combination of existing off-the-shelf components, the 428 CJ, conservatively rated at 335 horsepower, instantly transformed the Mustang into Ford's street performance savior. The new Cobra Jet V-8 also served as a main motivator for Mercury's Cyclone Spoiler and a potent option for the Cougar Eliminator, introduced in 1969.

After seeing a pre-production Cobra Jet Mustang run early in 1968, *Hot Rod*'s Eric Dahlquist concluded that "the CJ will be the utter delight of every Ford lover and the bane of all the rest because, quite frankly, it is probably the fastest regular production sedan ever built." Rascals that they were, Ford admen put Dahlquist's comments to use as they saw fit, substituting "fastest running Pure Stock in the history of man," a line used near the end of his article, for "fastest regular production sedan ever built" in their advertisements.

Whatever the translation, the Cobra Jet Mustang was a winner on the street, as suddenly was Ford under the direction of newly hired General Manager Bunkie Knudsen, who in February 1968 brought his performance-packed résumé over from GM. Blue Oval performance offerings became plentiful during his short tenure. Fairlane Cobra. Talladega. Mach 1. Boss 302. Boss 429. A new-and-improved, even more powerful Cobra Jet variety, the 385-series 429 CJ, superseded its FE forerunner (in all models except Mustangs) for 1970—just after Henry Ford II chose to reverse his earlier earth-shaking decision and fire the over-aggressive Knudsen, just before Bunkie's replacement, Lee Iacocca, chose to pull the plug once more on the Better Idea breed of performance.

Much like Ford, Chrysler Corporation movers and shakers apparently cared very little about image early in the '60s, choosing instead to concentrate where it mattered most—under the hood. And looking a lot like Ford, Chrysler's most potent performance products then were aimed at the track—witness the 413 and 426 "Max

Wedge" super stockers of 1962 and 1963 and the 1964 426 "race hemi," the far-from-conventional fire breather that taught everyone a lesson in volumetric efficiency at Daytona that year.

If pumping aviation fuel into your Mopar wasn't for you, Chrysler in 1964 did introduce a "street wedge" version of its race-ready, 13.5:1 compression 426 Max Wedge V-8. The "426-S" V-8, rated at 365 horsepower, could propel a 3,700-pound '64 Plymouth Sport Fury from 0–60 in 6.8 impressive seconds, according to *Motor Trend*. Quarter-mile performance was listed as 15.2 seconds at 95.5 miles per hour, numbers easily comparable to the GTO. Yet the 426 street wedge Dodges and Plymouths of 1964-65 were easily lost in the Tiger's shadow, thanks entirely to lagging images and weak promotion.

Mopar muscle began gaining real notice in 1966 after the arrival of the legendary 426 "street hemi," Chrysler's white-hot descendant of its '50s Firepower V-8s. New that year as well was Dodge's Charger, a suitably sexy, high-profile home for those optional 425 hemi horses. Yet another muscle-oriented Dodge, the R/T—for "road/track"—debuted in 1967, as did Plymouth's GTX, both sporting humble doses of go-fast imagery, along with decent loads of real performance thanks to a standard 375-horsepower, 440 cubic-inch wedge V-8. Costing less with fewer standard cubes, the 383-powered Plymouth Road Runner and Dodge Super Bee arrived in 1968—from there, the race was really on.

Plymouth's pony car, which actually predated the Mustang, didn't begin qualifying for supercar status until big-block power became a Barracuda option in 1967. Same for Dodge's A-body, the Dart. Then in 1970, the meanest 'Cudas were joined by equally tough counterparts from Dodge wearing Challenger sheet metal. When armed with the 426 hemi in 1970 and 1971, these two mighty Mopar E-bodies ranked right up with some of the quickest musclecars ever built. The still-hot 340 small-block V-8 carried on as a reasonably formidable weapon of choice for 'Cuda and Challenger customers after the hemi and 440 were dropped after 1971, but it just wasn't the same.

By 1972, Mopar muscle had been stripped of most of its might, as had all but a select few rivals. What began in 1964 with Pontiac's GTO quickly wound down in the early '70s into a weak-kneed mire of fuel-conscious, emissions-choked, painted-up impostors. And average Joe would never look at performance driving the same way again.

Chapter Two

BUCKETS O' BOLTS
Mechanical Milestones & Techno-Trivia

Automobiles, as a whole, tend to be lifeless things; they don't have a heart, they don't actually respond to tender, loving care (although proper maintenance does occasionally help), and they certainly shouldn't be identified by a pronoun. Like "she." Real fine or not. C'mon, folks, these are machines, nothing more nothing less. Right?

Today, maybe so. Even in an age when reality has become virtual, Americans no longer seem to possess the same imagination we once did. Why should we when we can simply punch one up on a diode screen? While society has certainly developed a strong taste for technical wizardry, it has somehow lost the lust for most things mechanical. At least greasy things mechanical. Young people today couldn't care less about tinkering with gadgets like carburetors. Okay, bad example since carbs are essentially extinct; hopefully, you get the picture. If carburetors had survived, they already would've been long-since overshadowed by the personal computer as the major distraction for the modern young American—probably rightly so now that it takes a computer geek to work on a modern American car.

So what if it sounds fuddy-duddy, times were different 30 years ago. Young people did use their hands (not just their fingers) along with their minds. And, although the things they worked with were mechanical, there was a unique, all-too-warm relationship present—dare we say it?, a love between a boy and his car.

Most boys (and some girls) in the '60s and '70s weren't in love with just a car, it was a supercar, a special breed that deserved, as well as required, special care. Along with being a machine, the supercar was also an extension of many things truly personal; a sense of freedom, a celebration of youth, and even one's sexuality.

Owning, maintaining, and showing off a performance automobile wasn't just a job, it was an adventure. And an attitude. Maybe that's why so many fuddy-duddies in Washington hated the supercar so. It was just too much fun. As it was, many more penny-pinchers in Detroit also, at best, only tolerated high-performance sales in the '60s. As Carroll Shelby wrote in 1966, "the top officials of Detroit's auto companies hate cars." These executives didn't even bother to wave good-bye in the early '70s once this devilish breed was finally exorcised, both from the streets and our collective consciousness.

But to car lovers the loss was not soon forgotten. Motor vehicle ownership would never be the same again. Nor would motor vehicle operation for those who truly loved to drive. Life, however, didn't stop rolling with the supercar's demise. After all, these were still just buckets of bolts, remember? Beloved bolts, but bolts nonetheless. And main bearing seals. And ring gears. And wrist pins. And pressure plates. The supercars we all knew so well and cherished so fondly did represent the sum of many parts. And, boy, were most of those parts greasy.

Pulling all those components together to help put the muscle in musclecar was a full-time job three decades ago, and one that changed almost every day as progress progressed. Some cynics said Detroit in those days didn't always progress until it was finally forced to do so, and that may well have been the case involving certain arenas in the '60s. Primarily so concerning efficient emissions controls and driver safety. Related to that latter category

No, that's not an optional vacuum cleaner below the headlight on this '66 4-4-2. It's the intake duct for the ram-air equipment, part of the legendary W-30 performance package introduced that year.

Opposite: When the legend fits, wear it. Muscleheads can argue all day long as to which engine was king of the performance mill hill, but Chrysler's 426 street hemi still stands as perhaps the era's best recognized performance powerplant. It had real muscle—probably about 500 ponies—and a truly terrific macho image, thanks both to its massive underhood presence and such high-profile, head-turning add-ons as this "Shaker" hood scoop, made part of the Hemi 'Cuda deal in 1970.

were brakes, which couldn't quite keep up with the increasing power they were asked to rein in.

If automakers truly were guilty as charged of showing little concern for highway safety it was in this area. Brake design advancements had always lagged far behind underhood developments, dating back to the horsepower race's earliest escalations in the '50s. The situation was simple: if it ain't broke in the public's perception, don't spend all that retooling money to fix it. Any complaints about substandard braking in those days were commonly drowned out by all the raves over how powerful this country's top-performing automobiles were becoming. Apparently few curbside critics then cared that stopping a performance car was every bit as important as getting it rolling in rapid fashion. Working in this atmosphere, all Detroit's designers had to worry about was simply keeping up with the Joneses. As one understandably unnamed engineer told *Motor Trend* in 1958, "our company's brakes are as good as the rest of 'em, so why should we get all excited about radical, expensive new designs?"

While that outlandish attitude didn't quite carry over into the '60s—at least not so boldly—the stop-and-go gap such thinking helped create remained, meaning most musclecar drivers were always at a disadvantage when it came time to reverse the process initiated once

Disc brakes were slow in coming to the arena where they were needed most: the high-performance market. By 1969, front disc brakes were standard equipment on most musclecars. But earlier muscle machines had to settle mostly for mundane drums. Exceptions included this '67 Formula S 383 Barracuda from Plymouth.

rubber started melting on the road. Almost all early muscle machines of the mid-'60s came standard with not much more stopping power, if any, than the low-performance family sedans they were based on. And engineers could've added optional truck-size drums at the corners all day long and they still wouldn't have defeated the real enemy of confident braking under duress—fade caused by poor heat dissipation.

From the beginning of time, the prevailing attitude among brake designers has been bigger must be better—of course a true conclusion. Larger linings, wider drums with increased diameters, more total swept area did help stopping reaction better compete with its not-so-equal opposite action. But the long-pervasive drum brake design always has and always will feature one major inherent inadequacy. Heat build-up inside those drums during hard braking will forever produce brake fade as gases formed in the heat of friction actually serve to reduce friction forces between linings and drum surfaces. Not even a power booster can transform a heavy foot into stopping power once high heat takes over.

Solutions included special metallic linings, first used by Chevrolet's Corvette in 1956. While these shoes did resist fading when overheated, they almost didn't work at all when cold—not a worry on the racetrack, but a distinct disadvantage to the driver hoping to avoid running that first stop sign on the way to work in the morning.

Chevrolet also added finned drums to its heavy-duty brake packages, with the idea being to keep things cooler the same way a radiator lowers coolant temperature. Yet another improvement involved manufacturing drums out of aluminum instead of cast-iron—the former dissipates heat more efficiently than the latter. In 1958, Buick became the first major automaker to offer aluminum drums (fronts only) as standard equipment.

Of course, the real next step involved disc brakes, a concept almost as old as the automobile itself. Since their caliper-mounted friction pads and rotors are fully exposed to cooling airflows, disc brakes do not overheat as easily as drums, thus brake fade is nowhere near as formidable. There is a trade-off, though. Disc brakes aren't "self-energizing" like their drum counterparts—when a brake shoe comes in contact with the inside of a rotating drum, the reactive force helps squeeze that shoe even tighter against the drum's wall, effectively multiplying pedal pressure into additional stopping power. Without this "free" power, early American disc systems for heavy, high-horsepower cars required a booster to keep pedal effort within acceptable ranges.

The first successful American disc brake application came in 1963 when Studebaker made Bendix-supplied front discs standard for its sporty Avanti. Two years later, Chevrolet, with the help of Kelsey-Hayes, included four-wheel disc brakes as part of the standard Corvette deal. Chevy also offered four-wheel discs as a rare (and expensive) Camaro option in 1969. Optional front discs had become a Chevy musclecar option in 1967.

Ford's first front discs came in 1965, as did Plymouth's as part of its nicely balanced Formula S Barracuda package. Standard front discs didn't begin proliferating until the supercar scene was on its way out, with Chevy's '69 SS 396 among the first to offer these in real numbers. By then, many Detroit watchers were wondering why such a move had been so long in coming. Unwanted additional expense, of course, was the determining factor, as it always had been whenever brakes were concerned.

Take for example Chevrolet's first SS 396, which in 1965 featured large drum brakes borrowed from the full-sized Impala. These warmly welcomed heavy-duty stoppers were just one part of the "Z16" Chevelle's fully loaded standard package. When a true production SS 396 appeared in 1966, it came with typical Chevelle drums to help bring the base price down to where more buyers—say, 70,000 more—could reach it. Standard braking power was sacrificed in favor of market penetration, a move not missed by press critics.

Wimpy brakes, however, didn't deserve all the blame for the way most early supercars failed to slow down with the same ease that they went fast. Stopping power is not only a function of bigger, better brakes, it's also a product of how much rubber meets the road. All things remaining equal on the mechanical side of the braking equation, more tread always means more stopping power.

More tread also means better traction and handling. Effectively transmitting truckloads of torque into sure-footed traction requires truckloads of rubber, as many loads as you can get. Additionally, the basic rule of handling involves keeping as much available tread on the road at all times, especially so in tight turns where resisting lateral g-forces is the key to separating the nimble men from the squirrely boys.

Nearly all early supercar tires failed to hold up their end of the deal when it came to maximizing performance of the engine, brakes, and chassis. First and foremost, early-'60s tires were far too "skinny," they just didn't offer enough tread width, maybe 4 or 5 inches at most in standard passenger car applications. As they had in the '50s, the best "performance" tires of the day carried about 7 inches of tread.

But to create this width, manufacturers had to make these tires quite "tall," as all designs were then a product

of basically the same "aspect ratio," a measurement of section height compared to tread width. Thirty-five years ago, most tires ran in the 82 range, meaning sidewall height was 82 percent of tread width. Thus, with the aspect ratio remaining constant, widening tires meant also increasing overall height. While these bigger tires did offer increased traction and stopping power, they didn't do much for handling. A taller sidewall, compounded by the internal structures of the day, resulted in a tire that tended to "bend" sideways more in a turn, which allowed the tread to partially lift off the road when it was needed down there the most.

As with brakes, improvements in tire technology to better match power increases were at first slow in coming. Early efforts dealt mostly with traction upgrades through the use of special rubber compounds. Certain compounds were "stickier," like the butyl-rubber recipe used by the Atlas Bucron tire. Load or speed rating was also important as performance tires of course had to hold up under rapid acceleration, lateral stress, and the high temperatures created by high speeds. Goodyear's Blue Streak was among the best tires of the early '60s as far as overall performance was concerned.

The first really big step toward improving tire performance came from Firestone late in 1966. The product

Probably the first big breakthrough in performance tire technology in the '60s involved the emergence of the "wide oval," a Firestone development the helped put more rubber where it was needed the most—on the road. Early 70-series performance tires were soon overshadowed by even wider 60-series treads.

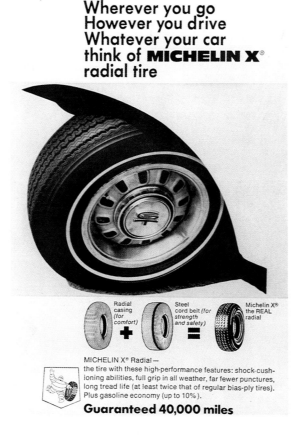

Wherever you go
However you drive
Whatever your car
think of MICHELIN X®
radial tire

Radial casing (for comfort) + Steel cord belt (for strength and safety) = Michelin X® the REAL radial

MICHELIN X® Radial— the tire with these high-performance features: shock-cushioning abilities, full grip in all weather, far fewer punctures, long tread life (at least twice that of regular bias-ply tires). Plus gasoline economy (up to 10%).

Guaranteed 40,000 miles

was called the Super Sports Wide Oval, and for good reason: this new tire was as wide as anything ever seen on the street and looked very much like an oval in cross section, its short sidewalls bulging out instead of running nearly straight up and down. With a high load rating and an aspect ratio of only 70 percent, the Wide Oval offered two more inches of tread width and a 23-percent larger "footprint" compared to the best 14-inch tires then on the market. All this while at the same time keeping low to the ground where a performance tire should.

Optional wide-oval 70-series tires were soon seen on many supercars, as were suitably wider wheels to allow this new trend in rubber to perform as it should. Maximum rim width went from 6 inches to 7, and Corvettes in 1969 even started using 8-inch-wide wheels. By that time, many manufacturers were offering fatter 60-series tires for both 14- and 15-inch-diameter wheels. G60 treads were the widest, highest-load-bearing tires offered through Detroit during the supercar era. While the factories never offered 50-series tires, the aftermarket sure did, and were they ever fat. Today, we even see what amounts to 40-series rubber on some factory performance machines, although the aspect-ratio designation since has been changed to a metric measurement.

By 1968, manufacturers were also upgrading internal affairs. For decades, tires had been of bias-ply construction: cords beneath the tread ran at an angle from side to side. Goodyear then introduced its belted bias-ply tire which added a reinforcing fiberglass belt around two-ply polyester cords, resulting in both improved traction and longer wear.

At the same time, the belted radial-ply tire was starting to make the scene, mostly in Europe. With cords running straight across from rim bead to rim bead radially around the circumference, this new breed promised to improve handling as sideways flexing didn't produce the corresponding tread warping inherent in earlier designs. Unfortunately, steel-belted radial tires didn't begin effectively infiltrating the U.S. market until well into the '70s, after the musclecar had all but vanished. A few survivors, like Pontiac's Trans Am, did benefit from radial technology.

As the '60s came to end, many supercars were wearing wider tires that markedly improved overall performance, although traction remained a tough call in most ultra-high-performance situations. Three hundred or more horses could still melt a wide-oval in 1970, just as it can in the case of today's high-tech rubber. Efficiently transforming excessive torque into confident traction will always represent the prime challenge in the performance arena, however long real performance stays with us.

Concerning handling, the best '60s treads did the best they could working in concert with what was then state-of-the-art chassis technology. Rapid acceleration and pure brute force always did receive the most attention from the engineering fraternity back then. Upgrades on the supercar's dirty side were done primarily to better beef things up to resist the tortures of high torque loads. In most cases, rubber-stamp modifications included increasing spring rates, stiffening shock valving, and thickening the anti-sway bar up front.

Geometry or physics lessons were rarely called into play, at least when mass-production was the goal. Discounting a few highly specialized models like Shelby's early Mustangs and the Boss 302, Detroit's muscle machines were treated to few other suspension modifications aimed at actually improving the way these cars went rapidly in lines other than straight. Tooling costs were again the prime stumbling blocks. With an eye toward keeping things both simple and cheap, basically nothing was done concerning roll centers, reducing unsprung weight, or lowering centers of gravity. In most cases, any lowering done in the mainstream was primarily a product of bolting on shorter, wider tires.

Status quo was the order of the day underneath. Nothing exotic there, just good ol' American meat and potatoes: typical short/long parallel A-arms with coils up front and conventional solid axles sprung by either coil springs or longitudinal leafs in back. No expensively engineered independent rear suspensions or lightweight tube A-arms were used. Rumors in 1964 did have Ford offering an optional IRS setup similar to the Corvette's for the Mustang, but such a costly arrangement never appeared.

Much cheaper was an easily installed innovation used by Oldsmobile in 1964. As part of the new 4-4-2 package, Olds threw in a standard rear sway bar. Measuring 0.875 inch in diameter—the same as Oldsmobile's standard front unit—this stabilizer helped reduce body lean and kept the rear treads more firmly planted.

Working in concert with a typical heavy-duty chassis, which also included a hefty 0.937-inch anti-sway bar up front, the 4-4-2's rear sway bar instantly transformed Oldsmobile's first mid-sized muscle machine into a leader of the road course pack. The '64 4-4-2, in *Car Life*'s opinion, "was the best handling of any GM car we've been exposed to (except the Sting Ray) and far superior to its identical cousins from the other divisions. There is, in our judgment, hardly a better handling passenger sedan produced in this country."

Long a regular feature from Olds, a rear sway bar was used in great numbers by AMC as well. Chevrolet's first SS 396 came standard with one in 1965, and did again beginning in 1970. Buick that year also made a rear stabilizer part of the desirable GSX package.

By then, supercar handling had advanced as far as it could within the parameters inherent in the mass-production practices of the day. All-in-all, the best of the breed in the early '70s did a decent job of holding the road for such heavy automobiles. Anything more by way of expensively modified underpinnings would've probably been overkill, not to mention a hard sell—in more ways than one. Supreme handling 30 years ago always translated into a less civilized ride; those bone-rattling springs and shocks giving all-new meaning to "seat-of-the-pants response." No ifs, ands, or sore butts about it, musclecars were often as hard on their drivers as they were the competition.

Of course, the real heart of the supercar's competitive nature, the instrument of torture for both tires and brakes, was found under the hood. The meat beneath all those potatoes was the engine, which continually produced far and away more motive energy than the average driver could possibly ever use in average driving situations. If worried industry leaders had thought horsepower was galloping out of control in 1957, they would not have been happy with what would arrive a decade later. By 1968, muscle mills churning out 300 to 350 horses were seemingly as plentiful as sandals in San Francisco.

Mechanical milestones that laid the groundwork for this proliferous proliferation surely must include GM's first modern OHV V-8s of 1949 and Chrysler's original hemi-head V-8 of 1951, engines that helped kick-start Detroit's postwar horsepower race. Perhaps more important from Average Joe's point of view was Chevrolet's small-block V-8, the high-winding, low-price OHV wonderment born in 1955.

As the first V-8 to offer rich man's speed at a working man's price, Chevy's 265-cubic inch small-block deserves credit for establishing the marketability of mass-produced muscle. And once proven, the "Hot One" just continued getting hotter. Optional fuel injection and a boost to 283 cubic inches came in 1957, followed by another jump to 327 cubes five years later. By 1963, the Corvette's 327 "fuelie" (regular production option L84) was pumping out 360 horses; 375 in '64.

That same year, the L76 327—basically an L84 small-block with a big four-barrel in place of the F.I. equipment—was producing 365 horses, enough power to make the new '64 Chevelle SS a real Tiger-tamer had Chevrolet followed through with L76 A-body production as promised early in the year. Only a handful of 365-horsepower Chevelles were built under mysterious circumstances after the L76 option briefly appeared on the A-body books before being unceremoniously canceled. GTO owners never even blinked.

Putting the muscle into a musclecar chassis always meant prefacing all hardware with "heavy-duty." The beef was there, but the basic technology remained meat and potatoes. One minor exception involved Oldsmobile's trend-setting use of a standard rear sway bar as part of its 4-4-2 package. *Oldsmobile Division, General Motors Corporation*

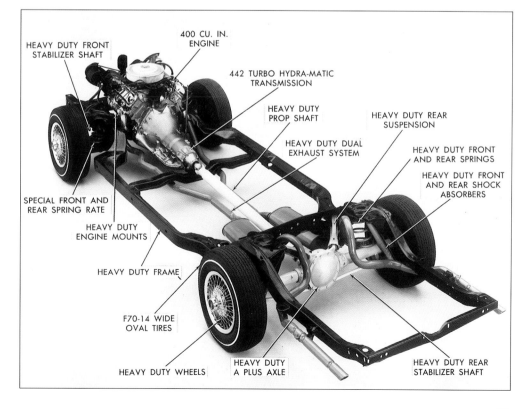

HEAVY DUTY FRONT STABILIZER SHAFT

400 CU. IN. ENGINE

442 TURBO HYDRA-MATIC TRANSMISSION

HEAVY DUTY PROP SHAFT

HEAVY DUTY REAR SUSPENSION

HEAVY DUTY DUAL EXHAUST SYSTEM

HEAVY DUTY FRONT AND REAR SPRINGS

HEAVY DUTY FRONT AND REAR SHOCK ABSORBERS

SPECIAL FRONT AND REAR SPRING RATE

HEAVY DUTY ENGINE MOUNTS

HEAVY DUTY FRAME

F70-14 WIDE OVAL TIRES

HEAVY DUTY WHEELS

HEAVY DUTY A PLUS AXLE

HEAVY DUTY REAR STABILIZER SHAFT

Hottest of Chevy's carbureted '60s small-blocks (outside Corvette ranks) was the L79 327, introduced to the passenger line in 1965. Fitted with big-valve heads, this high-compression 327 was rated at 350 horsepower, hopefully enough to help a '65 Chevelle SS hang in there with its GTO cousin. Even more potential was unleashed in 1966 when the L79 was made a Chevy II option, as shown here beneath an SS Nova's hood.

Opposite: Even as big-block ponycars began to thunder away with the attentions of the compact performance crowd, Chevrolet in 1967 was still investing considerable effort in a small-block Camaro capable of slugging it out with the best of them. Given away only by its 15-inch Rally rims and black striping, the '67 Z/28 was a certified street racer armed with a 302-cubic-inch hybrid V-8 created by bolting a 327 crank into a 283 block.

As if Chevy's 302-cubic-inch hybrid small-block created exclusively in 1967 as the Z/28 Camaro's standard power source wasn't hot enough already, engineers in 1969 put together this rare cross-ram option featuring twin four-barrel carbs mounted diagonally on a special intake. Mopar Max Wedges are best known for this cross-ram arrangement. *Roger Huntington Archives, courtesy Dobbs Publishing*

Stoplight challengers did learn a lesson or two once Chevrolet began offering the L79 327 in 1965. Listed as an option for both the Chevelle that year and the compact Nova in 1966, the L79 used free-breathing big-valve heads to help unleash 350 rarin' to run horses. The L79 represented Chevy's hottest non-Corvette small-block until 1970, when the Sting Ray's LT-1 350 V-8 was made the Z/28 Camaro's new power source. Probably the most formidable small-block of the supercar era, the LT-1 rated at 370-horsepower beneath a fiberglass hood, 360 between pony car flanks.

Before the LT-1, Z/28s had relied on a hybrid small-block created by bolting a 283 crankshaft into a 327 block, this swap job done to put displacement up as high as possible within the Sports Car Club of America's 305-cubic inch maximum legal limit for Trans-Am racing competition. According to *Sports Car Graphic*'s Jerry Titus, destroking the 327 "resulted in a happy and extremely potent screamer." With the L-79 heads, 11:1 compression, a 0.486-lift/346-degree solid-lifter cam, and an 800-cfm Holley on an aluminum intake, the Z/28's 302 V-8 was rated at 290 horsepower. Most agreed this number was a major understatement.

As hot as Chevy's "mouse motor" small-blocks had become in the '60s, the true stars of the show were the "Rats," the 396, 427, and 454 big-block Mk IV V-8s.

Chevrolet's big-block history dated back to 1958, when engineers took what was initially a truck design and created the 348 "W-head" V-8, an engine used only in top-performance applications in passenger car ranks. In 1961, the 348 was reborn as the famed 409, which by 1963 was cranking out 425 horsepower when fed by twin four-barrel carbs. Chevy sold its last 409 early in 1965.

The reason for the 409's fall from grace involved the emergence of the all-new Mk IV big-block, introduced by Chevrolet head Bunkie Knudsen at GM's Mesa, Arizona, proving grounds in February 1965. Mk IV roots

The L78 396 was a relatively rare piece in 1966—3,099 went into SS 396 Chevelles that year. Making this particular '66 L78 SS 396 much more rare is its extra-heavy-duty Muncie M22 "Rock Crusher" four-speed and cowl-plenum induction setup. Only a handful of the latter were sold over dealer counters in 1966. M22-equipped SS 396 sales numbered a mere 12 that year.

Opposite: A high-priced, low-production promotional ploy sprung in 1965, Chevrolet's SS 396 Chevelle returned in 1966 as a mass-market musclecar. From that year up until 1971, Super Sport Chevelles all featured big-block V-8s, no small-blocks were offered. Standard in 1965, the 375-horsepower 396 was the top SS 396 option in '66, listed under RPO L78.

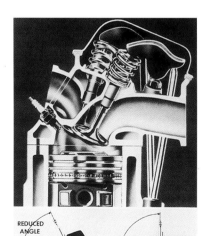

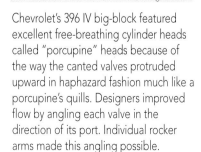

Chevrolet's 396 IV big-block featured excellent free-breathing cylinder heads called "porcupine" heads because of the way the canted valves protruded upward in haphazard fashion much like a porcupine's quills. Designers improved flow by angling each valve in the direction of its port. Individual rocker arms made this angling possible.

ran back to the Mk II 427 "Mystery Motor," designed by Engineer Dick Keinath in July 1962. Key to Keinath's work was the Mk II's intriguing cylinder heads, later called "porcupine" heads because of their staggered valves which protruded up from the combustion chambers like a porcupine's quills. Working in concert with big valves and large ports, those canted valves helped the Mystery Motor's heads flow like nothing ever seen.

Dyno test output for the NASCAR-prepped 427 was about 520 horses, enough power to help a group of Chevy stockers storm through Daytona 500 qualifying at record paces in February 1963. Two years later, Knudsen unveiled Chevrolet's Mk IV derivative of the Mk II 427, downsized slightly to 396 cubic inches. Three versions were offered: a solid-lifter 425-horsepower street killer for the Corvette, a socially acceptable 325-horsepower boulevard cruiser for the new Caprice Custom Sedan four-door hardtop, and the 375-horsepower variety, RPO L37, for the Chevelle.

Nearly identical to the Corvette's solid-lifter 425-horsepower 396 save for a tamer hydraulic cam, the L37 big-block was a performance mill from top to bottom. Its beefy four-bolt main bearing block featured a bulletproof bottom end, and the crank and rods were forged steel. Pistons were 11:1 impact-extruded aluminum pieces, while intake chores were handled by a big Holley four-barrel on an aluminum intake. When joined by a long list

of standard heavy-duty hardware included as part of the Z16 package, Chevy's first 396 guaranteed the new SS 396 Malibu would be a sure-fire winner. "No doubt a long line will form for these cars at Chevrolet dealerships," concluded *Car Life*.

When the second-edition SS 396 appeared in the fall of 1965, the tame 325-horsepower 396 was the standard big-block, with the hottest option being the 375-horsepower L78. The often rare L78 396 would remain the top performance power source for the Chevelle SS up through 1970. Camaros were first fitted with the 375-horsepower Mk IV V-8 beginning midyear in 1967, as were Novas starting two years later. Chevrolet in 1969 also introduced the aluminum-head L89 option for the 396 (L78 only), which late that year was bored out to 402 cubic inch—a fact label-makers simply ignored as Camaros and Chevelles in 1970 still wore "SS 396" badges.

Before the 396 became the 402, the Mk IV big-block had been enlarged in 1966 to 427 cubic inch for Corvettes and full-sized models. But this engine wasn't available to F- and A-body buyers due to GM executives' insistence that their smaller cars use engines no larger than 400 cubic inches.

That limit be damned, a few Camaros and Chevelles were built in 1969 with the Corvette's 425-horsepower L72 427. Performance products chief Vince Piggins simply

Chevrolet's supreme Camaro came in 1969 by way of the somewhat-mysterious COPO paper chase. Central Office Production Order paperwork represented an easy way around red tape since such requests didn't require upper management approval. Thus, ponycar buyers were able to purchase a '69 Camaro equipped with the race-ready ZL-1 427 big-block, a supposedly taboo combination considering GM execs had limited these cars to engines no larger than 400 cubic inches.

The exotic ZL-1 427 featured cast-aluminum cylinder block and heads and was given a token output rating of 430 horsepower. Chevrolet built only 69 ZL-1 Camaros in 1969, 22 with automatic transmissions like this one.

ran an end run around GM's displacement restrictions by using Central Office Production Order (COPO) paperwork. Usually meant for things like volume fleet orders, COPOs did not require management approval. Thus, putting an L72 into a Camaro was as simple as specifying COPO number 9561; the same application in Chevelle sheet metal was labeled COPO 9562. A third code, COPO 9560, belonged to the truly exotic ZL1 Camaro, a race-ready pony car armed with an all-aluminum 427. Token rated at 430 horsepower, the ZL1 427 ran well into the 500-horse range.

COPO use became moot in 1970 when GM dropped its displacement limit, allowing Chevrolet engineers to offer the new 454 Mk IV V-8 as a Chevelle option. SS 454 Chevelles that year came in two flavors, the 360-horsepower LS5 vanilla thriller and the 450-horsepower LS6 rocky-road roller.

Everything about the LS6 was savagely serious. It featured a four-bolt block (the LS5's main bearing caps used only two bolts); a tuftrided, forged steel crank; magnafluxed forged rods; and TRW aluminum pistons that squeezed the fuel/air mixture at a 11.25:1 ratio. The solid-lifter cam featured a 0.520-inch lift and 316 degrees of duration. Closed-chamber heads incorporated huge rectangular ports and big valves to breathe

even better than the previous porcupines. A 780-cfm Holley four-barrel on an aluminum intake topped things off. An additional list of mandatory heavy-duty hardware completed the deal, which added about a grand to a '70 SS 454's bottom line.

After establishing itself as one of the supercar era's greatest powerplants, the LS6 failed to return for an encore performance in 1971—beneath a "domed" SS 454 hood, that is. A low-compression 425-horsepower LS6 454 was offered as a Corvette option that year, the last for the truly hot 454. After briefly carrying on in LS5 form into the "smog motor" years, Chevy's biggest Mk IV big-block was finally canceled after 1974.

Ford's first entry in the muscle mill parade had come in 1960, when engineers Dave Evans, Don Sullivan—whose career dated back to the development of Ford's first V-8 in 1932—and John Cowley teamed up to create the 360-horse 352 Interceptor Special V-8 package. Featuring 10.6:1 compression, a solid-lifter cam, and streamlined exhausts, this ready-to-roll "Police Interceptor" big-block was a member of Ford's FE-series family, born in 1958. As luck would have it, the FE block offered much room for expansion, a fact quickly demonstrated in rapid fashion. Displacement jumped to 390 cubic inches in 1961, 406 in 1962, 427 in 1963, and 428 in 1966.

COPO codes could have also been used in 1969 to order a 427-powered Chevelle. Although wearing various Super Sport adornments, the COPO Chevelle was not an SS, but an L72-powered Malibu. The iron-block L72 427 made 425 horses.

Ford's "FE" family of big-block V-8s included this triple-carb 406-cubic-inch monster, introduced in 1962 and offered again briefly in '63. Notice the huge, streamlined cast-iron exhaust headers. In 1963, the 406 was enlarged to 427 cubic inches and the three two-barrels were deleted in favor of twin four-barrels. *Roger Huntington Archives, courtesy Dobbs Publishing*

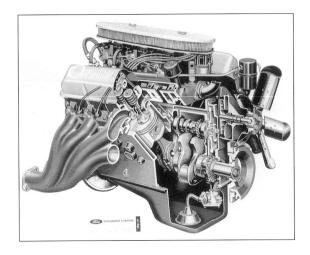

Initially available in 375-horsepower top-performance form, the 390 FE later in 1961 was pumped up to 401 horsepower by bolting on three two-barrel Holleys. Another midseason move the following year bumped FE displacement again to 406 cubic inches, with output increasing as well to 385 horses in single four-barrel trim, 405 with the triple carbs. All this monstrous horsepower

was made available to help move Galaxies along with great haste, which, as the late Carl Sagan might have opined, is never an easy task.

In 1963, FE displacement increased again with an eye toward NASCAR's 7-liter limit for legal competitors. Although a widened bore actually put cubic inches at 425, 427 became the advertised figure. NASCAR's 7-liter limit translated roughly into 427 cubic inch, and apparently Ford didn't want its new big-block finishing second to anything, whether on the track or otherwise.

Dearborn's 427 FE wasn't about to take a back seat to anyone, not with its aggressive solid-lifter cam, 11.5:1 compression, sewer-sized streamlined exhausts, and a beefy block with bullet-proof cross-bolted main bearing caps. Two 427s were offered, one with a single carb, another with twin four-barrels. Mounting a 780-cfm Holley on an aluminum intake, the 410-horsepower 427 hammered out 476 foot pound of torque. The 425-horsepower 427 was fed by a pair of 652-cfm Holleys. Torque output was 480. All this muscle made moving a Galaxie at warp speeds a piece of cake. When dropped beneath Fairlane hoods in 1966 and 1967, even more performance potential was unleashed.

In 1966, Ford began dropping its fabled 427 FE-series big-block into its mid-sized Fairlane line, but only as part of a limited run of plain-Jane, white-only, race-ready rockets. The following year, the 427 Fairlane appeal was widened with the big FE offered along with top-level XL trim and varying paint choices. The optional fiberglass hood is fitted to this '67 427 Fairlane 500—it had been standard in '66.

Unlike 1966, when the 425-horsepower dual-carb 427 was the only weapon of choice, Fairlane buyers in 1967 could also opt for the rare 410-horsepower 427 with its single four-barrel. This latter engine was the sole 427 offering early in 1968 before the NASCAR-inspired FE big-block was finally cancelled.

Engineers created the Cobra Jet V-8 by mixing and matching various hot, off-the-shelf FE parts with a 428 passenger-car block. Advertised output was a conservative 335 horsepower. Missing here on this '68 Torino's 428 CJ is the Thermactor "smog" pump, equipment added that year to meet newly instituted federal emissions standards.

Ford jumped full-force into the musclecar fray in 1968, introducing its 428 Cobra Jet FE big-block. More renowned as a Mustang option, the 428 CJ was also available for mid-sized Torinos and Fairlanes. Behind the rare '68-1/2 Cobra Jet Torino GT shown here is a '69 Fairlane Cobra, which relied on the 428 CJ as its standard power source.

Always a high-priced, low-production race-ready powerplant, the 427 finally faded from the scene early in 1968—by then it was only briefly offered in single-carb 410-horsepower form. Its replacement atop Ford's powerful pecking order was the 428 Cobra Jet, the last of the great FE-series big-blocks, introduced on April 1, 1968.

Inspiration for Dearborn's first Cobra Jet had come from Rhode Island Ford dealer Robert F. Tasca, Sr. He was no stranger to Ford performance, having promoted it wholeheartedly from his East Providence dealership since late 1961. But in 1967, Tasca's men found themselves trying to sell the new big-block 390 GT Mustangs, pony cars that didn't quite measure up to the competition. Tasca's solution was a 428 Police Interceptor transplant. A few other off-the-shelf hot parts helped create a 13-second Mustang.

Once Ford engineers got wind of Tasca's development, they decided to try a similar tack. On top of a 428-cubic inch passenger car block went 427 low-riser heads and a cast-iron duplicate of the aluminum Police Interceptor intake manifold mounting a 735-cfm Holley. Inside went a 390 GT cam, PI rods, and 10.6:1 pistons. Conservatively rated at 335 horsepower, the 428 CJ was

just the ticket to help Ford restore the faith on the street. Although the 428 CJ was popularized beneath the Mustang's hood, it was also offered as a mid-sized option in 1968, and the next year became the standard power source for the Fairlane Cobra.

While the FE-series 428 Cobra Jet would remain the top Mustang performance option through 1970, it was replaced that year in the Torino Cobra line-up by an all-new

CJ big-block based on the 385-series 429. Called "Ford's new clean machine" by *Motor Trend*, the 429 big-block was a product of Washington's increasingly more demanding mandates to reduce emissions. "Racing and research not only improve the breed," wrote *MT's* Dennis Shattuck, "they also clear the air." Ford's 385-series V-8 was first offered in 1968 in both 429- and 460-cubic inch forms.

In 1970, the Torino Cobra was fitted with a 360-horsepower 429 Thunder Jet V-8 in base form. Optional was the 429 Cobra Jet, rated at 370 horsepower with or without ram air. As it had for the 428 Cobra Jet, the Drag Pack option upped the 429 performance ante, transforming a Cobra Jet into a Super Cobra Jet. Along with a choice between a 3.91:1 Traction-Lok or 4.30:1 Detroit Locker rear end, Drag Pack equipment included a beefy four-bolt block, forged 11.3:1 pistons, a 780-cfm Holley four-barrel, and an external oil cooler, the last feature representing the easiest way to identify an SCJ at a glance. Advertised output for a 429 SCJ, again with or without ram air, was 375 horsepower. Both the Cobra Jet and Super Cobra Jet 429s carried over into 1971, not only for the Torino Cobra but also as a Mustang option in place of the retired FE-series CJ.

Baddest of the Ford big-blocks was the Boss 429. This 375-horsepower "semi-hemi" V-8, with its free-breathing, big-port aluminum heads, was homologated under Mustang hoods in 1969 as a legal NASCAR power source for Ford's long-nosed Talladega. Don't ask, just nod your head in mock agreement. Ford met NASCAR's 500-unit minimum production requirement be setting up a remote Boss 429 assembly line at the Kar Kraft works in Brighton, Michigan. There, various modifications were made to both allow the semi-hemi big-block entrance into the Mustang's engine bay and beef up the pony car platform to handle all that muscle. Kar Kraft built 859 Boss 429s in 1969, another 499 in 1970.

Basically an engine that had little business in polite society, the Boss 429 wasn't exactly compatible with regular production tuning, and "was kind of a slug in the Mustang," according to designer Larry Shinoda. The Boss 429 Mustang was brutally fast, but its race-ready nature made it a wholly uncooperative all-around performer on the street. For one thing, those huge ports flowed much too freely for low-speed, everyday operation. Not even its large 735-cfm four-barrel could shovel the coals fast enough to keep the big Boss hot and happy. But on NASCAR superspeedways or at the drags, the so-called "Shotgun" motor fired away with abandon.

Ford's small-block history dated back to 1962 with the birth of the Windsor V-8 line. Using an innovative technique known as "thinwall casting," Ford engineers had created one of the lightest, most compact V-8s then

on the market. First came the 221 and 260 Windsors, the latter chosen for its tidy merits by Carroll Shelby to power the first of his Anglo-American hybrid Cobras in 1962.

A bore job midyear in 1963 produced the 289, which in top "Hi-Po" tune was rated at 271 horsepower. Beefed throughout, the High Performance 289 featured a solid-lifter cam, a dual-point distributor, and free-flowing exhausts. It was introduced as a Fairlane option, then became the perfect performance boost for the new Mustang in 1964. The 271-horsepower K-code 289 remained on the pony car options list up through 1967, the year big-block power was first made available beneath the Mustang's long hood.

Dearborn's most outrageous big-block was the "semi-hemi" Boss 429, a 375-horsepower killer built for the street solely to homologate its use on NASCAR speedways. Ford offered the Boss 429 in Mustangs in order to meet NASCAR rules specifying a 500-unit production run for any and all legal racing engines. Here, a "Shotgun motor," as it was also called, is shoe-horned into a specially prepared '69 Boss 429 Mustang at the Kar Kraft facility in Brighton, Michigan.

CONTINUED ON PAGE 66

SOHC It To Me

Detroit's supercar engines of the '60s and '70s represented just the tip of the iceberg. Behind the scenes lurked many mechanized monsters, experimental powerplants that were both big on horses and innovation. Most were never intended for anything but the track, test or race. Others unbelievably almost made it onto the street.

Seemingly every engineer in the '60s was hot to copy Chrysler's trademark hemispherical combustion chamber design. Chevrolet's Mk IV big-block and Ford's Boss 429 featured similar chamber shapes—both engines were referred to as "semi-hemi" V-8s.

Overhead cams were even more popular among the experimental engineering crowd. Like the proven hemi heads, OHC designs dated well back into internal combustion's primitive days, with various pioneers discovering early on that fewer parts and less weight in the valvetrain department meant higher rev capabilities and greater performance potential.

OHC experiments were especially prevalent in GM engineering quarters. In 1969, John Beltz's boys at Oldsmobile took their four-valve-per-cylinder, hemi-head W-43 455 V-8, a perfectly streetable power source that could've feasibly found its way beneath a regular-production hood, and added dual overhead cams to produce the outrageous 700-horsepower OW-43 Can-Am racing engine. At Chevrolet, Zora Duntov had been toying with various OHC designs since mid-decade. And in 1966, Pontiac even introduced an overhead-cam six-cylinder as the standard powerplant for the Tempest.

Pontiac's OHC experiments had begun in earnest in 1963. Mac McKellar and Bill Klinger began concentrating on better ways for Pontiac to win on the street, resulting in various DOHC and SOHC V-8s of both 389 and 421 cubic inches. One of these, a 421 SOHC used three valves per cylinder. Pontiac engineering was also home to one of the experimental engine realm's closer calls, an episode where a wild animal of an engine almost escaped the tool room and made into the civilized world.

McKellar's men called it the Ram Air V, an all-out racing mill that made its Ram Air IV predecessor look meek in comparison. Roots for this radical big-block V-8 traced back to 1967 when John DeLorean, by then PMD general manager, put his engineering team to work pumping up Pontiac's 428 V-8 with a pair of "tunnel-port" heads.

Pontiac attentions in mid-1968 turned to SCCA competition, where Detroit's pony cars were galloping around the young Trans-Am circuit. Namesake or not, Pontiac's pony car was still technically ineligible for Trans-Am racing since its standard 400-cubic inch big-block V-8 was considerably larger than the SCCA's legal limit of 305 cubes.

To meet this requirement, Special Projects Group Engineer Steve Malone created a unique "short-deck" block with an equally unique center-feed forged crank and shortened stroke. Although sometimes called a destroked 400, that is too much of an oversimplification. In any case, Malone's first Ram Air V V-8 displaced 303 cubic inches, and wore tunnel-port heads. Per SCCA homologation specs, the division planned to build 1,000 Ram Air V Trans Ams for 1969.

Two other Ram Air V tunnel-port big-blocks were also developed; a 366-cubic inch NASCAR version and a 400-cubic inch counterpart originally considered as a GTO option. All three Ram Air V powerplants featured extra-heavy-duty blocks, rods, and cranks; free-flowing, individual-runner exhaust manifolds; and a 780-cfm Holley four-barrel on a special aluminum high-rise intake manifold. By most claims, output for the 303 Trans Am engine was about 430 horses. The NASCAR V-8 reportedly dynoed at 585 horsepower.

Itself a 500-horsepower bully, the 400 Ram Air V came the closest to making history as planned. Tightened budgets and changing corporate attitudes tripped up Pontiac's tunnel-port V-8s before they had a chance to prove themselves. The 303 short-stroker never made it onto SCCA tracks, at least not in a production-class Firebird in 1969. Nor did the 366 Ram Air V ever turn any heads on NASCAR's Grand National circuit.

But in 1970, anyone with a little inside info and about $2,000 could've walked away from a Pontiac parts department with a Ram Air V 400 in a crate under their arm. According to estimates, between 80 and 200 of these beastly big-blocks were sold. No Ram Air V Pontiacs were factory built—so close, yet so far.

Even more intriguing than the Ram Air V story, was Ford's earlier near-miss with its "Cammer," the 427 SOHC V-8. Called "Ford's 90-Day Wonder" by *Hot Rod*, the Cammer was rapidly developed under the watchful eyes of engineers Norm Faustyn, Joe Eastman, Mose Nowland, and Al Rominsky in early 1964. Inspiration for their haste? In February, Chrysler's new 426 race hemi had brutalized the field at the Daytona 500.

Within a few short months, Ford had a "Total Performance" response to Chrysler's hemi up and running. Atop a typical 427 side-oiler FE block went a pair of quickly engineered cylinder heads featuring hemispherical combustion chambers, huge round intake ports, roller rockers, and big sodium-filled valves. The clincher was the single overhead cam running the length of each head. To operate those two cams, a large T-shaped aluminum plate bolted to the block, supplying mounting points for cam drive hardware and more than 6 feet of timing chain—the short deadline ruled out a much more complicated gear-drive setup.

Pontiac's engineering crew in the '60s was especially fond of overhead cam experiments (an OHC six-cylinder did eventually make production). Shown here is a 1963 experimental OHC 421 big-block V-8. Two versions of this beast were built, one with typical two-valve combustion chambers and another using three-valve heads. Paul Zazarine collection

Oldsmobile's truly wild OW-43 455-cubic-inch V-8 was designed with Can-Am racing in mind. Induction was by four Weber two-barrel carburetors, while the hemi heads featured dual overhead cams and four valves per cylinder. The much more civilized W-43 version of this four-valve 455 hemi could have easily reached production. Oldsmobile Division, General Motors Corporation

Even though that apparatus looked clumsy, Ford's 427 SOHC was a wild winder. Maximum output of more than 600 real horsepower for the twin-carb variety came at a dizzying 7,200 rpm. When fed by one four-barrel, the Cammer pumped out around 580 horses. As *Car Life's* Roger Huntington saw it late in 1964, "I wouldn't be surprised to see [the 427 SOHC] dominating stock car racing next summer." Many others wondered what Chrysler would do to retaliate. In fact, Mopar engineers were indeed hard at work on a Cammer of their own, a DOHC hemi that would've surely trampled everything in its path—had it ever reached running stage.

As it was, the DOHC hemi was never completed, and Ford's 427 SOHC was left all revved up with no place to race after NASCAR rules mogul Bill France put his hefty foot down. Fearful of where such escalation would lead, NASCAR officials on October 19, 1964, announced a new set of rules to take effect January 1, 1965. Included was a statement claiming that legal "engines must be of production design only, thus eliminating overhead cams and hemispherical heads."

Chrysler's initial response involved a threatened boycott of the upcoming NASCAR season. Ford simply fell back on its pushrod 427, letting the SOHC instead do its thing in drag racing's factory experimental (F/X) class. The plot, however, soon thickened once Chrysler came back in 1966 with its street hemi, a production engine that could indeed legally do anything it wanted in NASCAR competition—and make everyone else like it.

Cammer production had continued on in 1965 as Dearborn engineers struggled to bring costs down in hopes of meeting another NASCAR mandate, this one establishing the maximum price of an eligible racing engine at $1,000. Estimates put Ford's early costs at $14,000 apiece for the first SOHC 427s, and the commonly quoted bottom line for a crated Cammer in 1965 was $4,500. These bloated figures aside, Ford racing men apparently had every intention of letting the SOHC loose on NASCAR in 1966. According to Roger Huntington, "a reliable source [told him] as far as Ford is concerned, [the SOHC] is a 'production' engine, and if [Dearborn] has to drop $250,000 selling [them] to racers for $1,000 to prove it, Ford will do so."

Additional efforts to legalize the Cammer for NASCAR competition came in the spring of 1966 as Dearborn leaked out news of a planned 427 SOHC option, priced at $1,963, for the Galaxie line. Ford then got the go-ahead in April after promising a production run of 50 SOHC '66 Galaxies. The catch? The overhead-cam 427 could race in NASCAR, but it would be penalized one pound per cubic inch.

Fed up at last, Henry Ford II immediately announced his company's pull-out from NASCAR racing, which both killed any possibility of seeing an SOHC street machine and effectively ended the once-proud Galaxie's high-flying stock car career. Then came the final hammer blow to the Cammer's coffin. In 1967, NASCAR simplified its rules, stating that "a minimum of 500 of a type of car and engine be titled pursuant to bona fide consumer transactions before they will be made eligible to compete." Quipped *Motor Trend*, "whether a purchase order from Holman and Moody for 500 SOHC V-8s would satisfy Bill France remains to be seen."

And that was that.

While contemporary reports put total 427 SOHC production at roughly 75 units, as many as 300 were probably built, nearly all of those going to Holman-Moody in Charlotte, North Carolina, where a few were installed in '65 Mustang A/FX drag cars. As for the rest, according to the late John Holman's son Lee, "when the Dearborn people decided the engine was no longer viable, those Cammers just sat in the warehouse until Ford had us sell them." The younger Holman remembers running magazine ads offering leftover SOHC motors for about $975. He also recalled more than one buyer taking home four or five Cammers before the supply played out in 1971.

You'll still occasionally see a 427 SOHC show up in a street rod or such. And they're still every bit as intimidating as they were three decades ago when they scared Bill France into legislating them out of existence.

Push came to shove in 1964 after Chrysler got the upper hand on the NASCAR circuit with its dominating 426 race hemi. To counter this escalation, Ford rushed its 427 SOHC "Cammer" V-8 into production. Chrysler turned right around and began work on an overhead-cam hemi. Chrysler's own Cammer, however, never made it to the running stage as NASCAR quickly banned OHC V-8s. Mopar Muscle, Dobbs Publishing

Pontiac engineers had hoped that this 303-cubic-inch short-deck V-8, the fabled Ram Air V, would find its way into SCCA Trans-Am competition as a Firebird power source. Plans were to offer this "tunnel-port" engine as a street-going Trans Am option, but the idea was shot down in 1969. Roger Huntington Archives, courtesy Dobbs Publishing

Ford's Cammer would have surely given Chrysler's race hemi a run for its money had the 427 SOHC made it past rulesmakers' red tape and onto NASCAR tracks in 1964 or '65. Here, engineers Norm Faustyn (left) and Joe Eastman, co-authors of the SAE paper detailing the Cammer's design, point out features of the SOHC V-8.

Ford's early high-performance small-block was the the K-code 289, a 271-horsepower Windsor V-8 first offered as a Fairlane power choice in 1963, then added to the Mustang's options list the following year. It was last offered in 1967. The generator appearing on this Mustang's Hi-Po 289 gives it away as the 1964-1/2 variety. Later renditions all used alternators.

CONTINUED FROM PAGE 63

Two years later, Ford's engineering crew unleashed a red-hot small-block in response to Chevrolet's 302-powered, purpose-built Z/28 Camaro. With SCCA Trans-Am competition being the goal, Dearborn in 1969 created the Boss 302 Mustang, a hunkered-down, hairy dog driven by Ford's better idea of a hybrid engine. The Boss 302 V-8 was produced by borrowing the excellent canted-valve heads from the 351 "Cleveland" V-8—then being readied for 1970 production at Ford's Cleveland engine plant—and bolting them atop a modified four-bolt 302 block filled with solid lifters and 10.5:1 compression pistons. Like its bigger Boss 429 brother, the 290-horsepower Boss 302 was built with racing in mind in 1969 and 1970.

Less costly than the Boss 302 and easier to live with on the street, the 351 Cleveland appeared in 1970 as yet another answer to America's air pollution problem. The Cleveland small-block was a real smoker in 300-horsepower trim, yet its emissions levels ran well within ever-tightening federal specifications. Ford offered the 351 Cleveland as a Mustang option; Mercury rightly chose it as the base engine for the '70 Cougar Eliminator.

The supreme Cleveland family member was the 351 High Output V-8, the '71 Boss 351 Mustang's one and only power source. Roll call for the 330-horsepower 351 HO included 11.7:1 compression, a solid-lifter cam, and a 715-cfm four-barrel with ram air. A Hurst-shifted wide-ratio four-speed, 3.91:1 Traction-Lok rear end, F60x15 tires, competition suspension with staggered rear

shocks, and power front discs completed the Boss 351 package, an impressive final salute to the rather short, yet definitely prominent Blue Oval performance bloodline.

Chrysler's high-horsepower legacy ran as long as any other's in Detroit, beginning with the Firepower hemi V-8's debut in 1951. Nothing else at the time produced pure power like the hemi, with its efficient hemispherical combustion chambers, centrally located spark plugs, and canted valves. All Chrysler's divisions except Plymouth used hemis in various sizes during the '50s before the corporation dropped these big, heavy engines after 1958 in favor of lighter, easier-to-engineer, equally powerful wedge-head V-8s.

Beginning in 1959, top power for the luxurious Chrysler 300 letter-series models was supplied by a dual-carb 413-cubic inch V-8 putting out as many as 405 horses. Exotic-looking ram-induction was introduced in 1960. Offering a "poor man's supercharger" effect, ram-induction featured twin Carter AFB four-barrels mounted outboard each valve cover on long, spider-like manifolds, with the Carter on the left feeding the cylinder bank on the right, and vice versa. In lighter Dodges and Plymouths atop either the 361 or 383 V-8s, ram-induction equipment helped make Mopars forces to be reckoned with in early super-stock drag racing competition.

In May 1962, both Dodge and Plymouth became seriously involved in the factory super-stock race with the introduction of the "Max Wedge" 413. Actually, Max Wedge was a street slang reference; "Max" coming from the "Maximum Performance" designation used in factory brochures, "Wedge" referring to the engine's wedge-shaped combustion chambers. Dodge's version was the Ramcharger 413; Plymouth's, the Super Stock 413. In either case, two totally uncivilized varieties were offered; the 11:1 compression 410-horsepower Max Wedge or the head-cracking 13.5:1 420-horsepower version. An even stronger 426 Max Wedge appeared for 1963 and 1964 in Stage II and Stage III forms. Maximum muscle was 425 horsepower in top racing trim, which was the only way a Max Wedge came. All were fed by two Carter carbs arranged diagonally on a cross-ram intake.

Another 426 wedge, this one not near as beastly, was offered to Dodge and Plymouth customers with a need for not nearly as much speed in 1964 and 1965. Obviously meant for the street, this 426 used a single Carter four-barrel to produce 365 horsepower, still a respectable amount, a fact not lost on many factory performance rivals whenever the light turned green. If anything, the 426 street wedge lacked a competitive image, unlike all those GTOs then roaming the roads.

It was another story at the drag strip, where Max Wedge Mopars had been kicking butts and taking names since their 1962 debut. The high-profile, highly successful

Max Wedge racing campaign was no accident, it was a direct result of Lynn Townsend's rise to power as Chrysler Corporation president in 1961.

"When Townsend came in, the good fortune was he had two teenage boys," said engineer and horsepower hound Tom Hoover to author Tony Young in 1990. "They were known to travel north Woodward Avenue late at night. They made it known straightaway to dad that [Chrysler products] were 'nowhere.' When Townsend let it be known it was time to change the image of our product, it was just like having the clouds separating and the sun shining through." The new president put Hoover in charge of Chrysler's competition performance program in October 1961, with the 413 Max Wedge being the first pet project.

In December 1962, Hoover's engineering team was assigned the task of building another new engine, this one capable of carrying the Mopar banner high around NASCAR tracks. The Max Wedge V-8s could dominate drag racing, but they quickly proved themselves unable to do the same in "roundy-round" competition. Henry Ford II had already denounced the 1957 AMA factory racing ban, and Townsend's men that summer had also announced they would step out of the closet as well, meaning there would then be no holds barred. One particularly historic result of this adjusted attitude was a monster of an engine that would rely on proven '50s technology to give birth to a powerful new legend for the '60s.

Hoover's first 426 hemi—like the Max Wedge, a race-only powerplant—was readied, per Townsend's directions, in time for the sixth running of NASCAR's Daytona 500 in February 1964. Unlike the hemis that had powered your aunt Sophie's DeSoto in the '50s, this totally re-engineered offspring was built from oil pan to air cleaner with bulletproof brute force in mind. In maximum performance form fitted with dual four-barrels on a cross-ram intake, the race hemi was rated at 425 horsepower, which, as Hoover later explained, "was purely an advertising number." "Most of the [later] street hemis," he continued, "would make 500 horsepower or better."

By 1964, that 425 output figure had become a popular token tag around Detroit: Ford had used it for its dual-carb 427 FE in 1963, as did Chevrolet that year for its top 409. Chevy tried it again in 1965 for the Corvette's new 396 Mk IV big-block. All these maximum-muscle engines producing the same power? Coincidence, no?

Coincidence, not at all. Someone somewhere in Detroit had determined that 425 horsepower represented the upper limit of tolerance for auto industry critics wary of just how little automakers cared about the dangers of putting too much power into the hands of the

people. Cross that line and you were sure to set off safety alarms everywhere. In Hoover's opinion, using the 425-horsepower rating "was purely a matter of everybody being in fear that they would be called to Washington to testify before some committee that would say, 'you dirty dogs are out there making more power for cars and that's the un-American thing to do.' We were really worried about that as far back as the early '60s. We were scared to death."

It was the competition who got the real scare once the race hemi had done its thing at Daytona in 1964. Hemis finished 1-2-3, with Richard Petty's winning Plymouth leading five other Mopars in the top 10. Ford's "Total Performance" teams, which had ruled NASCAR in 1963, could only watch as Petty went on to take seasonal honors by a wide margin. Soon after the Daytona whipping, the popular fashion statement around Chrysler had become a small button saying "Total What?"

The joke was soon on Chrysler, however, when NASCAR mogul Bill France banned the hemi in 1965, leading to a Mopar boycott and near complete dominance of the stock car season by Ford. France reasoned the 426 hemi was not a regular-production engine, thus it didn't meet his new requirements for legal competition on his racing circuit—with an intended emphasis made

Chrysler's "hemi-head" technology dated back to 1951. In 1964, the corporation dusted off the design and re-introduced it in the form of the all-out 426 race hemi. Lurking beneath Dodge and Plymouth hoods, the race hemi made quick work of its NASCAR rivals. Here, engineering vice president Paul Ackerman poses proudly with the race hemi in 1964. Two years later, the 426 street hemi would appear, kicking off one of Detroit's most powerful performance legacies. *Roger Huntington Archives, courtesy Dobbs Publishing*

When fed by a single four-barrel, Dodge's 440 V-8 produced 375 horses. Adding three two-barrel carbs on an Edelbrock intake upped the output to 390 horsepower. The chrome valve covers shown here are "non-stock" dealer parts-counter pieces.

Opposite: Originally introduced along with Plymouth's Road Runner in 1968 as a budget-conscious "econo-racer," Dodge's Super Bee could be loaded up with a whole host of Mopar performance options. By 1970, that hot hardware list included the 440 Six Pack big-block with its triple-carb induction. This '70 Super Bee is one of 196 built with the Six Pack option.

here on "his." In place of stock car success, the race hemi had to settle for drag racing victories in 1965.

The following year, Chrysler wowed the horsepower crowd by taking the hemi to the streets, making it a certified regular-production option in order to allow it entry back into the NASCAR racing fraternity. Although obviously "detuned" here and there to make everyday operation possible, the 426 street hemi still featured much of the race hemi's muscular make-up, including its laughable 425-horse advertised rating.

"If you missed the San Francisco earthquake, reserve your seat here for a repeat performance," began *Car and Driver's* first review of the street hemi, in this case a Plymouth. "Forget about your GTOs and your hot Fords—if you want to be boss on your block, rush down to your nearest Plymouth (or Dodge) dealer and place your order for a hemispherical combustion chamber 426 V-8. This automobile is the most powerful sedan ever, bar none."

It wasn't long before the 426 hemi was appearing beneath the hoods of almost everything Dodge and Plymouth offered, including a few four-door sedans. Belvedere, Coronet, GTX, Road Runner, Super Bee, even the E-body 'Cudas and Challengers of the '70s all felt the hemi's punch. Some 11,000 426 hemi cars were built between 1966 and the big engine's expected cancellation in 1971, with very few adjustments made to the mix. Dual inline carbs and that 425-horsepower rating carried over each year. Hemi updates in 1968 included a hotter cam, revised valvetrain, and a windage tray inside a 6-quart oil pan. Among other developments were hydraulic

lifters, which replaced the maintenance-intensive solid tappets in 1970.

Sure, the hemi was a heavyweight; it did compromise handling in all applications, especially so in the normally spry E-body's case. But as a horsepower churn, it had few equals in the supercar ranks, if any. And it does probably stand as the best-known, most revered musclebound mill ever. Bar none.

Almost lost in the hemi's shadow were Chrysler's wedge-head big-blocks, no slouches in their own right when it came to churning out horses. Biggest of the big was the 440, introduced in 1966 by boring out the 426 street wedge. In 1967, better-breathing heads, suitably generous single-carb induction equipment, and a warmed-up cam transformed this lukewarm mammoth into Plymouth's Super Commando 440 and Dodge's 440 Magnum, 375-horsepower big-blocks that were offered as standard equipment for the new GTX and Coronet R/T, respectively.

Two years later, the 440 Six Pack (Dodge) and 440 Six Barrel (Plymouth) debuted as the sole power source for specially prepared, stripped-down B-bodies. Wearing no wheel covers and featuring lift-off hoods, these Six Pack Super Bees and Six Barrel Road Runners were obviously built with specific duty in mind—perhaps short trips measuring no more than one quarter-mile? Beneath those huge fiberglass hood scoops were three Holley two-barrels on an Edelbrock aluminum intake, equipment that helped boost 440 output to 390 horses.

In 1970, the triple-carb 440 was offered, along with hood hinges, for all the top-performance B- and E-bodies. Like the hemi, it survived only up through 1971, although as many as three cars did escape into the wild with unauthorized tri-carb 440s in 1972.

Beneath the 440 in the Mopar performance chain of command was the 383 "RB" V-8, never necessarily a weakling in the '60s, but a lightly considered weapon of choice in most cases. That changed in 1968 when Plymouth's Road Runner and Dodge's Super Bee debuted. Standard for both these low-buck supercars was a special 383 four-barrel V-8 created by mixing and matching RB big-block parts. Heads, intake and exhaust manifolds, cam and valvetrain, and oil pan windage tray all were borrowed from the 375-horsepower 440. Output for this new 383 was 335 horsepower, just the ticket to make the Road Runner and Super Bee Detroit's best bang for the buck.

Another cost-conscious Mopar muscle V-8 also appeared in 1968, this one a small-block. The "LA" family 340, a descendant of the A-body's 273 and 318 V-8s, was an affordable, nicely potent lightweight alternative to the 383 big-block for Barracuda and Dart Swinger buyers who

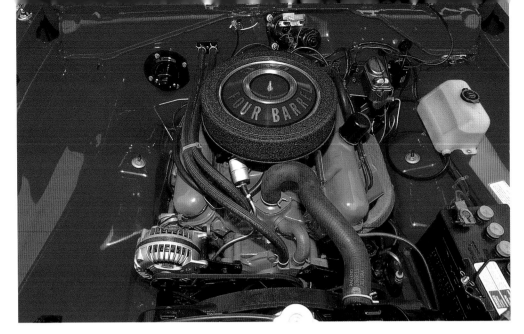

One of the best small-block buys of the musclecar era was Chrysler's 340-cubic-inch V-8, a compact, lightweight screamer conservatively rated at 275 horsepower. It would be the 340's honor to carry the Mopar muscle banner high into the '70s once the big, hairy hemis and 440s died out. This 340 is the heart of a '69 Dodge Dart Swinger.

The American Motors family of performance engines began with a 290-cubic-inch, 225-horsepower V-8, the standard power source for the new 1968 AMX. By 1970, the AMX's base engine had grown to 360 cubic inches and 290 horsepower. This '70 AMX 360 is also equipped with optional ram-air equipment, which sealed the open-element air cleaner to the hood's large, functional scoop.

Oldsmobile's first W-30 package began with the 360-horsepower L69 400 fed by three two-barrel carbs. Along with the fresh-air ductwork, the W-30 option also included a hotter cam and appropriate valvetrain gear. Because those ducts took up so much underhood space, the battery was relocated to the trunk—just where it should be anyway for a dragstrip-ready machine. That chrome air cleaner was hand-formed.

preferred their pint-sized supercars to handle curves as well as straights. Reworked heads were the key to the 340's ability to smoothly and easily produce 275 horsepower.

The supreme 340 small-block was the Trans-Am-inspired triple-carb variety offered along with the T/A Challenger and AAR 'Cuda in 1970. Beefed throughout and fed by a trio of Holley two-barrels on another Edelbrock aluminum intake, the 340 Six Pack/Six Barrel V-8 was conservatively rated at 290 horsepower. Destroked versions were used for Trans-Am racing.

The SCCA Trans-Am circuit basically became American Motors' prime proving ground in the late '60s. By 1970, a Javelin team would finish second behind Ford's Boss 302 Mustang, then take the title in 1971. Another AMC group also copped SCCA top honors the following year.

On the street, American Motors' hottest products were powered by derivatives of the same engine, the 290 V-8, introduced in 1967. Standard power for the new two-seat AMX in 1968 came from a four-barrel 290 rated at 225 horsepower. A bored-out 290, the 280-horsepower 343 V-8, was optional for the AMX and its longer Javelin teammate, which had debuted just months before. A bored-and-stroked 343, the big 390 V-8, appeared midyear along with the AMX to inject 315 horses into AMC's performance equation. The Hurst-built SC/Rambler of 1969 used this engine, mated to a ram-air hood. In 1970, another Hurst-influenced AMC product, the Rebel Machine, used an exclusive 390 four-barrel rated at 340 horsepower.

A stroked 343, the 360, was also offered from 1970 to 1974. And a stroked 390, the 401, remained at the top of the AMC performance pile in four-barrel form from 1971 to 1974. Maximum advertised output for the 401, listed before net ratings took effect, was 330 horsepower in 1971. The 360 and 401 at least gave American

Motors performance customers something halfway warm to play with in the emissions-controlled early '70s.

Also still performing reasonably strong in those "smog motor" years was Oldsmobile's W-30, one of Detroit's longest-running performance packages, having debuted in 1966 as part of a rapid escalation of 4-4-2 muscle. When introduced in 1964, the 4-4-2 was powered by a 310-horsepower 330 V-8. In 1965, the standard powerplant became the new 400 V-8, rated at 345 horsepower. The triple-carburetor L69 option appeared the following year to help bump output up to 360 horsepower, enough to rush a '66 4-4-2 through the quarter in a tad less than 15 seconds.

If that wasn't enough, the W-30 options group could've been ordered along with the L69 400 in 1966. Included in the deal was a hotter cam, stiffer valve springs, and a ram-air system made up of a hand-stamped air-cleaner force-fed through long ducts and twin plastic "vacuum cleaner" ram inlets mounted below the bumper. Also thrown in was a trunk-mounted bat-

tery and red plastic inner fenderwells, the latter pieces intended to save unwanted weight, just what you wanted while staging at the strip.

When the triple-carb option was dropped (by GM upper office decree) in 1967, the W-30 option was mated to a single-four-barrel 400. This time, the air inlets were moved up between the headlights, where they probably did more harm than good thanks to their radically reduced size. In 1968 and 1969, the large

W-30 intake ducts returned to their original position below the front bumper.

All that ductwork was done away with in 1970 when the W-25 fresh-air hood was made part of the W-30 package. Both mean-looking and fully functional, this fiberglass lid incorporated two large scoops at its leading edge to feed cooler, denser air to what was by then a 455-cubic inch big-block, the new standard power source for the 4-4-2. In base form, the '70 4-4-2 V-8 was rated at 365

Oldsmobile introduced its W-30 induction option in 1966, that year adding twin fresh-air ducts to the 4-4-2's tri-carb 400 V-8. The black, plastic intakes for those ducts can be seen on the '66 4-4-2 at left protruding through each bumper end just outboard of the turn signals. The intakes were moved up between the headlights for 1967's W-30, right.

In 1970, Oldsmobile made the 455-cubic-inch big-block the main power source for the 4-4-2 and topped it with the optional W-25 hood, a fully functional, tough-looking unit sporting two large, functional scoops. With these scoops on top, there was no longer any need for the W-30 big-block to use all that pesky plumbing. Shown here is a '70 W-30 (right) and a rare '71 W-30 convertible. Production of the latter was only 110.

horsepower; adding the W-30 equipment resulted in a tidy 5-horsepower increase for the force-fed 455. With very little tweaking, a '70 W-30 could drop into the 13-second bracket, performance that put it right up with the hottest-running supercars in the supercar era's hottest year.

Buick's efforts aimed at reaching that stratosphere began in 1965 when engineers dropped the 325-horsepower 401-cubic inch big-block beneath the new Gran Sport's hood. But while the 401 V-8 was a torque monster capable of transforming a classy Skylark into a deadly bird of prey, this engine was of Buick's antiquated "nailhead" lineage. That nickname referred to the 401's painfully small valves, which to some critics appeared not much bigger than the head of a nail.

Buick performance was modernized in 1967. Primarily the work of engineer Clifford Studaker, an all-new big-block was introduced that year with bigger valves, better breathing heads, and a truly beefy lower end featuring a crankshaft with 3.25-inch main bearing journals. This 400 V-8 featured lightweight "thinwall" construction—it outweighed Chevrolet's small-block V-8 by only 72 pounds and also tipped the scales at more than 100 pounds less than a Chevy big-block. Output for the GS 400 V-8 was advertised at 340 horses.

In 1969, Buick offered its first Stage 1 equipment package, which among other things included a hotter cam and a modified Rochester Quadra-Jet four-barrel fitted with a ram-air air cleaner sealed to two functional hood scoops by foam "doughnuts." The Stage 1 was given a token rating of 350-horsepower, a figure that could've been boosted even higher with Buick's optional Stage II cam, also new that year. Various other Stage II components appeared over the years, including the rare round-port cylinder head, released in April 1972. Only about 100 sets of these heads were sold.

While most Buicks never got a second look from the jet-set crowd, the "Stage"-equipped cars shocked many an uneducated curbside challenger. With headers, an aftermarket intake and carb, and a track-ready 4.78 rear axle, *Hot Rod's* testers managed to run a Stage II '69 GS well into the 12s down the quarter-mile. "If [the car] had a GTO sheet metal wrapper on it, you couldn't build enough of them," wrote *HRM's* Steve Kelly.

Like Oldsmobile, Buick turned to a 455 big-block in 1970, making the overlooked Stage 1 an even more surprising performer. With 360 *advertised* horsepower (compared to the base 455's 350 horses), the Stage 1 GS 455 was capable of handling anything else on the street in 1970, including 426 hemis and LS6 Chevelles. Many believe the '70 Stage 1 may well rank as the top supercar of all time. All Buick followers do.

From a Pontiac devotee's point of view, two names say it all: Super Duty and Ram Air. The former involved both PMD muscle's earliest supercar history and its last gasps, while the latter was actually "borrowed" by Pontiac from its customers.

The division's Super Duty legacy was officially born in December 1959 with the release of various performance parts aimed at NASCAR competition. Originally based on the 389 big-block, the Super Duty V-8 was producing as much as 368 horsepower by 1961. Late that year, an enlarged 421-cubic-inch Super Duty, rated at 373 horsepower, was offered in very small numbers to a few select drag racers. In 1962, an even hotter 405-horsepower 421 SD was included in a special run of race-ready Catalinas. After GM's anti-racing memo ended the 421 Super Duty's career early in 1963, a much more civilized version of the 421 V-8, the 370-horsepower HO (you guessed it, for High Output), survived as Pontiac's performance leader.

When the GTO was born in 1964, it featured a muscled-up 389 big-block wearing a pair of heads borrowed from the 421. Topped by a Carter AFB four-barrel, the Goat's 389 was rated at 325 horsepower. Adding Pontiac's trademark Tri-Power option, with its three Rochester two-barrel carbs, pushed output up to 348 horsepower.

In August 1965, dealers began offering a special "tub" that sealed those three little air cleaners to the hood's underside using a large foam gasket. On top, the GTO's previously ornamental scoop was made fully functional by unblocking its twin openings. Although not "officially" recognized, this dealer option represented the roots of Pontiac's Ram Air legacy.

1969 Buick Stage I.

No wonder Buick owners keep selling Buicks for us.

When Buick builds a premium performance machine, even enthusiasts start talking. Here's what you'll hear.

Stage I begins with a specially modified GS 400. Those hood scoops are completely functional. They ram cool, clean air into the carburetor.

The 400 cubic inch engine displacement stays the same. Increased output comes from a high-lift camshaft, a low-restriction dual exhaust system with bigger, 2¼ inch tailpipes and a modified quadrajet four-barrel carburetor with bigger throats.

At the rear wheels, a 3.64 Positraction rear axle.

You can select a specially-calibrated TH-400 automatic transmission that provides higher shift points and firmer shift engagement.

And don't forget that the heavy-duty rallye suspension and front power disc brakes are yours for the ordering.

That's Stage I by Buick for 1969. It's a lot to talk about.

It's something else to drive.

Wouldn't you really rather have a Buick?

In actuality, taking the generic reference soon to belong to the various ram-air hoods and scoops used by all Detroit's automakers and transforming it into the formal-noun "Ram Air" moniker for a family of PMD performance big-blocks wasn't exactly a Pontiac idea. Not originally.

Buick's fabled Stage 1 performance legacy began rather inconspicuously in 1969. Originally offered that year in 400-cubic-inch form, the Stage 1 big-block truly took off in 1970 when the 455 V-8 became the powerplant of choice for Gran Sport buyers.

Ram Air III 400 began receiving full coverage in shop manuals and on order forms. Previously, Ram Air IV factory identification had appeared in decal form in 1969. Other than that, a service bulletin sent out in February 1968 did mention the new Ram Air II 400, as did a Pontiac advertisement that year.

As for specifications, the Ram Air I 400 in 1967 was rated at 360 horsepower as a GTO option, 325 in Firebird applications. Revised heads with round instead of "D-shaped" ports keyed the March 1968 switch to production of the Ram Air II 400, labeled as a 366-horsepower big-block for GTO buyers, 340 for their Firebird counterparts. Wearing the same advertised output tag, the Ram Air III V-8 debuted in 1969 with D-port heads, a Power Flex fan and free-flowing "long-branch" cast-iron exhaust manifolds. The '69 Firebird's Ram Air III was advertised at 335 horsepower. Ram Air III 400s (UPC code L74) came standard in both of Pontiac's new 1969 supercars, the GTO Judge and Firebird Trans Am, with these muscle machines simply carrying "Ram Air" decals on their hoods.

A more specific "Ram Air IV" decal announced the underhood presence of the Judge and Trans Am's optional L67 400. A candidate for Detroit's greatest supercar powerplant ranks, the Ram Air IV was conservatively rated at 370 horsepower in GTO sheet metal, 345 in Firebird form. Features included a heavy-duty four-bolt block; exceptionally free-breathing heads with huge, round ports; revamped exhaust manifolds; a Rochester Quadra-Jet four-barrel on a special aluminum intake (in place of the L74's cast-iron piece); and a serious cam with a 0.520-inch lift and 308 degrees of intake duration, 320 on the exhaust side.

In 1970, the Trans Am's Ram Air IV was redesignated LS1 as the strongest F-body 400 joined its L67 GTO brother as a full-blown 370-horse fire breather. Factory paperwork even identified the LS1 as a "Super Duty" 400, although identification on the cars themselves remained "Ram Air IV." Also of note for 1970 was slight increase in valve lift—to 0.527 inch—for the Ram Air IV cam.

New for the GTO in 1970 was the optional L75 455 big-block. Although certainly torquey, the 360-horsepower 455 was not as hot as it looked as its long stroke inhibited high-rpm operation. In 1971, however, the low-compression LS5 455 HO received round-port heads similar to the Ram Air IV 400's. Even with a drop from 10.25:1 compression to 8.4:1, the 455 HO still rated at 335 horsepower, more than enough "real" muscle to keep the '71 GTO up among the leaders of the low-lead pack.

All those restrictive EPA specifications of the early '70s aside, Pontiac engineers still somehow managed to save their best for last, building an "emissions-legal" big-block for 1973 that would've still blown away most of Detroit's

Buick was already leading the way by 1970 as far as classy muscle was concerned. Then the Flint guys blew everyone away that year with their GSX, a high-profile performance machine that looked every bit as hot as it ran, especially when the optional 455 Stage 1 resided beneath that functional hood. Both this special-order '71 GSX (front) and its '70 forerunner are Stage 1 equipped. Red paint was not an "official" GSX color, it came only by special request.

This Tiger tale began in earnest in February 1966, when Pontiac engineers introduced a new 389 Tri-Power engine to go along with the dealer-offered ram-air tub of 1965. This "XS"-code big-block featured a stronger cam and stiffened valve springs along with that functional hood. Mandatory XS options also included an M21 close-ratio four-speed, heavy-duty fan, metallic brake linings, and a 4.33:1 limited-slip differential. Pontiac paperwork shows that 190 XS 389 V-8s were manufactured; perhaps as many as 185 made their way into '66 GTOs.

Although not labeled in any factory papers as such, the 1966 XS 389 was the division's first Ram Air V-8. Or at least it was the engine that began inspiring enthusiasts to start referring to Pontiac's top free-breathing performance mills as such. Customers, not PMD officials, coined the term. GTO and Firebird buyers in with the in crowd knew that the hottest of Pontiac's newly enlarged big-blocks in 1967 was a Ram Air 400. That reference then retroactively became "Ram Air I" once an even hotter "Ram Air II" 400 superseded its forerunner in March 1968. The progression continued in 1969 with the arrival of the Ram Air III and IV 400s, the latter being the supreme rendition of the breed. An outrageous, race-ready Ram Air V was built in small numbers but never made it into regular production, escaping instead into the wild only in crates by way of dealer parts counters.

Ram Air numbers terminology didn't begin appearing in Pontiac factory literature until 1970, when the unfettered atmosphere-choking supercar powerplants had it debuted five years before. Was it any wonder then that PMD people felt the LS2 455 was worthy of the name "Super Duty?" "Just when we had fast cars relegated to the museum sections, Pontiac has surprised everyone and opened a whole new exhibit," announced *Car and Driver* in its road test of an early '73 455 Super Duty Trans Am.

Everything about the 455 SD was super, from its new beefy block with reinforced bearing webs and lifter gallery, to its nodular-iron crank with big 3.25-inch main bearing journals, to its forged-iron rods that were shot-peened for hardness and magnafluxed to uncover any flaws. A heavy duty oil pump, 8.4:1 TRW forged-aluminum pistons, a Rochester Quadra-Jet, and free-flowing cast-iron headers were also included. Key to the mix were the cylinder heads, which were tweaked within an inch of their lives by the guys at Air Flow Research to maximize flow. These heads breathed better than anything Pontiac had ever produced, and probably did so in comparison to all rival products as well. All this and the 455 Super Duty passed EPA emissions testing, too. Almost.

Clever fellows as they were, Pontiac engineers noticed that EPA engine testing only ran for about 50 seconds. Accordingly, they developed a system that shut off the required exhaust gas recirculation valve after 53 seconds, allowing the engine to breathe in easier—and breathe out

unacceptable emissions levels. So equipped, the 310-horsepower 455 SD passed emissions testing with flying colors. Then the smog police found the rat they thought they smelled. Caught red-handed, PMD people were forced to remove these EGR inactivating systems and retest their engines by March 15, 1973. To pass these new tests, the 455 SD had to be fitted with a less-aggressive cam. The initial 0.480-inch-lift hydraulic stick was replaced with a tamer 0.401-inch unit, resulting in an advertised output drop to 290 horsepower, where it stayed for 1974 as well.

Initially offered for mid-sized models and pony cars, Pontiac's 455 Super Duty V-8s ended up finding their way only into 1,300 Firebirds in 1973 and 1974. Tests of the 310-horsepower 455 SD Trans Am put quarter-mile acceleration in the high-13-second range; great by '60s standards, simply stunning in relation to what was happening in the mid-'70s. Then just as fast as it came, the Super Duty went, a death that once and for all signaled the end of the road for truly super supercar performance. Could there possibly have been a better send-off?

Progress continued marching on after 1974, only the buckets of bolts then produced weren't anywhere near as beloved, at least not for car buyers with a real need for speed. The adventure by then was basically over as traveling to point B from A became nothing more than a job. And a boring one at that.

Pontiac's top-performance engines were initially named by customers, who took the generic term ram-air and formalized it. Pontiac men didn't make the Ram Air name official until 1969 or so. This 335-horsepower, Ram Air III 400 V-8 came standard with both the GTO Judge and Trans Am Firebird in 1969.

Chapter Three

LITTLE PONIES & BIG HORSES
One Size Didn't Fit All

They passed each other like proverbial ships in the night: one, a battle-hardened boulevard cruiser on its way to the salvage yard; the other, a spirited streetside schooner only then beginning a long, fruitful voyage. Early in 1965, Chevrolet sold its last 409, replacing the veteran mill with the all-new Mk IV 396 big-block, a full-sized power option that remained more than capable of putting the super in Super Sport. About the same time the venerable 409 was fading away, Ford's sporty Mustang was celebrating its first year on the road, a record year at that. Twelve months after Dearborn had kicked off Detroit's pony car race in April 1964, Mustang sales had surpassed 418,000, topping the industry's existing first-year sales standard, also established by a Ford, the Falcon, in 1960.

While all 409 Chevys built between 1961 and 1965 were high-powered thrillers, most early Mustangs were simply everyday transporters; budget-conscious cars that hid their mundane Falcon heritage well beneath a sporty facade. Standard buckets, a floor-shifter, and fresh styling did the trick, even if that base six-cylinder didn't. Yet one of the many market contributions made by the Mustang involved another new opportunity for buyers with a need for speed.

Once solely available in big, heavy cars—only because big, heavy cars were basically the only things Detroit built—American-style performance started rapidly becoming less homogeneous in the early '60s, due of course to the plain fact that the industry as a whole was doing the same. The Mustang in 1964 was simply the latest, greatest evolution in Detroit's trend toward smaller cars, a new marketing wave that had begun in

earnest with Chevrolet's compact Corvair in 1959.

GM's senior compacts had debuted in 1961, Chevy's Nova—a "sophomore compact?"—the following year. Hot on the heels of these bigger small cars came Ford's first intermediate in 1962, a downsized Galaxie of sorts using the existing Fairlane nameplate. Dodge and Plymouth also downsized that year, but their slightly shrunken Polaras and Furys were still very much full-sized flyers. An early intermediate of sorts, Dodge's A-body appeared in 1963 and picked up on a proven Pentastar image: Dart. Plymouth the next year added a glass fastback to its compact Valiant, creating Chrysler's own pony car, the Barracuda. Another new A-body family, GM's LeMans, Skylark, Cutlass, and Chevelle lines, rolled out for 1964, fully establishing Detroit's intermediate image in buyers' minds.

As Pontiac proved with the mid-sized GTO, all things being equal under the hood, a smaller, lighter car naturally tends to be faster than a larger, heavier counterpart—not even O.J.'s lawyers can beat those physical laws. It then follows that an even lighter car might promise even more performance potential. Enter the comparatively petite pony car.

Although somewhat slow in coming at first, the new small-car field pioneered by Ford's Mustang in 1964 soon blossomed into a full-fledged musclecar breeding ground once GM's counterparts, Camaro and Firebird, entered the fray. But even as it was widening the performance market's scope, the growing presence of various muscle-bound pony

Chrysler discontinued its letter-series legacy after 1965, but one more full-sized "letter-car" did appear, the 300H of 1970. This time, the "H" stood for Hurst, as the Hurst Performance people had once more teamed up with a Detroit automaker to create a special-edition performance machine. Special Hurst paint, a hood scoop, and decklid spoiler were part of the package. *Chrysler Historical Archives*

Opposite: Designers widened the Mustang's flanks in 1967 to make room for the ponycar's first big-block V-8, in this case Ford's 390-cubic-inch FE. Another new addition was an extra letter on automatic-transmission GT models, the red "A" signifying the transmission choice. All GTs used manuals; all GTAs, automatics.

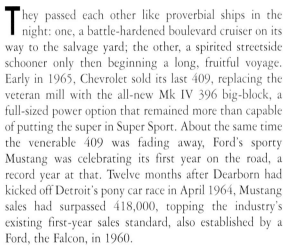

IT FEELS GOOD, LOOKS BETTER and GOES GREAT!

Take any one of Chevy's five '61 Impalas, add either the new 409-cubic-inch V8 or the 348-cubic-inch job and a four-speed floor-mounted stick, wrap the whole thing in special trim that sets it apart from any other car on the street, and man, you have an Impala Super Sport! Every detail of this new Chevrolet package is custom made for young men on the move. This is the kind of car the insiders mean when they say Chevy, the kind that can only be appreciated by a man who understands, wants, and won't settle for less than REAL driving excitement.

Here are the ingredients of the Impala Super Sport kit • Special Super Sport trim, inside and out • Instrument Panel Pad • Special wheel covers • Power brakes and power steering • Choice of five power teams: 305 hp. with 4-speed Synchro-Mesh or heavy-duty Powerglide. 340 hp. with 4-speed only. 350 hp. with 4-speed only. 360 hp. with 4-speed only • Heavy-duty springs and shocks • Sintered metallic brake linings • 7,000-RPM Tach • 8.00 x 14 narrow band whitewalls • Chevrolet Division of General Motors, Detroit 2, Michigan.

Optional at extra cost, as a complete kit only.

MAY, 1961

CHEVROLET

Impala SS

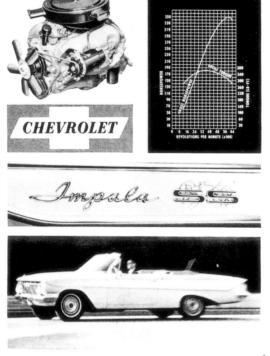

Chevrolet's original Impala SS, introduced midyear in 1961, was perhaps Detroit's first purpose-built sporty performer aimed at the common man. (Chrysler's 300 letter-series cars were certainly purposeful, but were priced far beyond the reach of Average Joe.) Only about 450 '61 SS Impalas were built, roughly a third of those with 409s.

cars was also helping pay Peter by robbing Paul. As musclecar buyers' attentions began tending more toward smaller offerings, full-sized bullies began losing ground, some more quickly than others.

Chevy's 409 wasn't the only performance pioneer to disappear in 1965; Chrysler also finally closed the book on its legendary letter-series legacy with the last of the revered 300s, the 300L. The Hurst-sponsored 300H (no relation to the letter cars) did appear in 1970. And the Fury GT was included as a member of Plymouth's Rapid Transit System that same year. Discounting these two quasi-supercars, the '65 300L represented Chrysler Corporation's final fling in the big-car performance field.

As for Chevrolet's counterparts, the 409's death didn't mean an end to full-sized force from the Bow-Tie boys. Obsolescence was the reason behind the "W-head's" cancellation. The modern Mk IV big-block offered both greater performance potential and increased versatility—unlike the 409, it could readily fit between the fenders of the mid-sized Chevelle (and, later, the Nova) as well as the big Impala. And as the perfect power choice for speed-hungry Super Sport buyers, the 396 and 427 Mk IV V-8s helped keep the Impala SS running strong almost into the '70s.

Chevrolet had first wowed the crowd with the Super Sport image in 1961. Introduced along with the 409 V-8, the SS trim package adorned an Impala with spinner wheel covers, special identification, and a sporty interior. Features included a spiffy steering wheel, a 7,000-rpm tachometer, and a Corvette-style grab bar on the dash. Chevy's existing hot V-8, the 348, was standard, with the rarin'-to-race 360-horsepower 409 four-barrel available at extra cost. A simply super package that was certifiably sexy and streetably civilized, the 409 SS truly did represent music to a musclecar man's ears.

And with an additional four-barrel in 1962, the 409-horsepower 409 made the SS pot even sweeter. But Chevrolet just couldn't resist diluting the SS to allow the most buyers in on the deal. An exclusive, performance-only package in 1961, the Super Sport trim option in 1962 was made available along with budget-conscious six-cylinders and yeoman 283 V-8s. Accordingly, SS sales jumped from 453 to 99,311 in 1962. After becoming a model line all its own in 1964, the Impala SS reached its peak the following year with production surpassing 243,000.

Although it didn't quite supply the same ring as "she's real fine, my four-oh-nine," the rare 425-horsepower 396 did help transform a '65 Impala SS into one of Detroit's strongest family cars. The optional L72 427, also rated at 425 horses, promised even more performance potential in 1966.

The next year, Chevrolet's SS 427 option group, RPO Z24, debuted as the top-performance Super Sport. Star of the Z24 show was the 385-horse 427 V-8, joined by a typical supporting cast: stiffer suspension, redline tires, and special badging. All in all, it was an impressive package. It was also the beginning of the end.

The SS 427 returned as leader of the Super Sport pack in 1968, when marketing men chose to strip the Super Sport Impala of model line status and put the SS image back on the options shelf, under RPO Z03. After only 38,210 Impala buyers checked off the Z03 option in 1968, the decision was made to offer the SS 427 exclusively. RPO Z24 production in 1969 was 2,425, small

enough to convince officials that marketing full-sized sportiness was no longer worth spit. Eight years and some 920,000 beloved Super Sports after it had begun, the Impala SS tale was unceremoniously canceled. Gone but not forgotten. Chevrolet chose to dust off the image—albeit for the four-door Caprice—for a brief encore from 1994 to 1996.

Chevrolet's corporate running mate, Pontiac, also remained heavily involved in the big muscle field in the '60s. PMD's Grand Prix, when introduced in 1962, was a sporty luxo-cruiser that could be equipped with decent muscle—radically so in the case of the 421 Super Duty GP, a truly bizarre combination of velvet and sandpaper.

Chevrolet's full-sized performance leader was the Impala SS, built from 1961 to 1969. Beginning in 1967, the flagship was the SS 427, offered as a complete package. In 1969, the SS 427 Impala was the only full-sized Super Sport produced. Chevrolet sold only 1,778 SS 427s in 1968, with one shown here. Power was supplied by a 385-horsepower Mk IV big-block.

Big-car Pontiac excitement was best represented by the Grand Prix, introduced in 1962. Class and sportiness were part of the deal, as was performance when a Tri-Power big-block was ordered. Wildest of the wild were the 16 Super Duty Grand Prix coupes built in 1962. The only known restored example of this rare breed, this '62 GP is secretly armed with the race-ready 405-horsepower 421 SD V-8.

Pontiac's Catalina 2+2 took over as the division's top-performing showboat in 1964. In 1965, the 421 V-8—an option the previous year—became the base 2+2 engine. This '65 2+2 convertible is also equipped with Pontiac's optional eight-lug wheels, among the most attractive sporty rims ever offered.

Only 16 of these hell-raising, high-class, 405-horse haulers were built—why is anyone's guess.

Discounting those rare super stockers, the much more streetable, 370-horsepower 421 HO Tri-Power Grand Prix was a real head-turner in 1963, able to do 0–60 in a startling 6.6 seconds according to a *Motor Trend* test. Concluded *MT*'s Bob McVay, the Tri-Power GP was "designed for the man who likes to go places fast in quiet elegance and luxury."

The list of hot Grand Prix varieties also included the Hurst SSJ conversion, an especially fast luxury car in 1970 when the optional 370-horsepower 455 big-block was installed. Hurst Products did the Grand Prix SSJ trick up through 1972. All told, less than 500 were sold, a major accomplishment considering the tangled paper trail required to put an SSJ together.

Much easier to buy was Pontiac's 2+2, a $291 per-formance option package for Catalina hardtops and con-vertibles first offered in 1964. The original 2+2 package

included a special interior with buckets and a console, a Hurst-shifted three-speed, and a 389 V-8. Fresh, exciting looks were also part of the package thanks to a Catalina redesign. Styling chief Bill Mitchell was justifiably proud of the results, telling *Motor Trend* late in 1964 that "this new design greatly enhances Pontiac's lean, aggressive look and youthful appeal. Even standing, it seems poised for action."

The 2+2 Catalina stood poised for even more action in 1965 as additional performance pieces became part of the standard package, now priced at $418.54. Added was a more exclusive image (front fender "gill" panels and chrome engine dress-up were thrown in), a stiffened suspension, and a 3.42:1 rear axle. Under the hood was the 421 V-8; an option in 1964, it was the only size engine included with the 2+2 in '65.

Three 421s were available, beginning with the 338-horsepower single-carb version crowned by a chrome low-restriction air cleaner. Boosting compression from 10.5:1 to 10.75:1, trading the four-barrel for Tri-Power, and adding dual straight-through mufflers resulted in the 356-horsepower 421. Beyond that came the triple-carb 376-horsepower 421 HO with its three, small, free-breathing air cleaners, special cam and valvetrain gear, low-restriction exhaust manifolds, and de-clutching fan.

Among additional options for the 2+2 group were even stiffer springs, a Safe-T-Track differential, transistorized ignition, quicker 17.5:1 (compared to the standard 24:1 ratio) steering box, heavy-duty radiator (with an oil cooler when an auto trans was specified), and those attractive eight-lug aluminum wheels with their finned aluminum brake drums. Buyers could also choose between a four-speed manual or three-speed Turbo-Hydra-Matic automatic, the latter a new replacement for GM's old four-speed automatic. Representing the first truly major update to the 25-year-old Turbo-Hydra-Matic design, the three-speed TH trans was more responsive, smoother, and more durable than its forerunner.

Beneath all this was an award-winning automobile that, in John DeLorean's words, was "the most improved car in the history of our division." *Motor Trend* supplied the award, honoring the entire line-up that year with the division's third "Car of The Year" trophy, this time "for styling and engineering leadership in the development of personalized passenger cars."

Additional publicity for the 2+2 came once more from David E. Davis' *Car and Driver*. And again his audacious plan involved a shootout with a "comparable" Ferrari, this time the 330 GT 2+2. A real one; Luigi Chinetti, Jr.'s. Veteran driver Walt Hansgen was chosen to do the flogging at Long Island's Bridgehampton road course.

Of course, Pontiac's 2+2 was another Royal Bobcat rendition, reinforced to its gills and loaded for Prancing Horse. Along with the 376-horsepower Tri-Power 421, close-ratio four-speed, and a Safe-T-Track differential (with standard 3.42:1 cogs) were various Royal Pontiac tweaks, which of course were not discussed to any great degree by Davis.

The *Car and Driver* editor was, however, more than willing to get a jump on his readers' poisoned pens. "For the benefit of those who are about to compose blistering attacks upon us for our Letters column," began his review, "our address is One Park Avenue, New York 16, and we have wives and mothers, so watch it."

From there, David E. pointed out how the two 2+2 models stacked up subjectively. "If the Ferrari was a woman, she'd be about 35 with an athletic figure and sad eyes. She'd be a lousy cook, sensational in bed, and utterly unfaithful." The Pontiac "would have an enormous bosom and the pretty-but-empty face of an airline stewardess. She'd be earnest but uninspired in both kitchen and boudoir, and your friends would think you were the luckiest guy in the world."

Amazingly (or probably not), the pair ran close on the track. "It doesn't just go around the corner," claimed Hansgen about PMD's 2+2, "it does a mighty fine job of it!" A fine job was also turned in on the quarter-mile, where the Catalina recorded a 13.80-second/106-miles per hour pass. Totally unbelievable were the 0–60 numbers—6.3 seconds for the V-12 Ferrari, a mere 3.9 ticks for the 376-horsepower Catalina. "The Pontiac—for a

Top 2+2 performance in 1965 came from the 376-horsepower 421 HO, a truly hot hauler topped by Pontiac's trademark Tri-Power induction. Along with those three Rochester two-barrels, the 376-horse 421 also featured a special cam and valvetrain and low-restriction exhausts.

street machine—is an excellent car by American standards," concluded Hansgen. "Man, if you ever need power, it's available!"

Clearly, the Royal power available to him was much more plentiful than that found by civilians in 1965. But that didn't mean the 2+2 did it all with mirrors. Even in standard form, it impressed many by the way it handled like a smaller car. And ample power was certainly available.

"Docile as a kitten in town, our 338-horsepower charger turned wild when we put our foot down hard," wrote *Motor Trend's* Bob McVay. Appearing much more believable, McVay's four-speed 2+2 test car needed 8.1 seconds to reach 60 miles per hour from rest, 16.4 seconds for the quarter-mile—nicely warm performance for a car that carried five comfortably, and also easily transported all five's luggage in that cavernous trunk. When it came to building full-sized excitement, few did it better than Pontiac.

Pontiac, however, didn't do it much longer after the second-edition 2+2 made the scene. With the need for full-sized speed rapidly fading away after 1965, the 2+2 quickly followed suit. After showing up for 1966 as a distinct model, the 2+2 made one last appearance, again as an options package, in 1967 before ending the equation.

Arguably the best in the '60s big-car performance ranks were Ford's Better Idea guys, if only because that was primarily all they concentrated on. Dearborn's full-sized fighters advanced upward right along with the company's horsepower curve, the latter a product of the ever-growing FE-series big-block V-8s. Ford's first '60s supercar was a '60 Starliner coupe armed with the 360-horsepower 352 Police Interceptor V-8.

The fabled 427 was created in 1963, putting Ford out in front, on the street, and around NASCAR speedways—led by Ned Jarrett's 15 wins in 1964, Galaxie teams tied Pontiac' three-year-old NASCAR seasonal victory record of 30. Equipped with the 425-horse 427 off the track, Galaxies were among Detroit's strongest-running muscle machines in 1964, and remained so, to some degree, in 1965, even with the lighter, less costly, more user-friendly GTO-class supercars running away with the youth market.

All 427 Fords were supercars for supermen. Standard features were burly; a knee-bending clutch and a bullet-proof top-loader four-speed were the only drive-line choices. Additional mandatory muscled-up hardware included bigger brakes and wheels (15-inchers instead of 14s), and beefed-up axle shafts, U-joints, and driveshaft. According to a *Speed & Custom* road test in 1964, a 425-horsepower Galaxie could burn down the quarter-mile in 13.96 seconds.

As hot as it obviously was, the 427 Galaxie was still no match for its mass-produced musclecar rivals as far as market survival was concerned. The 427 remained a rare option in 1966, but Ford's full-sized performance thrust then moved away from brute force toward a Grand Prix style of sporty luxury. If you can't beat 'em, try beating someone else.

Ford jumped back into the horsepower race in 1960, unveiling its 360-horsepower 352 Police Interceptor Galaxie. Performance levels increased each year from there as the FE-series big-block was both enlarged and strengthened. Here, Don White kicks up some sand with a 390-powered '61 Ford at the annual Daytona Beach speed trials. *Daytona International Speedway Archives*

According to ad copy, the '66 7-Litre Galaxie was "either the quickest quiet car or the quietest quick car." Much more pizzazz than performance, the 7-Litre featured standard buckets and a console with a floor shifter. Loads of dress-up flair, including mag-style wheel covers, was also part of the deal, as were power front discs. Standard beneath the 7-Litre's hood was Ford's newest FE V-8, the 428, which in this case delivered 345 horsepower. Behind the 428 was another new engineering piece, the C6 Select-Shift automatic transmission.

Discounting the handful of cars reportedly ordered with the dual-quad 427, the typical 7-Litre was barely able to break into the 16-second bracket for the quarter-mile. This big baby was certainly no supercar. Then again, it wasn't meant to be. Nor was its second-edition successor in 1967.

Dearborn did give full-sized performance one last shot in 1968 and 1969, offering its GT equipment group for the sporty Galaxie XL. Nice try, no cigar. Even with the optional 429 V-8, the "Michigan Strong Boy," as ads

Two years before, Ford's fearsome 427 Galaxies had held their own on Mainstreet U.S.A., even up against lighter rivals like the GTO. By 1966, however, Ford's full-sized performance presence was dwindling. The new 7-Litre Galaxie was much more bark than bite, its standard 428 FE big-block being best suited for turning pulleys on air conditioners and power steering pumps.

Ford's last stab at big-car muscle debuted in 1968. Called the "Michigan Strong Boy" in ads, the XL GT returned in 1969 with an impressive image and average performance. This '69 XL GT is fitted with the optional 365-horsepower 429-4V V-8.

called the XL GT, was more or less a sissified musclecar impostor. But it did play the part marvelously well—as comedian Billy Crystal might've seen it, better to look good than to run good.

By 1969, Ford had begun shooting most of its performance marbles into the Fairlane and Mustang's circles, the latter effort made much to the dismay of Lee Iacocca, who saw his baby in an entirely different light. "Within a few years of its introduction," he wrote in his autobiography, "the Mustang was no longer a sleek horse, it was more like a fat pig." Fattening up, however, was exactly what Dearborn designers had in mind to make room up front for Ford's big-block V-8, a power play inspired by GM's pony car performance escalations.

Simple sportiness with a wide appeal had been Iacocca's goal from the beginning. His vision involved a car young people would love. Hundreds of thousands of young people. "Seventy-eight million of 196 million citizens haven't yet reached their twentieth birthday," explained Ford's new general manager, Donald Frey, in 1965. "The sheer weight of numbers makes the youth of this country a faction that just can't be ignored." To attract this faction, Ford had created a sporty everyday automobile that helped persuade a youthful driver into thinking he was traveling in fast company even if he wasn't.

Dearborn's design team at first teased the sports car crowd in 1961 with a two-seat, midengined Mustang I. And late in 1963, *Motor Trend* was still spreading "rumors that Ford will produce a sports car to compete with the Corvette." What Ford did, however, was take a narrowly focused ideal and transform it into a product far more appealing to far more people. Per Iacocca's insistence, the real thing had to have four seats, a conclusion Frey later labeled as the key toward making the Mustang a regular-production reality. "Up until that point," he said, "we had been thinking two-seaters. But [Iacocca] was right; there was a much bigger market for a four-seater."

When Dearborn's four-seat Mustang II hit the show circuit in October 1963, *Motor Trend's* critics couldn't believe their eyes. "It's a shame the Mustang name had to be diluted this way," whined an *MT* report.

Complaints notwithstanding, the Mustang II was right on—an easy-to-handle four-seater with a long hood, short rear deck, bucket seats, and a floor shifter, the latter two ideas copped from the Corvair Monza, which had already proven the appeal of affordable sportiness. As Frey put it, "that's how [the Mustang] started—watching Monzas." On April 17, 1964, it became the world's turn to do the watching.

Both *Time* and *Newsweek* commemorated the event with cover stories honoring the wildly popular Mustang and its maker, who wasn't at all adverse to accepting the credit. Iacocca was responsible for prying open Ford's purse strings for the project—itself grounds enough to earn him a major feather for his rapidly tightening hat.

Once on the street, the first Mustang ended up being many things to many drivers. Economical practicality was there by way of the standard six-cylinder. So too was optional V-8 power, beginning with the Falcon's 164-horsepower 260. Top choice came in June 1964 when engineers added the 271-horsepower High-Performance 289 into the mix.

Along with the "K-code" V-8 came appropriate reinforcements; quicker steering, rock-hard suspension, bigger 15-inch wheels, a stiff clutch, the top-loader four-speed and a choice of 3.89:1 or 4.11:1 gears in a brawny 9-inch rear end. Front disc brakes were waiting right around the corner when the Hi-Po Mustang was first introduced, and rumors even persisted of an optional independent rear suspension.

On the street, the Hi-Po Mustang was hot, doing the quarter in the 15s in most tests, as low as 14.68 seconds when fully maximized by a track-trained *Motorcade* tester, and down to an unbelievable 14-flat in an October 1964 *Car and Driver* test that begs the question as to who was holding the stopwatch. Then again, Hi-Po drivers will tell you that certain early run engines

built more "precisely" with maximum compression in mind did run quite a bit stronger than the rest of the K-code crowd.

For the most part, however, Hi-Po Mustangs did generally trail the GTO by a fair margin in accelerative ability. Nonetheless, the 271-horsepower pony car was lauded by *Car Life* for its "obvious superiority to the more mundane everyday Mustang." Continued the *Car Life* review, "where the latter has a style and a flair of design that promises a road-hugging sort of performance, and then falls slightly short of this self-established goal, the HP Mustang backs up its looks in spades."

Additional performance appeal enhancement came in April 1965 with the introduction of the GT equipment group, featuring a host of dress-up pieces and heavy-duty hardware, including front discs and a special handling package. With or without the optional Hi-Po 289, which was discontinued in 1967, the GT edition served as the Mustang's sporty flagship up through 1969 when it too was canceled, a victim of Ford's success with newer, more powerful pony car variations.

Regardless of what Iacocca thought, the Mustang was fattened up in 1967, allowing the 390-cubic inch FE big-block to fit beneath that long hood. While many purists cringed, the heavier, wider '67 Mustang was quick to impress others. *Hot Rod's* Eric Dahlquist liked the new look. "Detroit has cobbled up so many fine designs in the last 20 years that when Ford decided to change the Mustang, everybody held their breath," he wrote. "But it's okay people, everythin's gonna' be all right."

Although "everythin" may have been all right at first, word soon spread about the 390-powered Mustang's inability to compete with big-block pony car rivals from GM. As *Car Life* explained in reference to the '67 GT, "perhaps this superburger, if it is to be a superburger, needs a little more mustard." And not grey poupon. Optimistically rated at 320 horsepower, the lukewarm 390 GT V-8 just didn't have a taste for serious competition.

Then came 1968. Ford Motor Company performance began blossoming that year thanks mostly to one person: the man they called Bunkie.

In many respects, Semon Knudsen may well be considered the prime motivator of the musclecar era. He was most certainly the busiest. Bunkie had been there at Pontiac when Super Duty performance started warming up in 1959. He was in charge at Chevrolet six years later when the 396 big-block was born. And on February 6, 1968, Henry Ford II shocked everyone in Detroit—most thoroughly, Lee Iacocca—by hiring Knudsen as Ford Motor Company president immediately following Bunkie's resignation as GM's executive vice president. Knudsen had quit after determining he had been snubbed when Ed Cole was made GM president instead of him.

Now it was Iacocca's turn to feel the snub.

"Henry was a great GM admirer," he wrote. "For him, Knudsen was a gift from heaven. Perhaps he believed Knudsen had all that famous GM wisdom locked in his genes. In any event, he wasted no time making his approach. A week later, they had a deal. Knudsen would take over immediately as president at an annual salary of $600,000—same as Henry's."

On the fast track himself, Iacocca had every reason to question his future at Ford once the former GM hero vaulted over him. But Henry II, in Iacocca's words, "took pains to assure me that Bunkie's arrival did not mean my career was over. For a few weeks I considered resigning. In the end, I decided to stay. I was counting on the prospect that Bunkie would not work out and my turn would come sooner rather than later."

The man who later went on to save Chrysler was right. On September 11, 1969, Henry Ford II fired Bunkie. Fourteen months later, Iacocca took his place. The reason for Knudsen's short stay at Ford? "The press has often reported that I led a revolt against [him]," explained Iacocca. "But his failing had little to do with me. Bunkie tried to run Ford without the system. He ignored existing lines of authority and alienated top people. In the slow, well-ordered world of GM, Bunkie Knudsen had flourished. At Ford, he was a fish out of water. Henry had achieved a great publicity coup by hiring a top GM man, but he soon learned that success in one car company does not always guarantee success in another."

However, during his abbreviated term, Bunkie did manage to boost Blue Oval performance. "When Mr. Knudsen came from GM," wrote Eric Dahlquist, "he brought along a strong belief in the value of performance." He also was well aware of the value of a race-winning reputation. "Any opportunity you have to show off your product in front of prospective buyers is good," said Knudsen during a 1968 interview. "Racing certainly has a visible effect; our sales increase somewhat every time a race is won."

Almost immediately after his arrival, Knudsen had put Special Vehicles Manager Jacque Passino to work reviving Ford's go-fast image, with the goal being to take some of that Total Performance racing prowess and pass it on to the street. Knudsen's performance-conscious presence inspired the rapid production of a wide array of powerful products, led by the brutish Boss 429 and agile Boss 302 Mustangs, both introduced in 1969.

Clearly contrasting with Iacocca's ideas, Knudsen felt the Mustang was "a good-looking automobile, but there are a tremendous number of people out there who want good-looking automobiles with performance. If a car looks like it's going fast and doesn't go fast, people get turned off. If you have a performance car and it looks like a pretty sleek automobile, then you should give the sports-minded fellow the opportunity to buy a high-performance automobile."

The first such opportunity for Ford pony car buyers was already in the works when Knudsen arrived. On April 1, 1968, Dearborn debuted its street performance savior, the 428 Cobra Jet Mustang. Inspired by fast-thinking Ford dealer Bob Tasca, the CJ Mustang appeared with an understated 335 horses under its black-striped hood. "Probably the fastest regular production sedan ever built," was ever-present Eric Dahlquist's conclusion in his famous March 1968 *Hot Rod* review after watching a pre-production Mustang CJ run a 13.56-second quarter-mile.

Typical street-stock Cobra Jets weren't quite that fast, but still impressed as one of Detroit's hottest offerings in 1968. CJ Mustangs featured an impressive collection of standard performance pieces, including power front discs and a ram-air hood. Thrown in as well was the GT equipment group consisting of a heavy-duty suspension, F70 tires on styled-steel wheels, fog lamps, and chrome quad exhaust tips.

In 1969, the Cobra Jet was joined by the Boss 302, built with Trans-Am road racing in mind. On the other side of the coin, the Boss 429 was a beast best suited for traveling in a straight line, and probably not on the street.

A much better all-around performer was the Mach 1 "SportsRoof," also introduced in 1969. "Are you ready for

A one-hit wonder, Mercury's Cougar GT-E was offered in 1968 only with either the aging 427 or the new 428 Cobra Jet big-block as standard power. *Ford Motor Company*

Plymouth's ponycar performance progression was slow at first, as early Barracudas were targeted primarily at the sporting crowd. Even though it was a bit short on muscle, the '65 Formula S was an intriguing road machine.

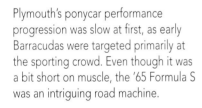

the first great Mustang?" asked *Car Life's* editors. "One with performance to match its looks, handling to send imported-car fans home mumbling to themselves, and an interior as elegant and livable as a gentleman's club?" Mach 1 imagery included a blacked-out hood with a non-functional scoop and racing-type tie-downs, color-keyed racing mirrors, bodyside stripes, pop-open gas cap, and chromed styled steel wheels. A special handling package went underneath and a complete choice of engines beginning with a 351-cubic-inch Windsor small-block came beneath the hood. At the top of the options list was the proven 428 CJ and the distinctive, functional "Shaker" hood scoop. Armed with a 335-horsepower CJ, a '69 Mach 1 became the "quickest four-place production car" *Car Life* ever tested: the quarter-mile went by in 13.90 seconds.

One of Knudsen's last contributions to the Mustang bloodline appeared a few years after his firing. Bunkie needed only one look at Chief Designer Gary Halderman's next-generation mock-up in February 1968 to O.K. yet another Mustang expansion for 1971. Of course, much of that additional mass was needed to handle even more horsepower beneath the hood. But the added size came at a cost. As Iacocca recalled, "in 1968, Knudsen added a monster engine with double the horsepower. To support the engine, he had to widen the car. By 1971, the Mustang was no longer the same, and declining sales figures were making the point clearly." Production for 1971 was more than 40,000 units less than 1970's, reflecting a downward trend that had been continuing steadily since 1966.

Also descending was the muscle Mustang's presence. Gone by 1971 were the race-ready Bosses, 302 and 429, replaced by the Boss 351. Replaced as well was the 428 Cobra Jet, superseded by the new 429 Cobra Jet, rated at 370 horses. The hot Boss 351 and 429 CJ

Mustangs themselves disappeared after 1971, leaving only a conventional 351 Cleveland small-block to keep Ford's performance pony car legacy running.

By 1970, pumped-up pony car rivals were as plentiful around Detroit as spent lottery tickets in a convenience store parking lot are today. GM's established F-bodies. Chrysler's all-new E-bodies. AMC's Javelin and AMX. The Mustang even had competition from within the corporation in the form of Mercury's Cougar, introduced in 1967, then instantly honored as *Motor Trend's* "Car of the Year."

Like its lower-priced Ford counterpart, the upscale Cougar line-up was initially led by a 390 GT variation. Next came the GT-E in 1968. GT-E power was supplied by the aging 427 V-8, offered only in 390-horsepower form for its last year on the planet. With the 428 Cobra Jet on its way, the previously pre-eminent FE big-block was discontinued in December 1967. Early GT-E Cougars hid a 427 beneath their dummy hood scoop; later renditions relied on the 428 CJ—either way the car's "7.0 Litre" badge applied.

Another hot-looking Cougar was added midyear in 1968. Using the GT-E's non-functional hood, the XR-7G was primarily an image machine in standard trim with its 210-horsepower 302, although 390s and 428 Cobra Jets were available. The "G" stood for Gurney, as in Dan, the man who drove the Trans-Am racing Cougars. On the street, an XR-7G came equipped with road lamps, racing mirrors, and hood pins, all the better to tie in the luxurious pony car with its track-tested alter-ego.

Yet another Cougar would make that road/track connection in more serious fashion in 1969 as Mercury unveiled its own Trans-Am-inspired counterpart to Ford's Boss 302. Like the Boss Mustang, the Cougar Eliminator featured a hot chassis and a sizzling image thanks to radiant paint schemes and purposeful spoilers front and rear. And, like the Boss, the Eliminator was also offered again in 1970, then was itself eliminated.

Before the Cougar's emergence in 1967, before the debut that same year of GM's Camaro and Firebird, the only competitor the Mustang faced early on was the Barracuda. Interestingly, stylist Dave Cummins' sporty small-car rendition from Plymouth actually debuted 16 days before Iacocca's pony made its big splash on April 17, 1964. Yet they don't refer to the still-running long-hood/short-deck crowd as "predator-fish-cars." Go figure.

Of course, the Mustang earned the right to inspire the new breed's name by waking up the sleeping masses like no vehicle before or since. Plymouth's first pony car, on the other hand, appeared almost secretly in comparison, and featured a unique fastback look that set itself far apart from Ford's established long-hood/short-deck ideal. The key to that look was the largest expanse of glass ever installed on an American car, a sweeping rear window that did its darndest to help buyers not see clearly the plain fact that this little automobile was not much more than a gussied-up Valiant. As for the choice of names, few at Plymouth apparently cared that, in the slang of the day, a "barracuda" was a very loose woman, maybe even loose enough to turn pro.

Not totally unlike its Ford rival, the Barracuda was a bit slow to make the grade as a true performance machine. As *Car Life* explained early in 1964, the car

"needs some development if it is to match with performance the promise of its racy good looks. As it is right now, it's just a novel little hardtop that won't swim away from anything." Chrysler engineer Scott Harvey, a rally driver himself, did help put together the Formula S package in 1965, but this sporty concoction concentrated more on handling—which it did well—than on underhood muscle. Not that the new four-barrel-fed 273 Commando small-block wasn't a welcomed upgrade. Its 235 hot-to-trot, little horses helped transform the '65 Barracuda "from a flabby boulevardier into a rugged middleweight," according to *Car and Driver*.

Again like the Mustang, Plymouth's big-block break didn't come until 1967, when the 383 Commando V-8 was literally shoehorned between the fenderwells of designer Milt Antonick's exceptionally sweet, restyled Barracuda body, now available both as a sexy fastback and polite "notchback" coupe. Even with a 2-inch wider engine bay, Plymouth engineers were forced to later re-invent their power steering pump to allow clearance on the driver's side. Air conditioning was an impossibility. Modified exhausts were also required, contributing (along with a milder cam) to a lesser-advertised output for the Barracuda's big-block. Normally pumping out 325 horses, the pony car's 383 was rated at 280.

Front discs, supplied by Kelsey-Hayes, were mandatory for the 383 Commando Barracuda, as was the desirable Formula S suspension package. The small-block Commando V-8 was still around, and its lighter weight was better suited for the established Formula S image, that being of a spry sports car. The 383 Formula S, on the other hand, was, in *Car and Driver's* words, "something of an oddball, more at home on a drag strip or a turnpike than on a winding mountain road." The big-block Barracuda was better than a second faster in the quarter-

Despite compromising the Formula S Barracuda's excellent chassis, Plymouth's 383 big-block V-8 was squeezed into the ponycar's engine bay in 1967 in an effort to better compete with the likes of Ford's 390 Mustang, Chevy's 396 Camaro, and Pontiac's Firebird 400.

mile compared to its 273-powered brethren—that was enough to convince many buyers that the 383 Formula S was indeed a supercar.

Plymouth engineers developed a wonderful compromise in 1968, introducing their 340 V-8, an exciting combination of big-block muscle and small-block sprightliness. Conveniently underrated at 275 horsepower, the free-breathing 340 was a direct descendant of the 273 small-block, so it fit easily between the Barracuda's fenders. Air conditioning could now be added. And with less cast-iron and more horses residing up front, the smaller-engined Formula S could really do its thing, both handling those winding mountain roads with ease and belting down the turnpike as quickly (often quicker) as many supercar rivals with many more cubes. Buyers who simply preferred bludgeoning the competition to death could still order the 383 Formula S in 1968.

In 1969, Plymouth's image-makers chose to segregate the lot, letting the Formula S (still with either the 340 or 383) exist as more of a gentleman's hot rod in one hand, introducing the bolder, less corner-conscious 'Cuda line for the other. Already popular on the street, the abbreviated name fit the new image perfectly, as did reams of black tape and twin, non-functional hood scoops. Street racers got just what they wanted from either the 'Cuda 340 or 383, a no-nonsense (well, maybe a little) ready-to-roll stoplight challenger. But there was more.

Most bystanders armed with tape measures knew two years before that Plymouth's first big-block pony car was only the beginning. "Is the 383 enough?" queried *Car and Driver* in its April 1967 Formula S road test. "The drag racing fraternity is already asking, 'why not the 440?' Indeed, the 440 ci block is essentially the same as the 383, so it would be a natural. For now, Plymouth is saying that a Barracuda 440 would be too much, but competition might change their minds." It did. The 440 'Cuda was introduced in April 1969. As you might have noticed, idea guys flopped the machine's identification order to better emphasize the big engine over the little car. For them, the job was as simple as reorganizing the tape labels on each front fender.

Engineers, on the other hand, had a much tougher time of it. Allowing the 375-horsepower 440 into the 'Cuda engine compartment meant fashioning a unique driver's-side exhaust manifold. It also meant leaving behind power steering and power brakes. And since a brake booster couldn't be installed, front discs were out of the question as well—power assist was always a mandatory must for disc brakes on more powerful or heavier cars. Optional air conditioning? Are you kidding?

A four-speed was also not used since engineers weren't confidant of the driveline's ability to resist torque

jolts—as many as 480 of them—created by bang shifts. Standard was the three-speed Torqueflite automatic backed by a Sure-Grip Dana rear end containing either 3.55:1 or 3.91:1 gears.

Clearly meant primarily to travel in quick, straight-line bursts measuring about a quarter-mile in length, the 440 'Cuda was indeed fast—5.6 seconds 0–60, 14.01 ticks through the lights—but that was about it. Calling it in some ways "a disturbing automobile," *Car Life* was quick to point out "obvious discrepancies between the superb way the 440 'Cuda goes, and the way it does other things. . . like, for example, stop." Steering was also predictably heavy, and promised an even sweatier workout if the track-ready quicker ratio was chosen. "Possibly the 1970 Barracuda will have suitable brakes and steering with the 440," concluded the *Car Life* test report. "But until they do the car will suffer."

As it was, those exact considerations had indeed been made a part of the engineering plan after Cliff Voss' Advanced Styling Studio began work on the next-generation Barracuda in February 1967. The all-new E-body would be able to house even the big 440 V-8 without sacrificing preferred accessories, like power steering and brakes. Air conditioning would also be possible with most

Things really got out of hand in the Plymouth ranks in 1969 when engineers literally stuffed their brutish 440 big-block between the Barracuda's fenders. Black-tape accents and twin dummy hood scoops were part of the 440 'Cuda package.

Opposite: Engineers had to create a special exhaust manifold for the driver's side to allow the 440 entry into the Barracuda's A-body engine compartment. Even then, there was still no room for a power brake booster, which in turn precluded the use of front disc brakes.

Dodge's Dart, a cousin to the Barracuda (both were A-bodies), received its first big-block late in 1967, although few buyers noticed. This very rare '67 GTS convertible is powered by a 280-horsepower 383 V-8. Production numbered fewer than 500.

big-blocks. Chrysler officials had big plans for the E-body, so much so they extended its realm into Dodge ranks, creating the Challenger as a running mate. Indeed, once on the streets in 1970, these two pony cars featured everything from tri-carb 440s and the vaunted hemi, to 383s and 340s—the muscle-bound list was almost mind-boggling.

Too bad the E-body performance tale was also short-lived. Although the 340 'Cudas and Challengers remained forces to be reckoned with for a few years more, the ever-present axe expectantly fell on the big-block bullies after 1971. Chrysler built its last E-body pony cars three years later.

While they were around, the smaller, more agile-looking E-bodies ran much closer to Detroit's established pony car ideal than their predecessors. Barracudas from 1967 to 1969 were more horse than pony, thanks to their

A-body heritage, a model line that also produced another family of "midrange" Mopar performance machines.

The A-body lifeline began with the refocused Dart in 1963. Dodge had first debuted the Dart nameplate on a slightly downsized rendition of its main line in 1960. Three years later, the image reemerged as a truly small car, a model originally very close in stature to the upcoming Mustang.

And, like the Mustang, early A-body Darts did offer simple sportiness by way of a GT options package, at first only available with a six-cylinder powerplant. The 273 V-8 came along in 1964, followed by the 235-horsepower 273 four-barrel in 1965. Then, just as Plymouth engineers did for the Formula S Barracuda, the Dodge boys late in 1967 added the 280-horsepower 383 big-block into the GT equation, creating the GTS, "S" for "Sport." It was a mysterious birth

to say the least. Other than a low-profile black-and-white ad, no official announcement of the first Dart GTS was made. Very few were built, leading most press mentions, then and now, to credit the 1968 version as being the first. Dodge paperwork that year did nothing to dispute that belief.

As part of Dodge's new "Scat Pack" promotion, the '68 Dart GTS received a lot more notice, both on paper and on the street. The GTS image was boosted somewhat by the optional "bumble-bee" stripes on the car's tail, a soon-to-be popular tie-in to the Scat Pack theme. Engine choices also expanded as the new 275-horsepower 340 was made the standard GTS power source, with the a 300-horsepower 383 available for a piddling $25 more. Even bigger news was made that year when Hurst began dropping 426 hemi super-stock V-8s into both Darts and Barracudas, and Norm Kraus, of Chicago's Grand-Spaulding Dodge, started marketing his 440-powered Dart GSS.

Picking up on what "Mr. Norm" started in the Windy City, Dodge's muscle builders did the 440 Dart trick themselves the following year, with a little help from Hurst's shoehorn experts, who obviously knew a little about ramming a square peg into a round hole. Hurst supplied the motor mounts, Dodge beefed everything

else up in order handle those 375 horses and nearly 500 foot pound of torque. Only about 30 '69 440 GTS Darts are known, all true rockets on wheels.

Back on earth, mere mortal drivers were treated to yet another brand of A-body performance in 1969. This time, the focus was affordability—"6,000 rpm for less than $3,000" was the description Dodge ads used for the new Swinger 340. For about $2,850, a Dart buyer got a Rallye suspension with D70x14 tires, the GTS hood, a Hurst shifter (when four-speed equipped), and 275 tried-and-true horses. All this added up to quarter-mile abilities in the high-14-second range. In *Car Life's* opinion, "the '69 Swinger has performance and is fun to drive—a lot more performance and fun than some of the intended performance and fun cars."

Affordable fun continued as a popular theme in 1970 when Plymouth joined the A-team, introducing its Duster, yet another Valiant with a fastback of sorts grafted on. Dodge pulled the same trick in 1971 for its Dart, adding a sweeping roofline to create the Demon. Having already proven it could throw some weight around, the 340 V-8 remained as the top A-body performance option in either case. Both the Duster 340 and Demon 340 were nicely priced (less than $2,800 in base form), definitely hot small cars, each able to do the quarter in less than 14.5 seconds. Pound for pound, these two fun machines may well have represented the most bang for the buck at the time.

Chevrolet's first moves to market lower-priced, small-car muscle came in 1963 when it extended its Super Sport image down into the year-old Chevy II lineup. The Nova SS in its first year was all looks and no action as a six-cylinder was the sole power source. Dealers did offer a V-8 swap in 1963, but at about $1,500, it wasn't for everybody, let alone anyone in the market for a budget-conscious Chevy II. A factory-installed V-8, the 195-horsepower 283, did come along as an official option in 1964, and a warmly welcomed 300-horsepower 327 was made available the following year.

When introduced in 1963, the Chevy II Nova Super Sport was all looks and no go—a six-cylinder was standard. An optional 283 V-8 did appear in 1964, followed by a 327 in 1965. Then, in 1966, the Corvette's 350-horsepower L79 327 became a Nova SS option, transforming the mild, compact Chevy II into a certified street sleeper. As demonstrated here, nothing at a glance gave away the true identity of a 350-horse Nova in 1966.

A truly tough SS 396 Nova debuted in 1968, making compact customers forget all about the L79 Chevy II. This '69 SS 396 is equipped with the optional L78 big-block, rated at 375 horsepower.

Then in 1966, Chevrolet borrowed the Corvette's 350-horsepower 327, RPO L79, and boldly dropped it into the Chevy II. The L79 Nova SS still stands as one of Detroit's greatest "street sleepers." Weighing slightly more than a ton and a half, the 350-horsepower Nova was both mean and nice. According to a *Car Life* review, "unlike some samples from the Supercar spectrum, [the L79 Nova] maintains a gentleness along with its fierce performance potential; its power/weight ratio is second to none and it is definitely better balanced than most." The little L79 could, with only a little help, run well into the 14s down the quarter-mile. Very few bystanders, however, noticed how hot the L79 Nova was. After appearing innocuously in 1966, less than a handful were built in 1967 before the combination was canceled.

Chevy's Nova flared up again early in 1968, this time thanks to the arrival of the hot 396 Mk IV big-block. And just as it was in SS Chevelle ranks, the 375-horsepower L78 variety was offered to help make the Nova SS 396 a real hauler, as in 13.8 seconds from start to the far end of the quarter-mile. L78 power once more transformed the little Nova into a secret weapon. And once again, it was over almost as soon as it started: the SS 396 Nova was dropped after 1970.

Not so secret was Chevrolet's response to Ford's pony car, a very close copy that finally hit the streets in 1967.

As early as 1962, Chevrolet Chief Designer Irv Rybicki had been talking to GM styling chief Bill Mitchell

about building a third small Chevy, this one along the lines of Dearborn's early Thunderbird. Mitchell was hot on the idea, but Bunkie Knudsen—who had become Chevrolet general manager in November 1961—didn't think the division needed another car line. By 1964, there would be five: Corvette, Impala, Chevelle, Nova, and Corvair. Then along came the Mustang that April. Four months later, word came down from the 14th floor giving the official go-ahead for a GM counterpart.

Bunkie had yet again moved onward and upward by the time Chevrolet's unitized F-body platform had taken shape. On July 1, 1965, he was bumped upstairs into GM's corporate maze; as he had done at Pontiac four years before, Pete Estes once more followed in Knudsen's footsteps, filling the vacated general manager position. And, as the GTO had earlier, Chevy's new pony car then became Estes' responsibility.

"I remember when we took [the F-body prototype] off the proving grounds for a test ride," Estes later told author Gary Witzenburg. "We had the whole thing camouflaged, all blacked out with cardboard on the quarter-panels and everything. But even then the fact that it was low and sleek and slender in the body prompted lots of questions. If a prototype car causes a big commotion, even looking like that, you really know you've got something. That was a hot car right from the start."

Clearly demonstrating its Mustang inspiration, with its really long hood and truly short rear deck, Chevy's new F-body still managed to turn heads with its fresh "Coke-bottle" body, a GM trademark. Initially called the Panther both inside Chevrolet and out, the F-body was finally

announced, via conference call, to the press nationwide as the "Camaro" on June 29, 1966. In his tele-communicated address, Estes called the car a "four-passenger package of excitement," and explained that "Camaro," in French, meant "comrade or pal." Whether that was exactly true or not mattered little since the name sounded good and began with a "C"—the latter seemingly representing at the time the sole criterion for creating Chevy nameplates.

As it was, GM name-callers generally felt that Panther inspired a much too "savage" image, something that would only serve to draw additional unwanted attention from Ralph Nader's auto safety crusaders. The Corvair had already done that enough.

With a more suitable, more socially acceptable image established, the real thing was unveiled to the media at a proving grounds press conference held September 12, 1966. Even with Washington's safety hounds watching, mucho performance was included as part of the Camaro's game. Hottest was the Super Sport with its special hood, striped nose, and wide-oval red-

stripe rubber. A Rally Sport package was also available, adding, among other things, hideaway headlights. The 295-horse 350-cubic inch small-block V-8 was the top SS power choice, inspiring the obvious reference, "SS 350."

Then in November, Chevy's purposeful 396 big-block, as expected, became a Camaro SS option, first in 325-horsepower trim, later in romping, stomping 375-horse form. Typically, the brutal big-block compromised the SS Camaro's balanced chassis and also commonly overwhelmed its brakes and steering capabilities. Nothing different here than in the case of any of Detroit's big-block pony cars. But when pointed in a straight line, an L78 Camaro could run away from almost anything in the supercar field, including, most importantly, Ford's first big-block Mustang.

Those who preferred all-around roadability could've opted for the nicely powered, better-handling, small-block Camaro SS, and perhaps added the RS package as well for a little more pizzazz. Customers with a real need for speed could check off RPO L78, bolt on a Muncie four-

Chevrolet's new Camaro was offered in a wide array of power levels in 1967, beginning with a base six-cylinder model. Initially, the top performance package was the SS 350 version with its small-block V-8. Not long after introduction, the SS 396 variety debuted, and again the top rendition was the 375-horsepower L78. This 1967 L78 SS 396 Camaro was originally sold at Yenko Chevrolet in Canonsburg, Pennsylvania.

speed, throw in a few heavy-duty chassis pieces, including perhaps a 4.11:1 posi rear gear, and let her rip. As Nader-baiters went in the '60s, they didn't come much more threatening than Chevy's 375-horse SS 396 Camaro. Even Ralph couldn't castigate what he couldn't catch.

Well, maybe he could. But while Nader and his cohorts were busy pushing legislation to bring Detroit's supercar strata back down to earth, Camaros were kicking butt and taking names all over town. Hell, in 1969 engineers, guided by performance products guru Vince Piggins, even dropped their animalistic 427s—both the iron-block L72 and the exotic all-aluminum ZL1—into their F-body pony car, all in the best interests of giving weekend warriors something to work with at the drag strip. Earlier, Piggins had also helped create a totally different breed for the road course crowd.

Also introduced in November 1966, the Z/28 Camaro was built to homologate Chevy's pony car for the SCCA's year-old Trans-Am racing circuit. The first of Detroit's "Trans-Am pony cars," the Z/28 featured a race-ready chassis and an exclusive 302-cubic-inch hybrid small-block. Originally a limited-edition, street-legal race car, the Z/28 by 1969 had become a truly popular road rocket, and today is still around to remind us of just how hot a Chevy can be.

While few musclecars can claim a career as long and successful as the Z/28's, only one has run unchecked from its birth in the '60s supercar days to the present. When Chevrolet rolled out a special-edition Camaro for 1997 to commemorate 30 years of Bow-Tie pony cars, it stands as somewhat of a misnomer in the case of the Z/28, which took a brief leave of absence in the '70s. On the other hand, when Pontiac people in 1994 put together an equally special anniversary model marking a quarter-century of Trans Am performance, they meant it. The T/A Firebird has been proving it all night every year since 1969, making it the only modern muscle machine (the "ineligible" Corvette notwithstanding) to run non-stop from its birth in the '60s supercar days to the present.

Like the Z/28, the Trans Am was created, as its name implies, with SCCA competition in mind. Having taken Pete Estes's place as Pontiac's chief in July 1965, John DeLorean wasn't about to let Pete's Camaros run away without a little supposedly friendly Firebird competition. As it stood, DeLorean had from the beginning envisioned PMD's pony car more as a true sports car comparable to Chevrolet's Corvette anyway. Why not let it maximize its sporty, racy appeal?

While still at Pontiac, Estes had been considering DeLorean's sporty proposals as early as 1963. An enthusiast as well as an engineer, DeLorean envisioned a fiberglass two-seater with four-wheel independent suspension and Euro-style six-cylinder power. Soon called "Banshee,"

DeLorean's XP-833 prototype had reached clay mock-up stage by August 1964, the same time Chevrolet was given the thumbs-up for its F-body project. DeLorean, however, wasn't interested in simply following Chevy's lead. Forget the F-body, he stood ready, willing, and able to make the Banshee a production reality by 1967. Designers were still working on his dream car as late as February 1966.

By then, a Pontiac F-body was already in the works. And in March 1966, GM Executive Vice President Ed Cole finally told DeLorean to give his Banshee dream a rest and "make a car out of the Camaro." Handicapped by the short time involved, PMD designers nonetheless did a nice job of creating their own pony car apart from the Camaro, thanks both to the addition of a purely Pontiac beak (measuring 5 inches longer than the Camaro's) and a few chassis tweaks thought up too late to be included in Chevrolet's F-body package. Pontiac's pony was better balanced thanks to an engine located farther back than the Camaro's. Also, radius rod traction bars were added in back to inhibit axle hop under hard acceleration.

For a name, label-hangers reached back into the '50s to a series of GM experimental turbine cars. The Firebird, PMD's F-body pony car, was introduced February 23, 1967. "You'd expect Pontiac to come up with a nifty new sports car like this," announced ads. "But did you expect five?" Pontiac's "Magnificent Five" for 1967 included two Firebirds fitted with the division's innovative overhead-cam six. Another, the "light heavyweight" Firebird HO, came with the 326 small-block V-8, while the top two models both were equipped with big-blocks, Pontiac's 400.

The base Firebird 400 offered 325 horsepower. Spending $616 more put a functional Ram Air hood on top that didn't change the advertised output rating but did allow those horses to breathe a little easier. Maximum output for the Ram Air 400 came on at 5,200rpm, 400 above the standard big-block. This translated into 100 miles per hour coming in 14.4 seconds down the quarter-mile according to a *Car and Driver* test.

Performance-oriented Firebird upgrades in 1968 included staggered shocks and multi-leaf springs in back to further battle axle hop. More advertised horses came under the hood, five more for the base 400, 10 for the Ram Air big-block. The L74 400 HO, also rated at 335 horsepower, was introduced, followed in March 1968 by the 340-horsepower Ram Air II.

Echoing advancements made by the GTO that same year, the restyled '69 Firebird wore a new monochromatic nose made of Lexan. Additional advancements behind that nose included the Ram Air III 400, still wearing the familiar 335-horse rating, and the outrageous, rarely seen

Ram Air IV, conveniently tagged with a conservative advertised output figure of 345-horsepower. Costing a whopping $832, the impressive Ram Air IV option was chosen by only 102 Firebird customers in 1969.

Another 55 Ram Air IV big-blocks were optionally installed in the new '69 Trans Am, which came standard with the Ram Air III 400. With either engine, the Trans Am was a real winner featuring an aggressive image that was both eye-catching and fully functional. The Ram Air hood rammed air, extractors extracted, and spoilers spoiled. It was a grand beginning for an exciting performance legacy. But it was also a humble start, as only 689 T/A Firebirds were built in 1969. Production delays also inhibited sales of an even better second-edition Trans Am in 1970, leaving the high-flying breed in a holding pattern in the '70s, that even with the presence of the superstrong, certainly rare 455 Super Duty variety in 1973 and 1974. By 1979, however, Pontiac was selling more than 100,000 of its spoilered and scooped Firebirds with those "screaming chickens" on their hoods. Almost two decades later, Pontiac continues building excitement.

No longer around today, since absorbed by Chrysler for its surviving, successful Jeep line, American Motors was a firm known far and wide in the mid-'60s for the decidedly unexciting cars it built. But by hitting the pony car trail in 1968, the company from Kenosha (as in Wisconsin) almost overnight traded its dull, small-car image for a high-performance reputation amazingly able to stand right up with the Big Three's.

The brainchild of George Mason, American Motors had been formed in April 1954 through the merger of Nash and Hudson. Then Mason died that October. George Romney, his replacement, essentially lucked out when his company's plainly practical compacts became just the ticket to attract bargain-hunters in the recession-riddled late-'50s. His sales successes in 1959 brought him a *Time* magazine cover, and in 1963 *Motor Trend* awarded his affordable Rambler a "Car of the Year" trophy. However, a rapidly changing, more youthful market quickly left AMC's boring econo-buggies in the dust as fun-loving buyers in the '60s no longer cared about puritanical practicality.

Fortunes quickly waned, to the point where 339 dealers abandoned AMC in 1965. But, as *Motor Trend* editor Donald MacDonald explained early in 1966, "it takes a heap o' dyin' to kill off a billion-dollar corporation, and AMC is not going to collapse before it reaches its 12th or 13th or 14th birthdays." Nevertheless, a much larger heap o' livin' was in order if American Motors executives had any plans to blow out many more candles.

Fortunately, the rigidly conservative Romney had left AMC in February 1962 to successfully pursue Michigan's governor's office. In his place as president came Roy Abernethy, who was more or less given an anchor and told to swim. Investors got the idea when their red-ink stained stockholders report was delivered in 1966 inside a plain brown wrapper instead of the glossy color cover used in 1965.

Still somewhat of a stick-in-the-mud, Abernethy at least let some new ideas flow in. And some real cash flow out. After he took over, AMC quickly spent $300 million over the next few years on its future; which, as rumors soon began claiming, would include racing projects. New model line retooling for 1967 alone cost $75 million, with $40 million of that going into the design of the new 290 V-8, a modernized power source that Kenosha-watchers felt didn't quite mix with the compact company's existing intentions. According to *Motor Trend's* MacDonald, the money spent on the 290 "has led to speculation that AMC is about to deep-six its anti-racing philosophy and turn to competitive events as a means of knocking down its avidly gathered reputation for economy."

Indeed, in 1967 Carl Chakmakian was put in charge of a modest AMC racing program. Added that year as well was the first of AMC's "Group 19" parts listings, which included various heavy-duty performance pieces. In 1967, only three Group 19 part numbers were listed; by 1969, they would fill a catalog.

These modest performance moves came along with an infusion of new blood up Wisconsin way. In 1966, figurehead Richard Cross had been replaced as the firm's chairman of the board by AMC's largest stockholder, Robert Evans. Not long afterward, Roy Chapin, Jr., was made executive vice president and basically given control of all "automotive activities." Was it any coincidence that Chapin, like AMC styling chief Richard Teague, was an avid sports car enthusiast?

Teague, in early 1966, had overseen "Project IV," an experimental vehicle program meant to prove that AMC could indeed build at least some excitement. Two of the four show cars included in Project IV were sporty, sexy things; the two-seat AMX and four-place AMX II, both inspired by Stylist Chuck Mashigan's original AMX-labelled concept initially developed in October 1965. A big hit on the auto show circuit in 1966, Teague's Project IV AMX featured a fiberglass body and flip-up "Ramble" seat in back for a third passenger. Uncharacteristically unconventional, especially by AMC standards, the AMX show car had everyone wondering just where the company was heading.

Evans had a clue. Called by Donald MacDonald "a little-known Detroit healer of sick companies," the new chairman of the board was out to shake things up in Kenosha. As MacDonald explained, "he, unlike AMC's present management, is not disposed to forgive Romney for past sins. He freely criticizes Romney's leadership on grounds that Romney failed to adjust to a changing market." As for future directions, "there is a strong suspicion in Detroit," wrote MacDonald, "that Evans has tucked away in the back of his mind a solution for AMC." All evidence then pointed to the regular production of a two-seat AMC sports car along the AMX show car lines. Evans "wanted the car very quickly," said Teague.

In the meantime, Chapin was voted the new chairman of the board and chief executive officer in January 1967 as Evans moved into a less visible director's position. At the same time, Roy Abernethy was put out to pasture. As a company official said a year later, the former president "had finally come around and was starting to think in terms of young cars—but by then it was really late in the game."

Meanwhile, rumors really started percolating concerning AMC's high-speed plans. "Is American Motors about to junk the auto industry's anti-racing resolution to which it has strictly adhered for 10 years?" asked an August 1967 *Motor Trend* report. "Until recently, AMC under George Romney and Roy Abernethy observed the letter and spirit of the [1957] AMA resolution. Now, however, things are changing under Roy Chapin, with the help of Robert

Alway striving to be different, American Motors introduced its two-seat AMX for 1968. The last two-seater was built in 1970, after which the AMX became an options package based on the longer Javelin platform. *Chrysler Historical Archives*

Evans." Mentioned in that report were various appearances by American Motors racers at drag strips and racetracks, one such machine driven by an AMC engineer "on vacation." "The next step in AMC's carefully planned program to create a performance image could be a pull-out from the antiquated AMA resolution," read *MT's* conclusion.

Creating that image by racing wasn't, of course, as simple as thumbing a nose at the AMA. As an unnamed AMC executive told Donald MacDonald in 1966, "you don't go into racing to do anything but win. To win, you have to spend millions of dollars and you've got to find the right combinations of drivers and crews. To find all that takes more than money—it takes time." To that, MacDonald pointed out that "Ford has already proved that if a company plans to make a run for the big loving cups, it'd better be prepared to go ahead with all the fervor and financial recklessness of a 16-month-at-sea sailor questing through San Diego's saloons."

American Motors's big run began late in 1967 with the introduction of the Javelin, a sporty pony car born out of the AMX experiments. Then on February 15, 1968, at the Daytona International Speedway, AMC officials debuted what Group Vice President Vic Raviolo called, "the Walter Mitty Ferrari." It may not have worn a fiberglass shell, but the new AMX did only include two seats. And, with a wheelbase measuring only 97 inches, it was also not much bigger than many European sports cars.

Performance, however, was purely American, with the 225-horsepower 290 V-8 coming standard, the 280-horsepower 343-cubic inch and 315-horsepower 390-cubic inch V-8s offered as options. Top performance came by way of AMC's "Go Package," available for both the Javelin and AMX. Included here was either the 343 or 390 V-8, power front discs, special suspension, and E70x14 redline tires, Twin Grip axle, heavy-duty cooling group with seven-blade flex fan and fan shroud, 140-miles-per-hour speedometer, tach, and space-saver spare tire.

All this added up to real American muscle. *Mechanix Illustrated's* Tom McCahill called AMC's little two-seater "the hottest thing to ever come out of Wisconsin." In a *Car and Driver* test, a '68 AMX ran 0–60 in 6.6 seconds, the quarter-mile in 8.2 more ticks, helping make the new machine "good enough to

become the sort of car by which other cars are judged." In AMC Vice President William Pickett's unbiased opinion, the AMX "will get a lot of attention from people interested in performance." Continued Pickett, "we are not getting the attention now. But this company has made a decision to go after the youth market."

Pickett's comments inspired an interesting analogy. As *Motor Trend* explained, AMC, "which appeared on the brink of disaster in recent months, is endeavoring to save itself by using the same formula that resurrected Pontiac 10 years ago. It's trying hard to build a performance image. Gone is all the talk about compact cars. And no latter-day George Romney flails away at the 'gas-guzzling dinosaurs' of the Big 3. Maybe full-bore competition is an ambitious goal for American Motors, whose performance image still has to be shaped before it can be polished. But if determination wins trophies, AMC's shelf might not be bare for long."

AMC muscle soon flourished, including not just AMX and Javelin pony cars, but other potent packages like the Hurst SC/Rambler of 1969, Rebel Machine in 1970, and the surprising, yet almost unknown '71 Hornet SC/360. Two-seat AMXs were built up through 1970, with an outrageous Super Stock drag racing version offered with Hurst's help in 1969. In 1970, the rare red, white, and blue Trans Am Javelin SST was born to mark American Motors's entry into the SCCA Trans-Am battles. And it was joined that year by a Mark Donohue-signature Javelin, Donohue being AMC's top Trans-Am pilot. On the SCCA sedan racing circuit, Javelin Trans-Am teams finished second in 1970, then rewarded Roy Chapin by copping the crown consecutively in 1971 and 1972. Back on the street, Javelins armed with 401-cubic inch V-8s continued promoting the "American way" with feeling up through 1974.

Like Chrysler's E-bodies, the Javelin disappeared after that. American Motors did survive, although it would never experience such wide-open success again before riding the Jeep down into Chrysler's hands. For nearly five years, however, its red, white, and blue brand of muscle helped this country's last great independent automaker ride high one last time.

And it was a pony car that led AMC to those heights.

Opposite: Although the two-seat AMX garnered the most attention from muscle watchers, its longer Javelin sibling was no weakling, especially when equipped with AMC's optional "Go" Package, which included power front discs, E70 Red Line tires, a special handling package, and either the 343 or 390 V-8 with dual exhausts. Twin black fiberglass hood scoops topped things off. This 390-equipped Go Package '69 Javelin also features the optional "Big Bad" paint scheme, roof spoiler and Hurst four-speed. Three Big Bad colors were offered, Big Bad Orange, Big Bad Blue and Big Bad Green. Color-matched bumpers were part of the Big Bad option.

American Motors commemorated its Trans-Am racing success in 1970 with a special signature edition of its Javelin honoring its SCCA driver, Mark Donohue. Production was 2,501. *courtesy John Conde*

Chapter Four

POWER TO THE PEOPLE
Performance Goes Back to Basics

Industry rivals wasted little time doing Pontiac one better following the GTO's introduction in 1964. Five years later, Chevrolet's SS 396 Chevelle took over as this country's best-selling supercar. But beating the GTO on its turf was one thing. There was more than one way to skin a Goat, and it didn't take Detroit's movers and shakers long to figure out a different approach to this mass-marketed muscle thing. The goal was to build hot performance and sell it like hot cakes. Going fast was no big deal, anyone could do that. But automakers soon realized they would need something more than just pure horsepower to turn customers' heads in an increasingly competitive market. How about something less?

These days, the concept is commonly called "best bang for the buck." Nearly 30 years ago, the idea was the same. "You order your car with every go, stop, and turn part available, but nothing else," explained *Car and Driver* in 1969. "No candy coating to kill the flavor because the flavor is the thing. And you haven't pushed the price out of sight with tack-ons which only serve to confuse the issue anyway. You've got yourself an Econo-Racer and it's sano."

Budget-conscious performance was nothing entirely new by the time the "econo-racer" term was coined. In 1967, Buick had tried that tack with its GS-340, a new twist on its Gran Sport theme using a less powerful, less costly 260-horse 340-cubic inch V-8 in place of the 340-horsepower 400 used by the big-boy GS-400. Introduced in February 1967, the GS-340, according to factory promotional paperwork, put "performance in the range of budget car buyers," but was "a lot of car for any car buff." While the exclusive exterior, available only in Platinum Mist and Arctic White, was dressed up noticeably with

high-profile accents (hood scoops, stripes, and Rallye wheels were all done in red), the GS-340's interior was taxi-cab Spartan with a bench seat and little else.

Including the $343 options package price, a '67 GS-340 started out at about $2,850, a fair price for fair performance. Buick came back in 1968 with its GS-350 as a lower-priced, small-block running mate for its big-block GS-400 brother, but the punch really wasn't there. Nonetheless, the division did move just as many small-block Gran Sports as big-blocks that year, the best ever for GS sales.

The true pioneer of the econo-racer breed, the first company to really sell America on the idea of budget muscle was one of Chrysler's divisions. In *Car and Driver's* words, Plymouth "realized it wasn't doing its big engines any favors by stuffing them into cars already overweight with gadgets and glitter."

As legend has it, *Car and Driver's* Brock Yates called Plymouth's product planning office early in 1967 with a suggestion. Whether it was Yates' idea or not, a plan then quickly formed for a new kind of muscle machine, a stripped-down, no-frills, high-thrills budget-bomb. Market research next proved what everyone already knew: the more you spent, the faster you went. In those days, the best bang came from the biggest bucks. There were many cars priced above $3,300 that could do 100 miles per hour in the quarter-mile; not one below that price that could score triple digits. That then became Plymouth's goal: 100 miles per hour in the quarter for less than $3,000.

Opposite: While Pontiac's GTO Judge idea began as a low-cost performer, in reality it ended up a much more costly machine. The only real concession to cost-cutting was the deletion of trim rings on the Rally II wheels.

103

While this big-block was based on the yeoman 383 V-8, it used heads, cam, and valvetrain from the GTX's 375-horsepower 440. With next to no muss and very little engineering fuss, Plymouth had produced a relatively cheap power source able to make 335 horses on command. Behind that went a standard four-speed—no wimpy three-speed box here.

Topping it all off was an image borrowed, at a cost of course, from a popular Warner Brothers kids cartoon. To beat wily GTOs, Plymouth turned to its Road Runner, a high-performance, low-cost alternative to big-buck muscle. Wise guys at Plymouth even fitted the '68 Road Runner with a cute "beep-beep" horn. And ads referred to the new supercar species by its Latin name, "acceleratii rapidus maximus." Customers of all ages loved it, both that horn and the super-cheap supercar behind it.

"Plymouth figures, and rightly so, that one way to win you over this year is to give you lots of car for your money," reported *Car Life*. "In the case of the Road Runner, Plymouth's idea is to give lots of *performance* for the money, and it does this partly by putting gobs of go-goodies into the car, partly by not charging tremendous amounts for it, and partly by keeping things simple." Base price was a few dollars more than the $3,000 goal, while early performance tests showed the Road Runner could do the quarter almost as fast as projected, faster with a few easy tweaks. It could definitely blow everyone away when equipped with the expensive 426 hemi option, but then that basically defeated the whole econo-racer idea, now didn't it?

Cutting costs in the case of the GS 340 meant cutting cubes and horses. The standard V-8 was a 260-horsepower 340. Price for the GS 340 options package was $343.

To meet this end, Plymouth designers kept non-essentials to a minimum. A bare-bones Belvedere sedan, with swing-out rear windows instead of roll-up units, was initially chosen as the base for their new model. Underneath went a beefed suspension. Beneath a slightly bulging hood went a clever combination of passenger-car power source and hot-ticket hardware.

Buick was among the earliest to try teasing customers with a more affordable muscle machine. The GS 340, introduced in 1967, was a little less costly compared to its GS 400 big brother, thanks to less engine under the hood and spartan appointments inside. The red accents were also part of the package.

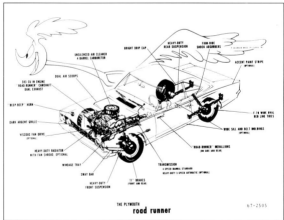

THE PLYMOUTH
road runner
67-2505

Calling the new Road Runner "the world's fastest club coupe," *Car and Driver* pointed out that "this is the first car since the GTO to be aimed directly at American youth and it very probably is dead on target. But just wait till ol' Nader hears about it."

Customers apparently got the word long before Ralph. Road Runner demand quickly skyrocketed, with 1968 production reaching 44,599. A classier hardtop ver-

sion sans pillars and with roll-up rear-quarter glass quickly joined the line-up in 1968, as did a sporty convertible in 1969. That year, *Motor Trend* awarded the Road Runner its "Car of the Year" trophy as sales soared even higher to 84,420, second only by a couple grand to Chevy's SS 396. And more than 12,000 above Pontiac's GTO.

Just as the GTO had four years before, the Road Runner quickly inspired competitors to try the econo-racer route themselves. Friendly competition first came from across the hall at Dodge, which in 1968 rolled out its similarly equipped, Coronet-based Super Bee, "a kind of inverse kinky name, but no less a real car," according to *Car and Driver*.

Dodge already had one solid performer with a reasonably low price tag, the 383 Dart GTS, introduced quietly late in 1967. Then in 1968, along came a second GTS offering a better balanced performance at an even lower price, about $3,150. Heart of this budget-conscious beast was Chrysler's new 340 small-block V-8, rated at 275 horsepower.

There was nothing complicated about this little engine that could. The 340 was simply a great combination of all the right stuff, parts that worked in concert to

Plymouth's Road Runner is recognized as the progenitor of the "econo racer" theme: it offered the highest level of standard performance for the best price. A buyer who wanted more muscle simply had to open up the wallet—the 440 and 426 hemi V-8s were available at extra cost. This '69 Road Runner features the standard 335-horsepower 383 big-block.

Plymouth made the Road Runner a more affordable musclecar by keeping frills to a minimum while concentrating on what mattered most—muscle. The long list of standard performance equipment was impressive. *Roger Huntington Archives, courtesy Dobbs Publishing*

produce maximum performance from minimal cubes. No maintenance-intensive solid lifters. No sky-high compression needing sky-high octane. No high-tech engineering to force its price up beyond the average Joe's reach. And no excess baggage to add to performance-robbing overall weight. It wasn't peaky and temperamental like the Z/28's 302 and Ford's Boss V-8. Nor was it hidden away and high-priced like Chevy's LT-1 of the '70s. The 340 wasn't Detroit's hottest supercar small-block, but it was easily accessible, and it was also an able competitor.

Lastly, the Mopar 340 represented one of the industry's earliest best bangs for the buck. Introduced in 1969, Dodge's Dart Swinger 340, marketed primarily for its affordable performance, was easily able to run well into the 14s at the strip. Its price? A few hundred less than

$3,000. Thrifty performance like this continued into the '70s as the Swinger's replacement, the Demon 340 and its Duster 340 counterpart from Plymouth both offered the same sizzling speed for not much more than $3,000—this at a time when many supercars were running well into the four-grand bracket.

Direct competition for the Road Runner came along in 1969 in the form of Ford's Fairlane Cobra. Commonly and erroneously identified as a Torino, the first Cobra was no such thing. Nor was the long-nose Talladega. Ford promotional people didn't help make this fact clear at all, instead they let their hunger for high-class hype take over while splashing "Torino" all over their NASCAR racers in 1969. In truth, the Talladega was essentially a Cobra with a nose job, and the Cobra didn't become a Torino until 1970.

Ford's response to the Road Runner was the Fairlane Cobra, a stripped-down screamer powered by a 428 Cobra Jet V-8 in base form. Like the Road Runner, the Cobra could become quite pricey as additional options were checked off. The ram-air hood and styled-steel wheels shown here were moderately costly extras.

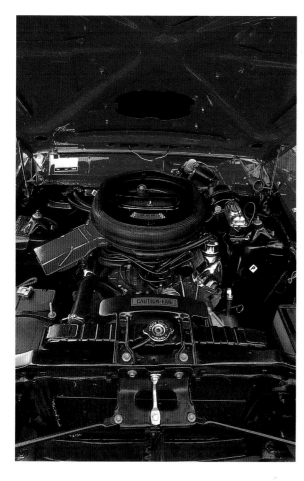

Like the Road Runner, the Fairlane Cobra came standard in 1969 with a four-speed stick and a competition suspension. Cobras with the standard manual trans (an optional automatic was available) were fitted with staggered rear shocks to help fight axle wind-up during hard acceleration.

Supplying the torque that commonly twisted that rear axle was Ford's 335-horsepower 428 Cobra Jet FE big-block. Again like the Road Runner, the Cobra could've been equipped with an optional ram-air hood—that attractive hood scoop in standard form was fully non-functional. It did, however, serve as a great place to mount those "428 Cobra Jet" scripts. Additional exterior identification included coiled-snake badges at the tail and on each fender. Early factory photos showed large decals, but these were apparently teasers.

Ford's Cobra were priced right in line with the econo-racer ideal: $3,183 for the fastback; $3,206 for the less popular formal roof. Typical add-ons of course could've raised that ante in a hurry. The ram-air hood cost $133; the Drag Pack with its 3.91:1 Traction-Lok rear end, $155; and 14x6 chromed styled-steel wheels, $116. With or without options, this back-to-basics machine represented a lotta go

for the dough, that is unless you felt mid-14s weren't worth three grand. After watching a '69 notchback Cobra quickly dispense with an SS 396 Chevelle in a side-by-side shootout, *Hot Cars* magazine's road tester was pleasantly surprised. "Like it or not, Chevy lovers, the Cobra is a threat," he wrote. "We also think [it] is going to do the job on a lot of Road Runners."

When *Car and Driver* did its own econo-racer showdown in 1969, both the Road Runner and Fairlane Cobra were present, as were Dodge's Super Bee, Mercury's Cobra Jet Cyclone, and Chevy's SS 396 Chevelle. "Decide which one your driving record can stand," concluded *Car and Driver* after the tire smoke had cleared. "For the price of a Porsche 912 minus most of a VW, you can have your choice."

A sixth supercar was also invited to *Car and Driver's* road test orgy. Only the GTO Judge supplied by Pontiac didn't quite pass tech inspection, failing both to meet 1969 emissions standards and to qualify as a regular-production example since it had a more radically cammed 1968 Ram Air engine in it. What had worked for Jim Wangers and Royal Pontiac in 1964 wouldn't wash five years later. PMD people "couldn't make up their minds whether our Pontiac was a prototype or a real car and the result was we couldn't get enough accurate test information about the car to put anywhere in the standings," explained the *C&D* report. So the Judge was held in contempt.

Initially born of John DeLorean and crew's plans for a real bare-bones econo-racer, the true production-line GTO Judge ended up a bit more in reality. Early plans spoke of a 350 HO small-block and even rubber floor mats in place of carpet. But once the ball got rolling, there was nothing more to say other than "here come da Judge." Introduced in December 1968, the final product featured splashy decals and a rear wing on the outside. The standard Rally II wheels did come without trim rings to at least look as if someone at Pontiac was trying to keep costs down somewhere.

Actually, the $332 asking price for the Judge package was much less than what a customer would pay if he tried to build this much excitement himself after putting down about $3,150 for a base '69 GTO. G70 rubber and the 366-horsepower Ram Air III 400 were standard issue, as was a stiff suspension. For another $390, a buyer could've added the hairy 370-horsepower Ram Air IV big-block and backed it up with a $195 Hurst-shifted four-speed. When *Car Life* tested a Ram Air IV GTO Judge in 1969, its fully loaded bottom line read $4,439—not exactly what anyone would've considered a steal. Then again, many of the '60s econo-racers were quick to reach the expensive stage once options started checking off. In Pontiac's case, the Judge just got a bit of a head start.

The vaunted 428 Cobra Jet V-8 was conservatively rated at 335 horsepower as the Fairlane Cobra's standard power source in 1969. Notice the black rubber "doughnut" on the air cleaner. It sealed the air handler to the hood's underside, allowing cooler, denser outside air to flow through the functional scoop to the carburetor below.

For Pontiac performance fans looking for a truly cheap way to rapidly go from point A to B, there was the enigmatic GT-37, called by Pontiac in 1971 "the GTO for kids under 30." Any GTO equipment save for the Judge package could've been added to the '71 GT-37, including the 335-horse 455 HO big-block V-8. The price for a nicely loaded 455 GT-37 was about $3,600, not a bad deal at all in 1971 terms.

Even more splashy than the Judge was Oldsmobile's 1970 entry in the low-buck muscle race. Olds since 1968 had been trying to fool those pesky insurance agents while still offering some decent performance at a decent price by offering a small-block "W-machine" to go along with its big-block W-30 4-4-2. The rare "Ram Rod 350" '68 Olds featured a hot W-31 350-cubic inch V-8 force-fed by the same ram-air ductwork used by the W-30 400. Output was 325 horses. Running separate from the high-profile 4-4-2, Oldsmobile's W-31 Cutlasses and F-85s were quietly offered up through 1970. When *Hot Rod's* Steve Kelley tried one on for size that year, he couldn't believe the way the small-block W-machine left the line much like its big-block brother. "On first tryouts," he wrote, "most of the group figured the 350-inch W-31 for the 455."

Dr. Oldsmobile, the mythical ruler of the Olds performance arena, even unleashed a detuned version of the W-30 big-block for 1969, undoubtedly as a sacrifice to the gods of insurance surcharges. Still fed by those two air ducts, the W-32 used a less-aggressive cam and was commonly rated 10 horsepower less than the W-30 at 350 horses. The W-32 400 was offered for only one year, probably because it was chosen by a mere 297 buyers in 1969.

Then in 1970, the good doctor tried the small-block route again, this time presented in a fashion far from quiet. For starters, the only color available for the new Rallye 350 was Sebring Yellow, a screaming zonker of a shade if there ever was one. On top of that, the wheels were yellow, even the bumpers were yellow thanks to a urethane coating. A blacked-out grille, fiberglass W-25 ram-air hood, contrasting black striping, and an optional rear wing only made the car all that more sleep-shattering. "It's Wurlitzer heavy," claimed *Car Life*.

But waking the dead wasn't the Rallye 350's sole purpose. "Beneath that gaudy paint and wing lurk bargains in performance and handling," continued *Car Life's* review. The Rallye 350 came standard with the FE2 heavy-duty suspension. Power was supplied by a 310-horse 350 four-barrel V-8. Offered on three F-85 and Cutlass models, the Rallye 350 carried a base price of $3,253. For that relatively tidy sum, a driver could go 0–60 in 7 seconds, and through the quarter in 15.27, according to *Car Life's* test. In conclusion, that test told

us "the world should know that you can get good handling, good mileage and good performance in a quality package for $3,200, shouldn't it?"

At least the world could get all that in 1970. Within a few short years, all that was left of the econoracer breed was the econo end of the deal. For the most part an impostor, the GTO Judge had retired by early 1971. The Cobra, based on the upscale Torino beginning in 1970, was discontinued at the end of 1971. Growing more expensive all along, Plymouth's Road Runner continued motoring along in reasonably sporty fashion up through 1974. The cartoonesque nameplate did return in 1975, only this time it was based on the less-than-sporty Fury, a somewhat bogus ending for a once-proud bird.

As it was, drivers by then found their bucks couldn't buy any bang of any kind, economical, expensive, or otherwise.

The W-31 Cutlass, offered from 1968 to '70, was the lesser known of Oldsmobile's revered "W-machines." The idea behind the W-31 was to keep costs down by both using a small-block 350 (in place of a big-block) and basing the package on a lower-profile Cutlass instead of the image-conscious 4-4-2. All this meant a W-31 driver would probably hand over less cash to his insurance agent since this muscle machine didn't appear near as much a threat to highway safety as its 4-4-2 brothers. *Oldsmobile Division, General Motors Corporation*

Opposite: Oldsmobile did its W-31 idea one better in 1970, introducing its high-profile, low-cost Rallye 350. Standard features included the radiant yellow exterior, matching bumpers, and a 350 small-block V-8.

A 310-horsepower 350 was the powerplant of choice for the Rallye 350. Topping it off was the fully functional, fiberglass W-25 ram-air hood. The foam gasket on the air cleaner is part of the W-25 equipment.

Chapter Five

GO SPEED RACER, GO!
Supercars from Super Stocks to Superbirds

Long, long ago, back when the rosy-fingered dawn first began illuminating the wine-dark sea, stock cars were *stock* cars. Sure, poetic license has always played a major role when defining the term. But when a race car embarked on a high-speed odyssey in stock-class competition three decades ago, it was based—loosely or otherwise—on a street-going counterpart. Or at least a machine manufactured, to some degree, by a Detroit automaker. That outside contractors might have tweaked the engine or fabricated race-required upgrades mattered not at all. When a Super Duty Catalina cruised past all comers on a NASCAR speedway in 1962, race fans recognized that Pontiac did indeed know how to build excitement. Loads of it.

As the saying goes, "Race on Sunday, sell on Monday." Loyal race fans see their favorite do its thing at the track, then turn right around and buy a street car of the same name. The sales ploy always has worked, and probably always will, only customers used to be able to bring home a real piece of the action, not just a caricature.

We among today's advertising fodder are still led to believe a tangible connection remains between the products we're asked to buy and those wearing the same logos taking checkered flags. For chrissakes, all those Monte Carlos running around Daytona have *V-8s* sending torque to the *back* wheels through, of all things, *Ford* rear ends. Try ordering that combination at your local Chevy dealer. Meanwhile, Chevrolet ads (or Ford's when they're winning everything) continue telling us we should buy one of their cars because their company wins NASCAR races. And you thought cupholders were the true measure of a new car's merits.

In many respects, it's a shame pro racing's stock classifications have long-since lost essentially all their

meaning. At least the SCCA circuit still has a top stock sedan series. Essentially everything else on race tracks out there today represents pure flights of fancy. On-track action once fostered the Walter Mitty in many of us, especially so when the cars we drove were race-winning "wannabes" themselves. Young drivers today don't even know who Walter is.

Then again, the reason behind this evolution involves the obvious fact that Detroit's offerings also lost all their competitive abilities in the '70s. Once the only way to fly in drag racing terms, NHRA stock-class competition by then had been all but completely overshadowed on the national level, first by the early funny cars in the late '60s, then by the burgeoning "Pro Stock" league. Stock-class drag racing today is a mostly nostalgic, minor league venue, as it should be since there aren't enough modern musclecars around to feed the system. Nor are such cars anywhere near as affordable or wrench-friendly as they once were.

Both unbridled competition and reined-in factory performance, combined with a constant concern for safety on the track, contributed to NASCAR's gradual departure from its "stock car" roots. Purposeful, battleship-like tube chassis designs began proliferating in the late '70s. And sheet metal went completely away from modified factory panels to fully fabricated forms in the '90s.

While certain recent Detroit styles (Thunderbird, Monte Carlo, Grand Prix) were created with an eye toward high-speed potential on NASCAR superspeedways, the closest these stock bodies get to the track is as homologation guinea pigs for the template shapes used to measure racing teams' "Reynolds wrap" shells. NASCAR's latest stock cars are all homogeneous tin boxes with a little bit of marque

One of the most impressive early entries in the factory super stock races was Pontiac's 421 Super Duty V-8, a 405-horse honker that became a regular-production option for Catalinas and Grand Prix coupes in 1962. The latter installation is shown here. Dual four-barrels and free-flowing, streamlined exhausts marked just the beginning of a long list of beefed-up, high-output Super Duty components.

Opposite: While the all-new Charger, introduced in 1968, looked sleek and slippery, its recessed grille opening proved to be a major stumbling block when the car took to NASCAR superspeedways. Dodge designers defeated this aerodynamic anchor in 1969 by adding a flush-mounted grille. Fixed headlights also came along as part of the Charger 500 transformation. Yet another change involved mounting flush rear glass in place of the standard "tunneled" window.

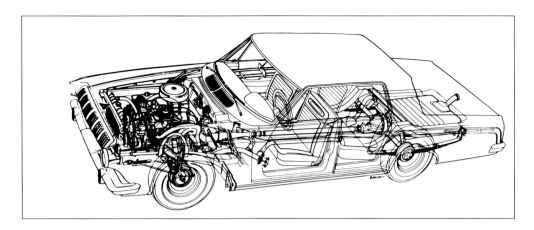

Above: Early '60s Mopar muscle was best characterized by the various factory super stock drag cars, which began flourishing in 1962 with the arrival of the 413 Max Wedge racing motor. In 1963, the Max Wedge V-8 was enlarged to 426 cubic inches. Notice the cross-ram dual fours; huge, header-like exhaust manifolds; and competition cutout exhaust plumbing (located directly ahead of the driver's seat) on this '63 Dodge super stock.

Detroit seemingly went mad with power in the early '60s, unleashing a wide variety of outlandish racing machines. In 1964, Ford contracted Dearborn Steel Tubing to help fabricate a run of strip-ready Thunderbolts, 427 Fairlanes beefed to the nines and lightened to help put one over on the competition. This particular Thunderbolt (right) is powered by a Mickey Thompson-designed hemi-head 427. The Mustang on the left is a Holman-Moody A/FX factory dragster, itself fitted with the exotic 427 SOHC V-8 fed by twin four-barrel carbs. Some '65 A/FX Mustangs featured Hilborn fuel injection.

Ford's Galaxies may have been big, but that didn't stop them from throwing their weight around at the dragstrip. To help lighten the load, various fiberglass panels were added beginning in 1962. In 1964, a distinctive "teardrop" hood became part of the lightweight Galaxie package. Beneath that scoop is the big-bully 427 "Hi-Riser." *courtesy Gold Dust Classics*

identification added at both ends to supply ad men ammo for their promotional campaigns. Even though these "hand-formed" boxes do say Chevy, Ford, and Pontiac on top, most race watchers really don't know what's inside.

Not so in the '60s. Beneath all those logos then was at least some portion of a machine that actually had been born in Detroit. The question at that time wasn't whether or not rac-

ing improved the breed, it was "which came first, chicken or egg?" Did racing really help Detroit build better cars, or did Detroit build better (translated: faster) cars to improve racing?

It all started so subtly. Various hot parts programs were springing up even as the '50s were closing up shop, all aimed at giving the rapidly growing professional drag racing circuit something better to play with; NASCAR, too. And as Detroit continued building more radical factory racers, racing's rules moguls kept responding with even more rules meant to help hold the reins on the runaway horsepower race and keep the competition as fair as possible. In drag racing, stock classes became super stock (S/S), then super super-stock (SS/S). NASCAR's earliest limitations included a 7-liter displacement lid, a nice fit for Ford's 427.

Next came Detroit's obvious escalation: body and chassis modifications to better package the horsepower being produced. In 1962, all automakers started jumping on the lightweight bandwagon as aluminum and fiberglass began replacing steel. Fenders, inner fenders, hoods, grilles, bumpers, brackets, and such were all put on diets and made regular factory options or dealer add-ons.

Ford built lightweight Galaxies from 1962 to 1964, first with 406s, then 427s. Super Duty Pontiacs featured aluminum noses in 1962 and 1963, and the latter models even had specially drilled frames, inspiring the name "Swiss Cheese" Catalina. Chevrolet's first Z11 package also included a few lightweight parts; even more in 1963. Mopar's Max Wedge monsters were given the lightweight treatment as well that year.

Runaway competition on the track soon translated into super stock escalations at the factory. Drag racing's officials had already responded again to Detroit's ever-loosening definition of "stock production" by creating

the relatively unlimited factory experimental (FX) class to serve as a catch-all for the growing group of super super-stocks. With the classifications door then wide open, America's automakers quickly turned to even more radical rides.

Hot on the heels of Pontiac's brutal Super Duty Tempest in 1963 came Ford's '64 Thunderbolt Fairlane, a purpose-built machine if there ever was one. Manufactured by Dearborn Steel Tubing, these little screamers were fitted with various lightened body parts and chassis beefs along with Ford's race-only 427 "Hi-Riser."

Outrageous, odd-looking, altered-wheelbase "super-FX" cars began appearing in 1965, sometimes wearing acid-dipped bodies and always using exotic power sources with or without Hilborn fuel injection. Altered Mopars had 426 race hemi V-8s, while Ford's Holman-Moody-built A/FX Mustangs were powered by both Hi-Risers and SOHC 427s. Already then in the works, drag racing's "funny car" class would quickly evolve from these early altered-wheelbase and "long-nose" variations on the factory-experimental theme.

Traditional super stocks carried on after 1965, although their presence did diminish greatly once race fans' need for speeds greater than 150 miles per hour began taking precedence. Ford's last great factory drag car came in the form of a more streetable 427 Fairlane for 1966. With NHRA S/S racing rules by then demanding a production minimum of at least 50 cars, Ford rolled out only 57 of these beasts off its Atlanta production line, all basically identical Fairlane 500 hardtops with Wimbledon White paint. Topping the 425-horsepower 427 was a scooped fiberglass hood tied down by four pins—hinges were deleted to save additional weight.

Factory super stock racers from Chrysler carried on into 1967 and 1968. Like the "WO51" and "RO51" 1965 S/S projects from Dodge and Plymouth, the WO23 and RO23 cars of 1967 were stripped-down, strip-ready cars powered by the 425-horsepower 426 hemi V-8. As before, the "O" in the vehicle identification number code signified super stock; the "W," Dodge; and the "R," Plymouth. The "23" referred to the body, a two-door hardtop. Reportedly, 55 examples were built of each, WO and RO. In 1968, Chrysler came back with a pair of wilder hemi super stocks, these prepared in conjunction with Hurst, this time using the smaller Dodge Dart and Plymouth Barracuda. Commonly quoted production for the Hurst hemi Darts was 80; 70 for their Barracuda counterparts.

Detroit's last all-out factory super stock came from Kenosha, again by way of Hurst. American Motors' '69 Hurst SS AMX featured a muscled-up 390 V-8 using heads massaged by Crane Engineering, 12.2:1 pistons, a Crane roller-rocker cam, Doug Thorley headers, and an Edelbrock cross-ram intake mounting two 615-cfm Holley four-barrels. These burly bruisers were as expensive as they were fast—the price was nearly $6,000. Only 53 were built.

Along with high-profile super stocks like the Hurst AMX and 427 Fairlane, Detroit also continually offered less-professional Saturday night warriors ample weaponry in the '60s. Many more machines were purpose-built with obvious intentions. Oldsmobile's top-performance package, the W-30, originally put the battery in the trunk in 1966 and 1967, just where it belonged for better weight transfer during jump starts off the line. And W-30 4-4-2s after that continued using those red plastic inner fenderwells, clearly made part of the deal to lighten the load.

Altered-wheelbase factory drag cars began flourishing in 1965, with Chrysler once again at the cutting edge. Better weight transfer during launches was the goal, thus both the front and rear wheels were moved ahead on cars like Dick Landy's '65 Dodge. Power came from an injected race hemi. *courtesy Gold Dust Classics*

Less exotic than its Thunderbolt forefather, the '66 427 Fairlane was still a purpose-built factory super stocker equipped only for drag racing. Beneath that lift-off fiberglass hood was a 425-horsepower dual-carb 427.

Aimed more at the weekend warrior, Plymouth's '69 Six Barrel Road Runner was built with one thing in mind—racing. No wheelcovers were included, nor were hood hinges—the fiberglass unit simply lifted off once pins were pulled at the corners. Beneath that huge scoop was a 390-horsepower 440 V-8 sporting three two-barrel carburetors on an Edelbrock intake. Dodge tried the same tack with an identically equipped Six Pack Super Bee in 1969. *Roger Huntington Archives, courtesy Dobbs Publishing*

Opposite: In 1969, Chevrolet built two special COPO Camaros equipped solely for racing: the ZL1 (COPO 9560) with its all-aluminum 427, and this version, COPO 9561, a less exotic combination featuring a typical cast-iron 427 big-block.

Heart of the COPO 9561 Camaro was the Corvette's L72 427 V-8. No aluminum heads or block here, just 425 unbridled horses to help haul this heavy big-block around with ease.

Chrysler in 1969 rolled out its Six Pack Super Bee and Six Barrel Road Runners for Dodge and Plymouth drivers who didn't mind lifting off (no hinges) their hoods by hand (four of them) or looking at bare wheels (no hubcaps) and lug nuts. Again, these mean machines were meant for one thing, and running down to the corner store for a Big Gulp Dr. Pepper wasn't it.

Why do you think Chevrolet engineers introduced those L89 aluminum heads for their 396 big-block in 1969? If you answered "to save unwanted pounds," you just might have won an expense-paid trip to the NHRA Nationals. For the serious racer, there was also the all-aluminum 427, the ZL1. COPO Camaros in 1969 used the ZL1, as well as the iron-block L72 427.

By 1970, however, factory-built drag cars were history as Detroit's attentions had turned to two other hot sales tickets; one that put customers into NASCAR seats of their very own, the other allowing entry into the world of SCCA road racing. The game was called "homologation," a derivative of the Greek "homologos," roughly meaning "in agreement." Homologation is the process by which a competition version of a regular-production automobile is legalized for sanctioned stock-class racing. Homologation was also the reasoning behind the birth of Detroit's "Trans-Am pony cars" and NASCAR-inspired aero-racers.

The former group hit the ground running in 1967. In March 1966, SCCA officials had staged their first Trans American Sedan Championship race at Sebring, Florida. During its first two years, the Trans-Am circuit

was a one-horse show as Ford's Mustang took top honors up against a pack of Plymouth Barracudas and Dodge Darts. But late in 1966, with the Camaro only a heartbeat away, Chevy officials had already recognized the need to beat Dearborn's pony car on its own turf.

Even with corporate killjoys watching, Vince Piggins' performance projects crew managed to create the Z/28 to homologate a Camaro entry in SCCA racing. At the time, SCCA sanctioning bodies demanded that a legal production engine's displacement not exceed 5 liters, about 305 cubic inches. No problem. Engineers maximized the Chevy small-block's efficiency by stuffing a 283 crank into a 327 block, resulting in the SCCA-

Chevrolet kicked off the Trans-Am ponycar race in 1967 with its Z/28 Camaro, at first a low-production, low-profile racer for the street. By 1969, the Z/28 had grown into one of Detroit's most popular musclecars, thanks in part to a go-fast image that worked in concert with all that performance potential.

approved 302 V-8, a rarin'-to-race engine offered only as the Z/28's exclusive power source. Although Chevrolet officially rated this hybrid small-block at 290 horses, seat-of-the-pants readings went much higher, some as lofty as 400 horsepower.

Simply named for its RPO code, the Z/28 also featured an impressive array of heavy-duty standard equipment. F41 sport suspension. Power front discs. Big 15x6 Rally wheels. Other than those wheels, no specific exterior identification was added save for black racing stripes on the hood and deck lid.

A Z/28 prototype was introduced to the press on November 26, 1966, at Riverside, California. Raves quickly followed. "With the Z-28," concluded *Car and Driver*, "Chevy is on the way toward making the gutsy stormer the Camaro should have been in the first place." The *C&D* test team also felt the new 302 was "most responsive American V-8 we've ever tested." At the track, the 302 Camaro supplanted the Mustang as Trans-Am champion in 1968 and won again in '69.

On the street in 1968, the Trans-Am Camaro was given a bit of an image boost as the soon-to-be-legendary "Z/28" emblems were finally added. After building only 602 Trans-Am pony cars for 1967, Chevrolet backed up that humble homologation run with another 7,198 Z/28s in 1968, followed by 20,302 the following year. Both a new body and engine came along midyear in 1970, when the Corvette's LT-1 350 small-block was made the Z/28's standard mill with a rating of 360 horsepower instead of 370.

Where was performance-conscious Pontiac while Ford and Chevy were battling it out in the late '60s? Unfortunately, no mixing and matching of available cranks and blocks from Pontiac's parts book could conjure up a competitive V-8 able to put an SCCA-legal Firebird on the Trans-Am circuit.

Canadian businessman Terry Godsall did field a Pontiac pony car team in 1968, basing his run on the belief that *all* Canadian Pontiacs were powered by Chevy V-8s—this fact allowed him to use the Z/28's 302 in his race cars within SCCA rules. In truth, *many* Pontiacs built north of the border were Chevy-powered—Canadian Firebirds were all built in Norwood, Ohio, using Pontiac engines. A scam? You betcha.

Pontiac's legit efforts to make the SCCA scene were well under way even as the Canadian ruse was taking root. Supported by upbeat engineers like Steve Malone, Bill Collins, and Herb Adams, John DeLorean rode herd over various pony car performance projects. Included was Adams's Pontiac Firebird Sprint Turismo. About the same time, world-class racer Jack Brabham was hired for another development project. Meanwhile, work also progressed on the SCCA-legal 303-cubic inch "tunnel-port" V-8.

Pontiac waited two years to follow Chevrolet's lead, introducing the fabled Trans Am in 1969. All '69 models featured the same blue-accented white finish and were fitted with hood scoops, fender-mounted air extractors, and a decklid wing.

Initial plans called for a hot "Brabham Firebird" package to appear for 1969. But Brabham's name was dropped in favor of a long-standing PMD tradition. The choice was clear: If SCCA racing was the goal, it was only right to name the car "Trans Am." Only this time, DeLorean couldn't just cop this title. A royalty fee was negotiated: $5 for every Trans Am Pontiac built. More than 25 years, 800,000 T/A Firebirds and $4 million later, PMD people are probably still shaking their heads.

Apparently no one at Pontiac figured the Trans Am would never die, at least not when they introduced the car in December 1968 at Riverside. All Pontiac wanted to do was build enough T/As to go Trans-Am racing, however long that roller coaster ride lasted. As it was, an SCCA career never got completely off the ground as planned in 1969, thanks to the 303 V-8's failure to make it into production.

But on the street, the car was a real winner. The "Trans Am Performance and Appearance" package, option code WS4, was priced at about $1,100 depending on transmission choice and body style, coupe or convertible. Imagery was plentiful, what with that blue-accented Cameo White paint, fender-mounted air extractors,

twin-scooped hood, and rear spoiler. According to Herb Adams, the Trans Am's 60-inch-wide rear wing created 100 pounds of downward force at 100 miles per hour.

In place of the stillborn 303 V-8, engineers turned to the proven 400 big-block as the '69 Trans Am's standard power source. The base engine was the 335-horsepower Ram Air III L74 400, with the L67 Ram Air IV available at extra cost. All eight '69 Trans Am convertibles were L74-equipped; four automatics, four manuals.

Early Trans Am reviews were mixed. "Trans Am my gluteus maximus!" began *Sports Car Graphic's* report. "What a gaggle of fibbers those name callers are in Pontiac, Michigan. This is no more a Trans-Am race car than the GTO is an 'omologated Ferrari or the Pontiac Le Mans is a race track in France. In the first (obscene language deleted) place, this pretender comes standard with a 400 cu. in. engine, and everyone in the world who knows what Trans-Am means also knows that 5 liters equals 305.125 cu. in.—no less and, very explicitly, no more."

"The decal said Trans Am, the car didn't." echoed *Car Life's* critics, whose "purist pride had been hurt." "The Firebird gets a racy name and a spoiler," they continued, "but it's still a long way from race-ready. Sorry. Tail foils and scoops may do something for the ego, but they won't keep a car in the turns."

Car Life testers didn't like the way the nose-heavy Trans Am handled. But even with its 58/42 front-end bias, the car's road-worthiness still impressed others. After beating Pontiac's new 'Bird severely about the beak and feathers, *SCG's* staff then regrouped and began praising the T/A generously, calling it "an animal; a souped-up, sharp-horned, hairy mountain goat. We can't imagine where Pontiac learned how to set up a suspension, but this one is a good illustration that a nose-heavy car doesn't *have* to be a tragic understeerer."

Like its Camaro cousin, the T/A Firebird was a limited-edition, hard-to-find machine in its first year. Then, like your best girl on a Saturday night, GM's complete F-body makeover wasn't quite ready for the new-car dance come fall 1969, leaving Chevy and Pontiac pony car buyers with updated leftovers until the "1970-1/2" models debuted the following February. Luckily, from a GM bean counter's perspective, the wait was well worth it, even more so in the case of the second-edition Trans Am, a real macho manhandler that quickly helped establish Pontiac's pony car performance legacy.

By then, competition in the Trans-Am pony car field was heavy, with everyone in the fray. Ford, the Trans-Am circuit's early champion, had at first watched as the Z/28 stole its thunder, then returned in 1969 with retaliation. Responding to Bunkie Knudsen's demands for "absolutely the best-handling street car available on the American market," chassis engineer Matt Donner created a lowered, competition-type suspension rolling on 7-inch-wide wheels wearing fat F60 rubber. Under the hood went the exclusive Boss 302 small-block, rated at 290 horsepower. Brute force, however, wasn't the focus. According to *Car and Driver*, the '69 Boss 302 was "without a doubt the best-handling Ford ever to come out of Dearborn and may just be the new standard by which everything from Detroit must be judged."

Larry Shinoda, the man who put the Boss in Boss Mustang—the name, the image, the slats, and stripes and spoilers were all his work—wasn't quite as quick to proclaim the '69 Boss 302 as the leader of the Trans-Am pony car stampede. A GM defector like Knudsen, Shinoda had followed his boss over to Ford to become its Special Projects director in May 1968, drawn by the challenge of helping Dearborn regain the attentions of the youth market. While at Chevrolet, he had also worked on the first Z/28, so he knew from whence he spoke when it came time to compare the two Trans-Am rivals.

"I've driven both cars and I really couldn't say the Boss 302 was dramatically better than the Z-car," he said. "In showroom trim, the Mustang was close, but I can't really say it was superior." Perhaps if there hadn't been so many stumbling blocks in Dearborn. . . .

Ford men, according to Shinoda, "knew very little about vehicle dynamics when [Knudsen and I] came on board. They never did testing on a skid pad. Initially they were saying that bolt-on aerodynamic stuff was bull, that you didn't need it. In fact, they even fought the rear wing because they were saying we've got a big enough spoiler already, which we didn't really have. And the front air dam? They argued about that, too. We finally had to show them how to use a skid pad, and how you develop your vehicle dynamics on it to get optimum handling."

Using such techniques, Chevrolet engineers had made the Z/28, in Shinoda's words, "one of the finest handling American cars ever built." As for the Boss 302, he could only say it was "quite good, especially compared to any Ford product." On SCCA tracks, the vote was split as the Camaro won the Trans-Am championship in 1969, the Boss Mustang in 1970. On the street, Ford sold 1,934 Boss 302s in 1969, followed by another 6,138 in 1970, decent numbers but still behind the Z/28.

Shinoda's Boss treatment also carried over into Mercury's stable in 1969. First shown in prototype form at the Los Angles Auto Show in October 1968, the Cougar Eliminator emerged as a regular-production reality six months later. Like its Boss cousin, the Eliminator came in various eye-popping finishes, and looked exceptionally purposeful with its chin spoiler and rear wing. A competition handling suspension with attractive slotted

With a flashy image supplied by designer Larry Shinoda, Ford's Boss 302 Mustang looked every bit as fast as it was. Although handling was the Boss 302's forte, that 290-horse canted-valve small-block beneath the hood was certainly no slouch. This fully loaded '70 Boss 302 is decked out with all the goodies: front chin spoiler, rear wing, window slats, and Magnum 500 wheels.

Exclusive to the Boss 302 Mustang in both 1969 and '70 was the specially created small-block V-8 of the same name. The Boss 302 engine used Ford's new Cleveland heads, then being prepared for an all-new 351-cubic-inch small-block to be introduced in 1970. The Shaker ram-air scoop on this Boss 302 was in option in 1970.

develops along a body's surface at speed. Splashy graphics, radiant paint schemes, and optional spoilers also came along in the deal. So too did mismatched rubber, a Detroit first: rear tires were G60s, fronts were E60s. Equally new and different was the cutout exhaust system. Exhaust flow went into the mufflers, did a U-turn inside to exit out the front, then cut a sharp arc outward and rearward again to reach the atmosphere, race-car style, just in front of each rear wheel.

Like its Z/28 and Boss 302 rivals, the T/A Challenger and AAR 'Cuda were fitted with an exclusive engine created solely for this application. New SCCA rules in 1970 allowed Trans-Am racers to meet the 305-cubic inch requirement by destroking a standard production V-8. Thus, these two Mopars hit the streets with a 340 small-block topped with three Holley two-barrel carbs. Beefed throughout, the 340 Six Pack (Dodge) and 340 Six Barrel (Plymouth) V-8s were rated, probably conservatively, at 290 horsepower.

Although impressive on the street, the AAR 'Cuda and T/A Challenger were high-priced disappointments on SCCA tracks. A second-edition T/A Challenger was briefly mentioned for 1971, but by then Trans-Am racing was old news. Chrysler, Ford, and Chevrolet dropped out of the circuit that year, and Dodge's '71 T/A never appeared.

With the Big Three gone, American Motors took full advantage of the situation and dominated the token Trans-Am field in 1971 and 1972. Having been in the SCCA race since 1968, with little to show for it, AMC had enticed Roger Penske and Mark Donohue over from Chevrolet with a $2 million carrot. The company released two street-going commemorations of this deal that year, the image-conscious Mark Donohue signature Javelin and the traditionally red, white, and blue Trans Am Javelin SST.

AMC only built 100 of the latter, all featuring a 325-horsepower 390 with the "Go Package" (power front discs, Twin-Grip axle, handling package, special cooling, ram-air, etc.), a four-speed with Hurst shifter, 3.91:1 gears, 14x6 five-spoke wheels, and front and rear spoilers. Although not anywhere near as prominent as the other Trans-Am pony cars, the T/A Javelin was still a fun ride. While it lasted. Even though AMC Javelins did keep the Trans-Am legend alive into the '70s, the real glory was in the past. Trans-Am racing fans would never get such a great taste of the action for the street again.

The NASCAR faithful first got their own taste in 1969 when Detroit began building more street machines aimed at legalizing competition-ready counterparts. In this case, the sanctioning body was big Bill France's. And Bill's basic homologation requirement was by no means Greek to Detroit's automakers: simply build 500 regular-

Mercury's Cougar Eliminator was the Boss 302's cousin, offering similar chassis features and dress-up imagery, but with a wider choice of power sources. This 1970 Eliminator is powered by a Boss 302. The 351 Cleveland small-block and 428 Cobra Jet big-block were also available.

Plymouth's Trans-Am pony car entry came in 1970 wearing flashy imagery and showing off a pronounced forward rake thanks to the different size tires used at each end—a Detroit first. As for the AAR 'Cuda's name, that acronym referred to Dan Gurney's "All American Racers."

wheels wrapped in F70 Polyglas Goodyears was standard, as was a 290-horsepower 351 Windsor small-block V-8. Optional power varied greatly, from the 428 Cobra Jet, to the Boss 302, to the 320-horsepower 390 GT. Cobra Jet and Boss Eliminators were fitted with even heavier suspension hardware, and a rear sway bar was also optional.

Chrysler finally entered the Trans-Am pony car race in 1970. More compact and agile than its A-body forerunner, Plymouth's all-new E-body Barracuda offered real potential as a road racer, as did its Challenger running mate from Dodge. First offered to the public in March 1970, the Challenger T/A left little doubt about its intentions, as did its AAR 'Cuda counterpart—"AAR" in reference to Dan Gurney's "All American Racers." Both featured fiberglass cool-air hoods, each wearing a distinctive, radical scoop; the Challenger's setting up above the restrictive boundary layer of air that naturally

Dodge's '70 Challenger T/A mirrored the AAR 'Cuda, using the same cutout-style exhausts and mismatched rubber—the latter long-since replaced by modern tires here. While both these Mopar street racers used fiberglass ram-air hoods, the scoops varied greatly. The T/A Challenger's scoop was "elevated" above the hood to avoid the restrictive boundary layer of air that normally forms at speed along a car's surfaces.

Both the AAR 'Cuda and Challenger T/A used the same exclusive small-block, a 290-horsepower 340 V-8 fed by three two-barrel carburetors. This is the Dodge version, thus the "Six Pack" logo. Plymouth always used "Six Barrel" in reference to its tri-carb engines.

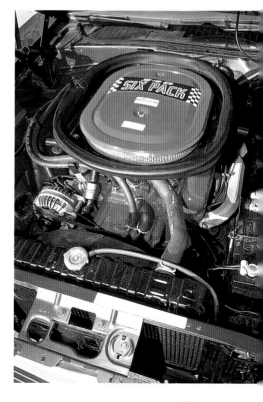

production examples of any given engine or body style and you could race them all day.

Various liberal interpretations of "factory stock" had been keeping France busy trying to stay one step ahead of crafty competitors since NASCAR's inception in 1949. He always envisioned fair competition, an ideal that grew tougher to police in the early '60s. It hadn't taken the big boys long to get back in the game after the AMA "racing ban" of 1957, and they were determined to bring their own ball. After years of various rules changes, NASCAR finally established the 500-unit minimum production requirement in 1967.

While this production standard helped make things easier on France's end, it also served to lead Detroit in a new direction. Brute horsepower wasn't the only key to speed. Physical laws being relatively constant, 500 or more horses could only do so much anyway with a stock

body possessing all the aerodynamics of a parachute. A "wall" apparently existed at about 175 miles per hour as all that power simply couldn't beat the wind.

FoMoCo drivers breached that wall first when the sleek Fairlane and Cyclone fastback bodies appeared in 1968. Left in the dust, the Dodge boys found their new Charger body was only sleek-looking as its recessed grille and tunneled rear window created ample drag at high speeds.

Dodge's solution was the Charger 500, introduced in the fall of 1968. Taking its name from France's production requirement, the '69 Charger 500 was put together at Creative Industries in Detroit. Using the grille from a '68 Coronet, the Creative fellows transformed the Charger's recessed front cavity into a flush nose, complete with fixed headlights. In back, they fabricated a steel plug to fill in the rear window tunnel. The end result was an additional 5 miles per hour on top end.

Mercury's counterpart to the Talladega was the Cyclone Spoiler II, which relied on basically the same tricks to cheat the wind at high speeds. Two versions were offered in 1969, the blue-accented Dan Gurney Special and the red-trimmed Cale Yarborough Special.

Opposite: Although '69 Ford Talladegas are commonly referred to as Torinos, there's nothing Torino about them, as was the case with the '69 *Fairlane* Cobra. Not helping the situation was official Ford factory paperwork which used the "Torino Talladega" moniker, leading Ford racing teams to also paint the misnomer on the quarterpanels of NASCAR versions. On the track, these odd concoctions with their aerodynamically superior extended snouts used 427s and Boss 429 V-8s. On the street, all '69 Talladegas came with 335-horsepower 428 Cobra Jets backed by C6 automatics.

Creative Industries—by hook or crook—actually fell a bit short of France's production requirement. Estimates today commonly list only 392 Charger 500s for 1969. Nonetheless, Dodge was given the green flag. On the street, Charger 500s were powered by either the 375-horsepower 440 or 426 hemi.

But while it appeared promising, the Charger 500's early announcement, made before the end of the '68 NASCAR season, only helped inspire a threatening response. While Dodge was showing off its new aero-racer in Charlotte, Dearborn's racing chief, Jacque Passino, was heading across town to Holman-Moody, where Ralph Moody had built a similar machine based on Ford's Fairlane.

Using longer Cyclone fenders, Moody had fashioned a wind-slicing extended nose. Hot on the idea, Passino took Moody's idea back to Dearborn for Bunkie Knudsen's approval. Special Vehicle Engineer Bill Hollbrook then supplied a suitable moniker, suggesting the car be named after the superspeedway then under construction in Alabama near Talladega.

To meet NASCAR's 500-model minimum, Ford dedicated most of its January 1969 production run at its Atlanta plant to the new Talladegas. Using the '69 Fairlane fastback body as a base, workers added special fenders with stamped steel extensions welded on, a flush-mounted Cobra grille and a sloping header panel between the grille and hood. Along with reducing frontal area, the revised nose also brought the car's leading edge nearer to the ground, inducing wind over, not under. This helped NASCAR versions stay exceptionally stable while busting the 190-mile-per-hour barrier.

NASCAR-minded modifications on the street-going Talladegas also included rocker panels that were cut and re-rolled 1 inch higher than stock sheet metal. This barely noticeable hocus-pocus allowed race teams to lower Talladega bodies that extra inch over their racing frames while still maintaining NASCAR's rigidly enforced minimum ride height, which was measured in ground clearance.

Counting prototypes, Ford built 745 '69 Talladegas. All were essentially identical, save for paint. Three shades were offered: Wimbledon White, Royal Maroon, and Presidential Blue. Inside, a mundane bench seat interior was done only in black. Powertrain choices numbered

one: the 428 Cobra Jet mated to a C6 automatic transmission. Early racing versions used the 427 tunnel-port V-8 until the new Boss 429 was ready. Curiously, the "semi-hemi" 429 was homologated for NASCAR competition in 1969 beneath Mustang hoods—France's rules stated that 500 cars or engines be built, they didn't say the two had to live together.

Mercury also manufactured a kissin' cousin to the Talladega in 1969, the Cyclone Spoiler Sports Special, or Cyclone Spoiler II. Looking quite similar with its long, dropped snout and rolled rockers, the Spoiler II in fact differed much in detail, only because the Cyclone and Fairlane bodies themselves weren't identical. Spoiler IIs also were fitted with a less formidable 290-horsepower 351-cubic inch small-block V-8. They were flashier as well, thanks to a rear wing, more prominent striping, and contrasting roof paint. Two images were offered, the blue-accented "Dan Gurney Special" and its red "Cale Yarborough Special" running mate. Supposedly, the Gurney models were meant for dealerships west of the Mississippi; the Yarboroughs for out east. But each ended up in the other's "zone."

Like the Charger 500, the Spoiler II apparently didn't quite play by the rules. Although a production figure of a shade more than 500 was published over the years, only 353 cars are actually known. As the theory goes, the difference was made up by Mercury's more-conventional, standard-shell Cyclone Spoiler models, themselves introduced that year in red Yarborough or blue Gurney Special garb. Apparently no one noticed that among all those red or blue long-nosed Spoiler IIs lined up for NASCAR review were various stock-bodied red or blue Spoilers.

Much more noticeable on the street, the Spoiler IIs were completely overshadowed by their Ford counterparts on the track. Debuting at Daytona in February 1969, the Talladega onslaught overwhelmed Dodge's teams as LeeRoy Yarbrough's long-nose Fairlane ended up in the Daytona 500 winner's circle. Talladega pilots took 26 wins in 1969, giving Dearborn another manufacturers title. Charger 500s took 18 checkered flags, while Spoiler II wins numbered four.

Dodge quickly regrouped and returned in April 1969 with an even more aggressive wind-cheater, the Charger Daytona. The product of some serious wind-tunnel testing, the Daytona may well represent the wildest-looking machine ever launched by Detroit. To better beat the breeze, Creative Industries added a pointed steel beak with a chin spoiler, a fully functional modification that stretched the car by about a foot and a half. In back went a cast-aluminum "towel rack" wing towering over the rear deck. And like the Charger 500, the Daytona was also fitted with a leaded-in steel plug to allow flush-mounting of the rear glass. Reportedly, the new nose could produce nearly 200 pounds of downforce; the rear wing, 650 pounds. In racing trim, the Daytona was the first NASCAR competitor to surpass the 200-mile-per-hour barrier.

Again like its flat-nosed predecessor, Dodge's winged warrior was equipped with either 440 or 426 hemi power. Production this time was completely legit: 503 were built during a three-month run.

Not long afterward, Plymouth kicked off an aero-car project of its own. First born in June 1969, then temporarily canceled in August, the Superbird was rapidly readied for the 1970 NASCAR season. As in the case of the Talladega-Spoiler II relationship, Plymouth's winged street racer looked similar to its Daytona forerunner, but was very much a different bird. For starters, the Road Runner front clip wouldn't accept that nose graft as easily as the Charger's. Thus, a hood and front fenders were copped from the Coronet line for this application. Various other measurements differed, including the rear wing, which was taller, wider, and raked back more than the Daytona's. Yet another difference came on top, where the Superbird's roof was covered in vinyl to hide the seams around the flush rear window's mounting plug.

Hand-leading those seams was ditched to save time and money. Conserving became an issue when NASCAR rulesmakers adjusted their homologation requirements for the 1970 season. Rules then stated a manufacturer had to build either 1,000 street versions or a number equal to half of that company's dealers, whichever was higher. Plymouth was then faced with the task of creating nearly four times as many Superbirds as Dodge did Daytonas. In the end, 1,935 were built; 1,084 with 440 four-barrels, 135 with hemis, and an additional 716 with the 440 Six-Barrel V-8.

With Ford growing disinterested in racing, the two winged Mopars took command on NASCAR tracks in 1970. Superbirds won eight races; Daytonas, four; with another victory coming from a Charger 500. Talladegas and Cyclone Spoiler IIs each scored four wins before Henry Ford II finally canceled his corporation's competitive programs late in the year. Bill France did the rest, instituting a carburetor restrictor plate rule for the high-flying hemi-powered Mopars to help keep speeds down to earth. This restriction then influenced Chrysler to give up on the Superbird—like the '69 Daytona, it was a one-hit wonder for 1970 only.

Stock cars were still stock cars after Detroit's aero-racers departed. But street racers would never be so super again.

Easily the most outlandish of the NASCAR-inspired musclecar lineup were Chrysler's winged warriors, Dodge's '69 Charger Daytona (front) and Plymouth's '70 Superbird. With their aerodynamic "beaks" and tall, "towel-rack" spoilers, these two high-flying Mopars could reach 200 miles per hour on NASCAR's superspeedways. In civilian sheetmetal, they both looked like they were going that fast even while standing still.

Chapter Six

WHEELER DEALERS (& ONE SNAKE)
How'd They Do It? Not with Volume

In 1965, any young speed-racer could have walked into almost any dealership and plunked down his pennies and dimes for some real horsepower. And if he'd waited a couple years, he could've scored even more ponies, although he would've also needed a few more wheelbarrows full of change. By 1968, American automakers were busy making performance like it was going out of style. Actually, it was. But while the gettin' was good, the factories were downright gettin' it. Performance didn't come any more muscular than it did from Detroit in the late '60s. If you still had a need for more speed you simply had to go elsewhere.

Factory men themselves looked elsewhere more than once, primarily when ultra-performance was the goal. Pontiac, then Chevrolet, was commonly seen in the '60s knocking on the door at Smokey Yunick's "Best Damn Garage In Town" down Daytona Beach way. While Yunick was known most for his racing exploits, some of his seemingly endless tricks did influence Bow-Tie performance offerings for the street. Another trickster, California's Bill Thomas, worked his Chevy magic in many ways, conjuring up everything from racing Sting Rays, to his totally wild 500-horsepower fuel-injected Cheetah, to 427 Camaro street dominators. Mickey Thompson, also on the West Coast, didn't discriminate; over his long and glorious career he built record-setting machines using GM, Ford, and Chrysler power.

Dearborn Steel Tubing near Detroit was home to more than one "factory" race car project, including Ford's ferocious Thunderbolt Fairlanes in 1964. Holman-Moody, Ford's "racing wing" in Charlotte, North Carolina, manufactured Blue Oval competition machines for everything from Daytona to Le Mans, with veteran Bill Stroppe in

California occasionally pitching in after having served Mercury's NASCAR campaign beginning in 1963.

But not everyone in the market for more than Detroit had to offer was in the hunt for a race car.

Ford fans in the mid-'60s who wanted a real hunk of Total Performance, not crumbs, needed only look as far as the Los Angeles International Airport. There in a hangar resided Shelby American, home from 1965 to 1967 of the GT 350 Mustang, Carroll Shelby's Corvette-killer. Built there as well that last year was the GT 350's big-block brother, the GT 500. Both were more than capable of letting the supercar world know what a hard charger the Mustang really was— just what Lee Iacocca had in mind when he turned to Shelby late in 1964.

The Shelby-Ford connection actually began almost three years before. Former Texas chicken rancher, former winner at Le Mans in 1959, Shelby in 1961 had set out in search of V-8 power for a Euro-Yankee sports/racer hybrid he wanted to build. He already had the car, Britain's AC Ace. Ford then supplied the engine, first its 260 small-block V-8 in 1962, then the enlarged 289 in 1964. The ultimate development in Shelby's quest to beat the world's best sports cars on their turf came in 1965 when he let loose his awesome 427 Cobra, easily the fastest "American production car" ever built in numbers greater than a handful. That it wasn't all American and didn't quite qualify as a production car shouldn't mask the plain fact that Shelby's big-block Cobra could toast the rump-roasts of any meat-eating muscle-monster out there in the mid '60s—or today, for that matter.

Having proven he could manhandle "America's sports car," Shelby was just the man Iacocca wanted to see. Even though he has always said he "wasn't real high

There was more than one source for performance outside Detroit in the '60s as various speed merchants were more than willing to pick up where the factory left off.

Opposite: "It looks like a Camaro . . . drives like a Ferrari!" Or so claimed Dana Chevrolet brochures. Based on an RS model, this '68 Dana Camaro features a fully functional fiberglass hood and a non-stock, custom-ordered lacquer finish applied at the dealership three decades ago. Practicality anything the customer wanted, Dana Chevrolet was ready, willing, and able to produce. In this case, the weapon of choice was the 435-horsepower L71 427. L88 components were also offered.

In 1966, Shelby American and the Hertz Rental Car company teamed up to put renters behind the wheels of GT 350 Mustangs. Most Hertz Shelbys were black; this white example is a rare bird indeed.

Shelby American's first GT 350 Mustang variants were more race car than street machine. The special run of R-models left no doubt whatsoever—that "R" stood for one thing, and running to the store wasn't it. Shelby's '65 GT 350-R was a stripped-down, gnarly beast ready to roll right onto an SCCA track. Such was also the case with the 1995 Cobra R, a 351-powered Mustang offered by Ford's Special Vehicle Team. All 250 SVT Cobra R Mustangs built came with white paint; no backseat, radio or air conditioner; huge four-wheel discs; and 17-inch wheels.

on the project," Shelby nevertheless agreed to help the Mustang run more competitively, a decision that both made pony car history and forced Shelby American out of its small shop in Venice into roomier quarters at LAX.

Introduced in January 1965, the first GT 350 was more racer than sports, with its "Shelby-ized" 306-horsepower Hi-Po 289; bellowing cut-out exhausts; stiff Koni shocks; bone-rattling, altered suspension; and gnarly, noisy Detroit Locker differential. No nonsense here. Also no available automatic trans, no paint choices, and no back seat. All '65 GT 350s wore Wimbledon White finishes, with Guardsman Blue racing stripes perhaps included as an option. And all were abusive brutes always able to give Corvette crybabies something to cry about.

Iacocca's men, however, didn't quite like it that rough, and they soon had Shelby smoothing out some edges. The standard '66 GT 350 was toned down a little. The '67, a lot. Dearborn stylists started to take over that year, adding a fiberglass makeover whether Shelby liked it or not. And the new, nose-heavy 428-powered GT 500 wasn't what Carroll originally had in mind at all. By then, he was ready to give the ball back to Ford.

As he told *Mustang Monthly* in a January 1990 interview, "big corporations tend to destroy the cars they create

and try to turn them into something other than the cars they created." Always Shelby's favorite, the first GT 350 was, in his words, "a no compromise car built to get the job done." But then political pressures forced him "to prostitute the cars" in 1967. "All of the corporate vultures jumped on the thing and that's when it started going to hell," said Shelby in 1971. "I started trying to get out of the deal in 1967, and it took me until 1970 to get production shut down."

After 1967, the Shelby Mustang project was transferred to the A. O. Smith Company in Livonia, Michigan. In 1969, a totally distinctive restyle turned heads, but couldn't turn back the clock. As *Car and Driver's* Brock Yates explained it, "the original Shelby GT 350 was a fire-breather. The GT 350, 1969-style, is little more than a tough-looking Mustang Grande—a Thunderbird for Hell's Angels. Certainly not the car of Carroll Shelby's dreams." Only through remarketed leftover 1969 models did the Shelby Mustang legacy manage to carryover into 1970.

Of course, both Yates and Shelby were biased, as well as a bit harsh. They did, from their perspectives, have valid complaints. But not everyone who bought a GT 350 or 500 wanted to race. Cars built after 1967 were still strong—Cobra Jet GT 500s rank among the quickest Ford supercars ever built—and the image was

Carroll Shelby had been out of the picture for three years when the last Shelby Mustang was sold by Ford in 1970. The final run of GT 350s and 500s were essentially slightly altered 1969 leftovers.

always well-received, Hell's Angel or not. All Shelby Mustangs—not just Carroll's favorite '65 and '66s—are loved and honored by the Ford faithful today, as they should be.

Carroll's unwillingness notwithstanding, Shelby American still stood as the biggest, most successful manufacturer of '60s supercars outside of Detroit. And Kenosha. No other independent firm came anywhere close to matching Shelby's productivity. Of course, no one else had big Dearborn dollars behind them, either. Yet many free-thinkers did do their own thing putting factory hardware to better, stronger use than the manufacturer originally planned.

The lesson taught by Professor Shelby wasn't missed. If he could build and market his own brand of Ford performance, so too could other individualistic power brokers relying on rival products. However, unlike Shelby American, which was an honest-to-goodness

manufacturer, these competing efforts to pick up where the factory had left off were all fronted by various horse-power-happy dealerships.

Hot-blooded Chevrolet dealers were plentiful in the '60s, probably because hot-blooded Chevys were even more so. Among this lusty list, certain names do stand head and shoulders above the rest. Yenko. Baldwin-Motion. Berger. Dana. Nickey. These dealerships were not only the places to go if you wanted the latest, greatest production-line performer, they were also home to various cars Chevrolet couldn't build. Officially, that is. Remember, before 1970 GM officials held a 400-cubic-inch lid on top of its performance intermediates, pony cars, and compacts. Accordingly, Chevelles, Camaros, and Novas could be fitted at the factory with the hottest 396 Turbo-Jet Mk IV big-block. They couldn't, however, use the Corvette's 427-cube rendition of the Turbo-Jet V-8.

Don Yenko (left) stands proudly with a '69 S/C Camaro at a Virginia dealership, one of many included in a network of Yenko Super Car sales sources. The sign above the car remains a controversy today. Yenko himself claimed as many as 500 Yenko Camaros were built in 1969, but only 201 are known—so where did that 350 number come from? No solid answer is available.

Don Yenko began offering 427-powered Camaro conversions from his Pennsylvania Chevrolet dealership in 1967, at first performing troublesome transplants in his own shop. In 1969, the job became easier thanks to a special run of Chevrolet-supplied COPO Camaros fitted with L72 427 V-8s. Yenko Camaros in 1969 were also adorned with ample exterior identification.

This restriction didn't stop Don Yenko. Easily the best-remembered among the superdealers of the '60s, he was the busiest at building his own forms of Chevrolet performance. A big-time Chevy racer himself, having copped four SCCA national titles, he first started dealing in modified Chevrolet muscle in 1965, making "Stingers" out of Corvairs. One of the 200 '65 Stingers built by Yenko Sports Cars—the performance division of Yenko Chevrolet in Canonsburg, Pennsylvania—scored its own SCCA national crown in 1966 with Jerry Thompson driving.

Next came the first Yenko Super Camaro in 1967. What Yenko did was take delivery of a V-8 F-body, pull out the 350 and drop in the Corvette's L72 427, along with lots of additional heavy-duty hardware and a little touch of extra imagery. Similar transplants were made in 1968, this time beginning with an SS 396 Camaro.

Then in 1969, Yenko simply went through the Central Office Production Order pipeline to request a run of factory-built 427 Camaros. COPOs didn't require upper office approval, so they represented the loophole needed to drive a forbidden model through unabated. COPO number 9561 supplied Yenko Sports Cars with the iron-block 427 Camaros Don's men needed to make their job easier—no more pesky transplants, at least not in Camaro terms. In 1969, Yenko's already attractive Super Camaro also became a real eye-catcher with special striping and more add-on imagery.

Yenko didn't stop there. Offered in 1969 as well were two other 427 Supercars, the Chevelle/SC and Nova/SC. Yenko 427 Chevelles were based on COPO 9562 models, while the mean Nova was another transplant job, and the very last. Few 427 Novas were sold, basically because they were just too nasty. Claiming it would do 0–60 in about 4 seconds, Don Yenko later described the car as "a real beast." "It was almost lethal," he continued. "In retrospect, this probably wasn't the safest car in the world."

Yenko came back in 1970 with a less-threatening Nova, the only product offered that year. Rising insurance costs had

The Yenko Super Car lineup in 1969 also featured a 427 Chevelle, again created by taking delivery of Chevrolet-built COPO models and adding the "sYc" touches in Canonsburg, Pennsylvania. The mag wheels appearing here were a Yenko option; most S/C Chevelles came with 15-inch Rally wheels.

Yenko Camaros, Chevelles and even a few Novas in 1969 relied on the Corvette's L72 427 Mk IV big-block V-8, rated at 425 horsepower by Chevrolet. Yenko's team used the more believable figure of 450 horses.

transformed his 450-horsepower Supercar Chevelles and Camaros from tough sells into nearly impossible sells, leaving him no choice but to kill those vehicles. His solution to the problem was the small-block Yenko Deuce, a 360-horsepower LT-1 Nova created through another COPO, number 9010.

As Yenko later explained, "insurance companies wouldn't insure a 427 Camaro, but a 350 Nova was a normal family car. All the customer had to tell his agent was that the car was a 350 Nova. It was none of the agent's concern that the 350 was the solid-lifter LT-1 Corvette motor. We built 200 of the cars and never heard a peep from the insurance companies."

From there, it was all downhill for the Yenko Supercar legacy. Yenko's Stinger Vega in 1971 was only proof that

Easily the most radical of the super Chevrolets built by "superdealers" were the Baldwin-Motion Phase III cars, most common of which were the Camaros. Corvettes, full-sized models, Chevelles and Novas were also offered in the late-'60s and early '70s. This '71 Baldwin-Motion Camaro gets its strength from a massaged 454 Mk IV big-block. *Jerry Shaw*

the end of the road had arrived. As for Don Yenko, he was tragically killed, along with his three passengers, when his Cessna 210 crashed in West Virginia on March 5, 1987.

Perhaps the most aggressive of Chevrolet's superdealers was Baldwin-Motion, which was actually a partnership between Long Island's Baldwin Chevrolet and Joel Rosen's Motion Performance speed shop. Rosen, a horsepower hound through and through, had begun his career doing hop-up work for a friend in 1957 in Brooklyn's Sheepshead Bay section. Six months later, he opened his own shop at Loch Sheldrake in the Catskills. Then in 1959, he moved back to Brooklyn, where Motion Performance resided until 1965. The next year, he moved to Sunrise Highway in Baldwin on Long Island.

In 1966, Rosen made his pitch to Baldwin Chevrolet management. "What I proposed was to offer buyers a new car built as they wanted it, instead of them buying a car to later modify," he recalls. The dealership folks loved the idea, and an agreement was quickly formed; Motion Performance would build the cars, Baldwin Chevrolet would handle the marketing. Presto, the Baldwin-Motion Phase III cars were born.

Phase III modifications were widely varied over the years, always including Chevy's hottest big-blocks combined

with many aftermarket goodies and often Motion's trademark three-barrel carburetor. Among the earliest projects was a '67 Camaro powered by an uncrated L88 427. But Rosen didn't discriminate—the Baldwin-Motion line-up was soon known as the "Fantastic Five" once the Phase III treatment was offered for Corvettes, Camaros, Chevelles, Biscaynes, and Novas. Camaros were the most popular. Featuring anywhere from 450 to as much as 600 horsepower, a fully loaded Phase III Motion machine could almost always dip well into the 11s at the strip. Setting records in a Baldwin-Motion Chevrolet was simply a matter of how much you were willing to spend.

Word quickly got around about the Baldwin-Motion partnership. Soon, Rosen was building Phase III models for Chevy freaks as far away as Australia. Expansion then followed as he opened a mail-order parts business and another division, Motion Minicar, a Volkswagen speed parts business run by Bill Mitchell. Motion Marine was also formed for those with a need for water-logged speed.

By 1971, the Fantastic Five had become the "Sensational Six" as Motion began offering an outrageous 454 big-block swap for Chevrolet's Vega, something *Motor*

Trend editors never possibly could've envisioned when they named the new compact their "Car of the Year." These hot conversions remained popular up into 1974, when the federal government finally stepped in, issuing a cease and desist order. Rosen then changed his tack, offering kits for "for off-road use only," as well as export sales, which remained relatively strong through the '70s.

Motion Performance then turned to cosmetics for the Corvette, introducing the customized Phase III GT, which echoed the looks of Chevy's Mako Shark and Manta Ray Corvette show cars. Another offering, the Motion Spyder, copied the IMSA racing image. Rosen was still making the custom car show rounds with his wild Corvettes as late as 1984. His Motion Performance company remains alive today at its same location on Sunrise Highway, now offering such things as fiberglass hoods and spoilers.

Undoubtedly the biggest of the Chevy superdealers—perhaps the biggest factory performance sales and service shop anywhere, anytime—was Chicago's Nickey Chevrolet. Founded in 1925 by Edward and John Stephani, Nickey Chevrolet by the '60s had grown into a huge 200,000-square-foot facility bragging early on of the world's largest inventory of "Genuine Chevrolet High Performance Parts."

Nickey's earliest racing involvement came in 1955, the year Chevy introduced the "Hot One" and then quickly took it to NASCAR tracks. In 1957, Nickey's Jim Jeffords bought Harley Earl's son Jerry's SR-2 Corvette, painted it purple and went racing. Jeffords' SR-2 was the first of three successful "Purple People Eater" Corvettes, racers recognized by two trademarks, their color and the backwards "K" used in the '58 Mk II and '59 Mk III logos. By 1970, any Chevy lover worth his salt knew that Nickey was spelled with a backwards "K."

Nickey Chevrolet's high-performance parts branch opened in 1957. Then in 1965 successful drag racer Dick Harrell was hired to head the performance shop. Two years later, he went off on his own, reappearing in 1967 to help Don Yenko engineer his Supercars. Harrell also went to work that year for Fred Gibb at Gibb Chevrolet in LaHarpe, Illinois. Gibb was the man who in 1969 requested Chevrolet to build the exotic COPO 9560 Camaro with its all-aluminum ZL1 427.

In late 1966, Nickey Chevrolet teamed up with West Coast race car designer Bill Thomas to create yet another Corvette-powered variation on the new Camaro theme. Nickey used the 425-horse L72 427, the 435-horsepower L71 and even the race-only L88. By 1969, the huge dealership on Irving Park Road was also offering pumped-up Novas and Chevelles, both with 427s and the Z/28's hot, little 302 small-block. In 1970, the 427 was joined by the 454 in either LS5 or 450-horse-

Nickey Chevrolet in Chicago also jumped into the 427 engine swap game in 1967, and like Yenko also eventually offered such deals to Camaro, Chevelle and Nova buyers. Along with the Corvette 427 beneath the hood, this '67 Nickey Camaro is equipped with four-wheel disc brakes.

Anything available on a Chevrolet's parts shelf could've been added to a Nickey Camaro, including the Corvette's L71 427 with its triple two-barrel carburetors. The single-carb L72 427 was also available.

Berger Chevrolet did a few performance transplants by request. And in 1970, the dealership offered this Super Nova. Features included a 300-horsepower 350 small-block backed by a four-speed and a 3.31:1 Positraction rearend. Hood pins, color-keyed racing mirrors, 14x7 SS wheels, and decklid wing were also added. Ever seen one? courtesy Dale Berger and Musclecar Review magazine

power LS6 tune. Of course, anything the customer wanted by way of aftermarket additions was also available through Nickey's extensive speed catalog. Then just as things really got good, factory muscle began fading from the scene, eventually taking Nickey Chevrolet with it.

Bill Thomas' involvement with Nickey wasn't the only Southern California contribution to the 427 Camaro game in 1967. Not far west as the crow flies (but a fair poke measured in terms of L.A. traffic time) from Thomas's Anaheim shop was Dana Chevrolet, located on Long Beach Boulevard in South Gate. This established dealership had just changed hands, with one of the new partners being Peyton Cramer, who had helped Shelby get his GT 350 Mustang project running just two years before. And when Cramer came to Dana, he also brought Don McCain, the man responsible for various successful Shelby drag racing campaigns.

Another addition to the team was Dick Guldstrand, who eventually became general manager of Dana Chevrolet's Hi-Performance Center. Today, Guldstrand is

well known for his racing exploits and long-time involvement in the ultra-hot Corvette conversion business, including the recent GS90. But before the Guldstrand name became forever entwined solely with Chevrolet's fiberglass two-seater, he was kept busy in South Gate overseeing the development of the Dana 427 Camaro.

Per brochures, "the Dana 427 is more than just a souped-up Camaro. It's the first sensible solution for the car enthusiast with a Ferrari taste and a Camaro bankroll." Like Yenko, Dana began with a basic SS 350 '67 Camaro, replacing the small-block with a 1966-spec, 425-horsepower L72 427. From there, options were typically plentiful, including Traction Master traction bars and both a Stage I and Stage II suspension package. Price for these two chassis updates was $235 and $275, respectively. A $2,000 Stage III option was meant for racing only and featured, among other things, a rubberized fuel cell in place of the stock gas tank. A customer could've also requested the '67 Corvette's L71 435-horsepower 427 with its triple carbs, a $150 option. A distinctive fiberglass hood with twin functional scoops was a $125 item.

Whatever the options, a Dana 427 Camaro was loaded for bear. Or pony. "No matter how many 'hot' cars you've driven, the first time you really uncork a Dana Camaro you're bound to be awe-stricken if not outright panicked at the sheer magnitude of the force unleashed," explained *Motor Trend's* John Etheridge. "At about T plus 1/2-second you begin to wonder if maybe you hadn't ought to have done it, a feeling which persists until you either chicken out and get off it or shift into 3rd gear." With slicks and open headers, Etheridge's test subject posted a 12.75/110-mile-per-hour e.t.

Just like its rivals from Chicago and Pennsylvania, the Dana Camaro was built in various forms in the '60s, all meant to meet each customer's individual whims. An L88 "Phase I" cam, the M22 "Rock Crusher" four-speed, power front discs, a Hurst Competition Plus shifter—it was all in there and more, as were many optional dress-up pieces. Often overshadowed by its Yenko, Nickey, and Baldwin-Motion counterparts, the Dana 427 Camaro was still one super car.

Berger Chevrolet's approach to the Chevy-powered fast lane differed greatly from the others. Pronounced "bur-jur," this long-running dealership in Grand Rapids, Michigan, was founded in 1925 by William Berger. Forty-one years later, Nickey's hot parts guru, Jim O'Connor, came over from Chicago and joined Berger Chevrolet, selling Dale Berger, Jr., on the idea of marketing Chevy performance in a big way. But unlike Nickey and the rest, Berger Chevrolet didn't jump head-first into the conversion kit game.

"We were not like Yenko," sales manager Mike Wawee later told author and Camaro enthusiast John Hooper. "We never had an assembly line to build the cars." "We were never too keen on conversions," added performance parts manager Jim Luikens in a 1987 *Musclecar Review* interview. "We'd do it to accommodate our customers."

As Luikens said, some specially requested big-block swaps were performed at Berger, and the company did market its image-conscious "Super Nova" in 1970. But the vast majority of the hot Camaros, Corvettes, and Chevelles rolling off the Berger lot in the '60s were stock Chevy machinery, not that that was bad. In 1969, Berger Chevrolet took delivery of as many as 50 COPO Camaros and another six COPO Chevelles. By then, performance cars were making up about 20 percent of the dealership's yearly sales. Whether it rolled right off the truck or was dealership tweaked or tuned, both the "by Berger" screw-on badge in back and "Prescribed Power" decal under the

hood meant your hot Chevy had come from one of America's top sources for Bow-Tie power.

Hot parts sales were Berger Chevrolet's main priority. To this end, Bob Delamar moved in after O'Connor left to head the dealership's High Performance Department. In 1968, Delamar hired Luikens, then working in a local grocery store's produce department, as his assistant. And when Bob went into business for himself in 1970, his right-hand man replaced him as manager. Under Luikens' direction, muscle parts sales soared; even as late as 1973, Berger was bringing in more than $1 million a year from hot hardware, making the Grand Rapids firm Chevrolet's number one performance distributor.

As Berger ads claimed, "Jim probably knows more about high performance parts than almost anyone inside or outside the factory. He can pull more specs out of his head than you can find in Motors, Chilton's and the factory manuals put together." And not only Chevy specs. Being a General Motors dealer, Berger Chevrolet was also the hot spot for anyone hungry for, say, a pair of Pontiac Ram Air IV heads or an Olds W-30 big-block in a crate. Berger's business concentrated on parts, genuine GM parts. According to Dale Berger, 80 percent of these sales consisted of factory pieces. Aftermarket items made up the other 20 percent.

While Berger Chevrolet's performance heyday ran longer than anyone else's, the power did finally wane after Luikens left Grand Rapids in January 1975 to join Joe Hrudka's Mr. Gasket company. As he told *Musclecar Review*, his replacement at Berger, Doug Koechnef, was "a really good guy" who later went on to a successful business career. "But in 1975 he just wasn't ready," continued Luikens. "From being the number one dealer in the U.S. in January 1975, by January 1977 it was gone, they had given up on it."

Dale Berger explained it a little differently in 1996, claiming Luikens "did do a great job while he was here," but his leaving, nor his replacement's actions, wasn't the reasons behind Berger's decline. "At its height, the performance business was like shooting fish in a barrel," said Berger, "all the kids were buying that stuff." Changing times, however, meant a change of direction. "The parts sales didn't drop because of Jim leaving," he continued, "they went to hell because the government started putting emissions controls on everything in 1974. Plus Chevrolet started raising prices on all the parts; the kids couldn't afford them anymore. A lot of young guys just started finding different things to do."

Like everyone else, Berger was out of the performance market by the late '70s. The dealership, however, continued on in healthy fashion. Family owned and operated through four generations now, Berger Chevrolet is

CONTINUED ON PAGE 140

135

After kicking off his aftermarket performance parts career with a slick three-speed shifter in the '50s, George Hurst then solidified his fame with his four-speed stick in the '60s. But automatic transmission drivers were not left out, as Hurst also introduced its "His and Hers" Dual-Gate in 1964. These auto shifters were later offered as options by both Pontiac and Oldsmobile.

Hurst also sponsored more than one exhibition drag racing tour, the most memorable featuring the "Hemi Under Glass" Barracuda. Making those wild wheelstands possible was a 426 hemi V-8 mounted behind the driver beneath that big rear window, thus the car's name.

The Hurst Touch

Many buyers in the '60s refused to sit still once they'd taken delivery of their GTO, Road Runner, or such. Off went those standard steel rims, replaced by, say, a set of chrome-encrusted Cragar S/S five-spokes, perhaps the most popular custom wheel of the '60s. As for under the hood, the quickest way to free up a few more horses was by dumping those stock exhausts for a set of headers—the choices here were wide.

But if you wanted to trade that often-clunky, standard-issue floor-shifter for a really hot stick, there was only one true choice. If you didn't have a Hurst shifter in your supercar, you were a mild-mannered loser. Hands down, nobody built solid, high-quality, quick-working shifters like George Hurst. Musclecars may have come and gone. And come again. The Hurst shifter, however, has always been there at arm's reach whenever the need for speed-shifting has arisen.

And, like superdealers such as Yenko and Royal, Hurst's multi-talented firm was also the home to various modified factory muscle machines, a group led most prominently by the long-running Hurst/Olds line. Oldsmobile wasn't Hurst's only partner in the muscle makeover business. Hurst modified supercars for Pontiac. For Dodge, Plymouth, and Chrysler. And for American Motors. George's firm also added its Hurst/Hatch T-top conversion to Buick's Indy 500 pace cars in 1975 and 1976. The last Hurst conversion, another Hurst/Olds, came in 1984, roughly 15 years after George Hurst had left the company he founded.

The Hurst story had begun right after 27-year-old George was discharged from the Navy in 1954. His first business was George Hurst Automotive in Philadelphia. Popular hot rodding engine swaps quickly became his forte, and he started designing various motor mounts to make these conversions a snap.

Later, he also designed a floor shifter for his '56 Chevy. Right after Christmas in 1958, he set out in his floor-shifted Chevy in search of buyers for his top-notch design. Exceptionally precise and durable, featuring much shorter throws than stock shifters, the Hurst stick was just the ticket for the speed-needy. These merits impressed the folks at Detroit's Gratoit Auto Supply; there, he took in several thousand dollars worth of orders. His shifter later also impressed the guys at *Hot Rod* so much, they later wrote all about it.

Back in Philadelphia, he took out a $20,000 loan to begin manufacturing his shifters. In 1958, he made his existing partnership with cohort Bill Campbell official, founding Hurst-Campbell, Inc. Anco Industries was formed the following year, later becoming Hurst Performance Products, Inc., Hurst-Campbell's sales division.

Hurst Performance's big break came in 1961 when Bunkie Knudsen and Pete Estes asked George Hurst in for a meeting in Pontiac. Estes had read *Hot Rod's* report on George's shifter and had a proposition. A deal was then inked and Pontiac began offering Hurst shifters as a parts-counter option. So, too, did Chrysler. And Ford. From there, the Hurst company shifted into high gear.

With annual sales of more than $20 million, Hurst-Campbell in 1965 expanded into a bigger building in Warminster, Pennsylvania. The Hurst Research Center, directed by Jack "Doc" Watson, was also opened in Madison Heights, Michigan, outside Detroit. About the same time, Hurst-Campbell bought out clutch-maker Schiefer Manufacturing and the Airheart brake company.

All the while, Hurst shifters were quickly skyrocketing in popularity. When the GTO debuted, it featured a Hurst stick as standard equipment, beginning a trend that soon spread throughout Detroit. As Jim Wangers later explained in *Automobile Quarterly*, "we quickly learned that one of the first things a new customer would do after purchasing a high-performance stick shift car was to take it down to the local hot rod shop and install a Hurst. I was finally able to convince both Estes and DeLorean that it meant more to Pontiac to be able to advertise the fact that our cars came equipped with a Hurst right from the factory than it meant to Hurst to say they were original equipment on a Pontiac. This was the first time GM had ever allowed a component supplier's name to be used in advertising."

All GTOs built up through 1974 featured factory-equipped Hurst shifters. Hurst/Olds models were also fitted with Hurst's Dual Gate automatic shifter, the so-called "His-and-Hers" stick, developed in 1964. The list of Hurst-equipped supercars grew fast, and Hurst shifters were even created for Volkswagens.

In 1965, Hurst began branching out, introducing a custom wheel called the "Dazzler." Essentially unbreakable, contrary to so many lesser rivals then on the market, the Hurst wheel debuted in California during a special press conference on January 5, 1965, and then was further promoted as part of Pontiac's GeeTO Tiger giveaway contest. Despite its merits, the Hurst wheel never did get rolling.

That same year, George Hurst patented another innovative design, the "Jaws of Life" rescue apparatus. As important a contribution as this was, Hurst is much more renown for the 1966 hiring of Linda Vaughn as one of various "Hurst Golden Shifter Girls." Every bit as affable as she was eye-popping, Vaughn soon became the parade-ground ambassador for not only Hurst but the entire supercar realm. Few people who handled one can forget a '60s Hurst-shifted performance machine. No one has ever forgotten Linda Vaughn—even without any hands-on experience.

The next big news for Hurst came in early 1968, when Doc Watson built a special Olds 4-4-2 for his boss using the Toronado's 455 big-block V-8. GM couldn't build this combination itself because of the ever-present 400-cubic inch limit for mid-sized models. Hurst, however, convinced Olds executives to let him do the trick instead, resulting in a special run of Hurst-modified 4-4-2s, the first Hurst/Olds.

Converted to Hurst/Olds specs in an abandoned foundry near Oldsmobile's Lansing assembly line, these cars all featured specially prepared 455s fed by ram-air ducts located beneath the front bumper, Turbo-Hydra-Matic automatic transmissions (on all but the first one built) and special contrasting silver and black paint. Hurst, of course, wanted his trademark gold and black, but the Olds assembly line was not set up for the gold paint.

CONTINUED ON NEXT PAGE

In 1965, George Hurst tried his hand at the custom wheel game. The Hurst wheel venture, however, never got rolling.

Hurst teamed up with Oldsmobile in 1968 to build the first of many specialty muscle machines. The original Hurst/Olds featured exclusive black and silver paint and a 455 big-block V-8 force fed by Oldsmobile's W-30 ram-air ductwork. In 1969, the second-edition Hurst/Olds was given a special fresh-air hood, negating the need for those bumper-mounted "vacuum-cleaner" scoops. A new gold-on-white paint scheme was also introduced.

Hurst shifters were manufactured for many cars, including Volkswagens. And many American manufacturers would eventually offer Hurst sticks as factory options. Undoubtedly the most recognizable of these was the Mopar "Pistol Grip" shifter. This one was installed in a '70 Dodge Coronet R/T.

Hurst/Olds models continued rolling in proud fashion into the '70s, and were even offered again in 1983 and '84. At left is the 1973 variety; behind it is a 1974.

And, contrary to the long-told legend, these cars were not converted to 455 power in Hurst's hands, they were delivered that way, something done—definitely against the corporate grain—easily enough on the Lansing line since the 455 and standard 400 were essentially identical at a glance. Had Ted Lucas, Dale Smith, Bob Stemple, and cohorts been caught pushing this taboo installation through in 1968, Oldsmobile's secretary surely would have disavowed any knowledge of their actions. And Stemple would've never got the chance to later take the chairman's seat atop GM.

Hurst also got involved with Chrysler Corporation in 1968, helping both Dodge and Plymouth wedge the 426 hemi into a limited run of Dart and Barracuda super stock drag cars. Two years later, Hurst did the 300H, a 440-powered '70 Chrysler that briefly brought back a few memories of the famed letter-series cars of 1955-65.

Another Hurst/Olds package was produced in 1969, this time with gold accents. The Hurst/Olds was offered again in 1972-75, 1979, and 1983-84.

Hurst's American Motors connection also began in 1969 with the SC/Rambler— "Scrambler" to you—a somewhat odd-looker with its red-white-and-blue paint scheme (the "A" layout; there was also a "B") and angular ram-air hood scoop. Yet

beneath all that '60s garishness was some serious performance supplied by a 315-horse-power 390 V-8 linked to a four-speed with a—you guessed it—Hurst shifter. Additional standard equipment included a Twin-Grip differential with 3.54:1 gears, power front discs, quicker steering, and a special handling package with staggered rear shocks.

Hurst was in cahoots with American Motors twice in 1969, the second instance involving an all-out race car, the Hurst AMX S/S. This strip-ready AMC featured a special 390 with dual four-barrels on a cross-ram intake, a trunk-mounted battery, acid-dipped body panels, and enlarged rear wheelwells—the better to house slicks perhaps?

A third Hurst/AMC product, this one a much more polite street machine, picked up in 1970 where the Scrambler had left off. Although not all were painted the same, the early Rebel Machines showed off another patriotic paint scheme, as well as a Scrambler-like boxy hood scoop. Beneath that ram-air scoop was a 340-horsepower 390 V-8.

Yet another Hurst conversion debuted in 1970, this one based on Pontiac's Grand Prix. These attractive SSJ models could be equipped with 455 V-8s and American Racing mag wheels. Hurst's SSJ was marketed again in 1971, and apparently a few more were sold in 1972.

By then George Hurst had changed his course. Hurst-Campbell had gone public in 1968, instantly attracting the Sunbeam Corporation, which acquired controlling interest by buying out Bill Campbell's stock in 1970. George Hurst then left soon afterward to pursue other business ventures.

In November 1981, Sunbeam was bought out by Allegheny Intereaction, which sold Hurst to Richard Chrysler, of Cars and Concepts in Detroit. Chrysler had started out in 1966 as a menial "floor-sweeper" at Hurst, eventually rising to management before leaving to found Cars and Concepts.

Early in 1986, Hurst was bought once more, this time by Mr. Gasket's Joe Hrudka. Sadly, George Hurst's story came to an end about the same time; he died at age 59 on May 15. His legacy can't be missed. In its heyday Hurst gave horsepower hounds hot GTOs and Oldsmobiles. Race cars from Dodge and AMC. Clutches and wheels. Exhibition dragsters like the "Hemi Under Glass" and the twin-engined "Hurst Hairy Oldsmobile." Hurst gave us taxi cabs and emergency equipment. Hurst still gives us shifters.

And last, but by no means least, Hurst gave us Linda Vaughn.

Among Hurst's many muscle machines was the AMC SC/Rambler, a patriotic performer offered in 1969. An all-white version was also available for those who preferred a little less color.

Beneath the Hurst SC/Rambler's boxy ram-air hood scoop was a 315-horsepower 390 V-8. Heavy-duty cooling and a Hurst-shifted close-ratio four-speed was also included. SC/Rambler production in 1969 was 1,512.

A more "formal" Linda Vaughn upstages the Hurst-created SSJ Grand Prix, shown here with optional mag wheels. Hurst also performed that sunroof trick for Buick in 1975 and '76. Pontiac Historical Services

CONTINUED FROM PAGE 135

still moving Bow-Ties like nobody's business on 28th Street in Grand Rapids, making it the only firm among the '60s superdealer group that has continually operated in the same location to the present.

Undoubtedly ranking as Dearborn's top superdealer, Tasca Ford also operates today from its original address, 777 Taunton Avenue in East Providence, Rhode Island. But in this case, the run has not been continuous as Tasca traded Ford for Lincoln-Mercury late in 1971, selling luxury instead of performance in nearby Seekonk, Massachusetts, up until 1994. The famed Tasca name then was reunited with the Blue Oval over the same lot on Taunton Avenue that had once been the East Coast mecca for the Ford faithful.

The big man behind Tasca Ford, Robert F. Tasca, Sr.—the "Bopper" to his friends—got his start as a 17-year-old "grease monkey" at Sandager Ford in Cranston, Rhode Island, in May 1943. By 1949, he'd climbed all the way to sales manager, and in November 1953 opened his own dealership in East Providence, where it still stands today. Although sons Robert, Jr., Carl, and David run the

show now, the Bopper continues to make sure satisfaction remains Job 1. As one employee put it, "Bob Tasca will do whatever it takes, whatever the cost to satisfy a customer—he will not quit until that guy leaves here happy."

Tasca also always has been willing to do whatever it takes to sell Fords. Early promotions in 1960 included adding luxury touches to certain models, which he soon found wasn't enough in a market quickly filling up with young, spirited buyers. "I was trying to sell Fords on beauty," recalled the Bopper in 1992, "and I found out that beauty helped, but I needed performance. That's why I went from making them pretty to sell them, to making them pretty and making them go."

In late 1961, Bob Tasca formed a special high-performance division, managed by Dean Gregson, who had been working for Bob since September 1956. Early purposeful playthings included a 427 Thunderbird in 1965 and the "505" Mustang, an outrageous 505-horse pony car that, according to Tasca, helped inspire the Boss 302. And in 1969, Tasca's own personal driver was a street-legal, 11-second Boss 429.

Tasca Ford's team assembles outside the dealership in April 1967 to welcome racer Mario Andretti. To the right of the street-going GT40 Mk III is Robert F. Tasca, Sr. Left to right, starting from Tasca, are performance division manager Dean Gregson, Jim Almonti, Ralph Natalazia, and Joe Conetti. The gold '67 Mustang to the left of the GT40 is the car Tasca mechanics modified with a tweaked 428 big-block—it inspired Ford's '68-1/2 Cobra Jet Mustang. The Cortina beneath the billboard was campaigned by Gregson in SCCA racing. *Robert F. Tasca, Sr. collection*

Most impressive were Tasca Ford's drag cars; first a '62 406 Galaxie, followed by a 406-equipped Fairlane, reportedly the forerunner to Dearborn's racing Thunderbolts of 1964. A full-fledged drag race team began competing nationally in 1963 with driver Bill Lawton and a lightweight Galaxie, then claimed an NHRA national championship the following year with Tasca's own Thunderbolt. Lawton made it consecutive NHRA titles in 1965, this time driving an A/FX Mustang.

In 1966, Tasca Ford debuted its Holman-Moody-built "Mystery 9" Mustang, which quickly changed names as its e.t. dropped, first to "Mystery 8," then "Mystery 7?". By 1969, the Tasca team was running a fuel funny car with a blown Cammer, a machine that didn't exactly meld with the Bopper's pet adage, "race on Sunday, sell on Monday." Early Tasca track machines were more easily associated with the civilian cars race fans bought after watching checkered flags fall. Seeing a supercharged funny car win a race meant very little to the average buyer.

Tasca spent $300,000 at the track between 1962 and 1968. Winnings included the number two national sales rankings among Ford dealers. By 1963, upwards of 60 performance cars a month were rolling off Tasca's lot, equal to about 40 percent of total sales. Included were AC Cobras as Tasca was New England's first Shelby dealer. In 1965, the Bopper's lot was the place to be if you wanted to see anything hot wearing a Blue Oval.

However, the tide soon subsided. As Bob told *Super Stock* in 1968, "we did well from '63 to '65, when the market was a young one. [Then] younger people [became] disenchanted with Ford's performance on the street, and stopped buying. Consequently, we had to cut back the racing budget that year." Reportedly, Detroit in 1966 sold 634,434 high-performance automobiles, defined as those with engines rated at 300 horses or more. Ford's share? Only 7.5 percent. "Shameful for a 'Total Performance' company," said Tasca to *Hot Rod's* Eric Dahlquist in 1967.

Not even Bob Tasca could teach a new horse old tricks, a task he encountered once the supposedly pumped-up '67 Mustang GT began rolling off the truck. As Dean Gregson told Dahlquist, "we found the [390

Bob Tasca, Sr., (center with glasses) and Carroll Shelby battle it out on a slot-car track at Tasca Ford in 1965. Tasca was the first East Cost dealer to offer Shelby American's Ford-powered Cobra. *Robert F. Tasca, Sr., collection*

Tasca Ford's crew toyed with various modified models over the years, including this '70 Torino Cobra. Minor Tasca tricks included a trunk-mounted electric fuel pump and relocated upper shock absorber mounts up front.

Tasca Ford, in East Providence, Rhode Island, was the East Coast mecca for Blue Oval performance in the '60s. Most importantly, it was the birthplace of the famed Cobra Jet Mustang. A Tasca-modified '67 Mustang ended up inspiring Dearborn to build a regular-production counterpart, leading to the 428 CJ Mustang's debut in April 1968. This '68-1/2 Cobra Jet Mustang was originally sold at Tasca Ford—its original dealer badge is still visible near the driver's side taillight.

Mustang] so non-competitive, we began to feel we were cheating the customer. We had to do something about it."

Their solution came by luck; first bad, then good. In the former's case, a Tasca employee grenaded the 390 in a '67 GT coupe while street racing one night after hours. As a fix, mechanics fortunately discovered what happens when you add reworked heads and a 735-cfm Holley four-barrel to a standard 428 Police Interceptor short block—bam, instant 13.39-second street-killer. Great luck continued when local police discovered Tasca men demonstrating their good fortune on the street one evening. As Gregson later recalled, "they stopped us and told us if we didn't get that car out of town in 10 minutes, they'd throw us all in jail."

Labeled "KR," for "King of the Road," Tasca's 428 Mustang inspired *Hot Rod* to ask readers if Ford should build a factory counterpart. Once a few thousand positive responses began piling up on Henry Ford II's desk, Dearborn engineers responded. Following Tasca's lead, they simply mixed and matched a collection of existing FE parts to create a better big-block, which debuted on April 1, 1968, to save Ford's bacon on the street. Passing on Tasca's name, Ford instead chose "Cobra Jet" for its new 335-horsepower 428, leaving the KR label for the CJ-powered GT 500 Shelby Mustang.

In Bob Tasca's words, "the Cobra Jet began the era of Ford's supremacy in performance. It was, in my opinion, the fastest production-built car in the world at that point, and I'm not talking top speed. I'm talking fun, fast, get up and go."

Tasca's inspiration of the Cobra Jet Mustang was the last great contribution the dealership made to Ford's performance image. In its heyday, Tasca Ford was selling about 100 factory hot rods a month, along with about $6 million in Autolite parts a year. But by 1969, the handwriting was on the wall. In 1971, Dearborn asked him to drop Ford and move over to Lincoln-Mercury. Thirteen years later, Tasca Lincoln-Mercury had become the world's leading Lincoln-Mercury dealership.

And now it's Tasca Ford again.

What Bob Tasca did for Total Performance, Mr. Norm's Grand-Spaulding Dodge did for Mopar muscle. Beginning in 1962, Grand-Spaulding was Chicago's home to Dodge performance. Ramcharger 426s, hemis, 440 Six Packs, Super Bees, Daytonas. You name it, it was sold there, along with all the parts and loads of tuning know-how. And what engineers designed in Detroit, Mr. Norm's men proved on the track. Whether it was at nearby U.S. 30 in Indiana or across the country at Long Beach, California, Grand-Spaulding Dodge drag cars were always out in front. And the center of attention. When "Mr. Norm The Hi-Performance King" spoke,

young performance buyers listened. By the end of the decade, Grand-Spaulding had become *America's* home to Dodge performance.

"Mr. Norm," alias Norman Kraus, is the son of Harvey Kraus, who in 1936 opened a small gas station at the corner of Grand and Spaulding in Chicago. Brothers Norm and Lenny began working at their father's station as teens in the late-'40s. They started selling used cars in an adjacent lot soon afterward. Then, when placing a newspaper ad in an effort to dump a badly used '56 V-8 Chevy, they found they needed a name that would fit in the restrictive space. Thus came the line, "Call Mr. Norm."

The name stuck. And after calls came flooding in to Mr. Norm for that beat-up stickshift Chevy, the Kraus family recognized a new opportunity and started grabbing up all the V-8 stickshift cars they could find. As the '50s came to a close, the Krauses found themselves in the performance car business—used performance cars, that is.

In the '60s, Dodge officials approached Norm and Lenny Kraus about picking up a new-car franchise. They were at first not interested. Then in 1962, they saw what Dodge had planned for the future, including the 413 Max Wedge super stock machines. They changed their minds and in October opened the doors of Grand-Spaulding Dodge.

Local ads were soon portraying Mr. Norm as "The Ram Charger King." Horsepower-hungry Dodge boys (and maybe a few girls) were soon flocking into the dealership where the motto was "Kids are King." Mr. Norm's doors were always wide open to younger buyers, leading some to call Norm Kraus "the pied piper of performance." In 1968, *Senior Scholastic*, a publication aimed at high school students, even described Norman and Leonard Kraus as "the world's oldest teenagers." The brothers didn't mind, that's exactly the way they felt. Most of their customers were young and enthusiastic, which only served to heighten their enthusiasm for their work. And keep them young as well.

"Performance was for fun and that's what I always promoted," said Norm Kraus. His customers instantly became members of "Mr. Norm's Sport Club," with an official club newsletter beginning service in November 1964 to keep all informed of the latest fun goings-on; match races, in-house special events, etc. Later, he came up with "Kill Stickers"—tombstone decals with names of rival cars on them; Mustang, GTO, etc.—and "Street Chutes," dummy drag parachutes that allowed Mr. Norm's customers to at least pretend they were finishing a record quarter-mile run. And when they pulled their "ripcord" to impress their friends and neighbors curbside, what do you think was emblazoned on those chutes?" Why, "Mr. Norm's Hi-Performance Headquarters," what else?

One of this country's hottest performance dealers resided at the corner of Grand and Spaulding in Chicago. Mr Norm's—Norm Kraus to you—Grand-Spaulding Dodge sold Mopar muscle like it was going out of style in the '60s. A decade later, Grand-Spaulding itself went out of style. *courtesy Motorsports Racing Apparel*

Such shenanigans were all part of the youthful enthusiasm that helped Grand-Spaulding Dodge popularity skyrocket. Reportedly, sales volume doubled each year for the dealership's first seven in existence. Grand-Spaulding was, by 1966, Dodge's leading performance-car dealership. Two years later, it was among the division's top 10 in total sales. And in 1972, Mr. Norm's became the nation's number one Dodge dealer. A second Mr. Norm's location in suburban Buffalo Grove soon became the number two Dodge dealer.

Many things Grand-Spaulding did, Dodge did too. In 1967, Mr. Norm's men started shoehorning 383 big-blocks into Darts, something factory men said couldn't be done since the proximity of the driver's side exhaust manifold and stock steering apparatus would fry the grease in the latter. No problem: a simple heat shield took care of that problem, and customers had themselves a new hot street machine. Late in 1967, Dodge quietly introduced its Dart GTS, powered by a 383.

Next, Grand-Spaulding began offering 440 Darts, the so-called "GSS" conversions. In 1969, Dodge did its own 440 Dart conversions. One car Dodge didn't follow

suit with was the '72 Demon GSS with its supercharged 340. Its 13.9-second quarter-mile performance represented, by then, more speed than most automakers, including Dodge, cared to offer.

Behind the blown GSS was Gary Dyer, Grand-Spaulding's racing and performance director. Already an experienced drag racer, Dyer hooked up with Norm Kraus in 1964, a year after Mr. Norm first got his feet wet at the drags. Grand-Spaulding's drag race team quickly developed from there, as did Dyer's control of both race car construction and street performance development. With Dyer doing some of the driving along with various other hot-shoes, Mr. Norm's rampaging Dodges were soon known nationwide. In 1965, the dealership's cars ran off 65 straight match race wins.

Match racing remained Grand-Spaulding's forte, basically because winning in regular classes didn't achieve what Norm Kraus had in mind—beating your own customers at the track served no purpose. But beating the right competitors—big name stars like the factory-backed Ramchargers or Pontiac pilot Arnie Beswick—demonstrated that Grand-Spaulding's way was the right one. "Everything we learned at the track," explained Mr. Norm, "we made available back at the dealership, and to the over 10,000 members of the 'Mr. Norm's Sport Club.' When we win, the fans win, too."

However, not even Grand-Spaulding Dodge could keep winning forever. So many things have changed around Chicago since those heady days of high-performance. Well, the Cubs are still the same. But the White Sox's Comiskey Park—*old* Comiskey Park—no longer stands next to the Dan Ryan Expressway. U.S. 30 radio commercials—"where the g-r-r-reat ONES-S-S-S RUN, RUn, Run, run. . . ."—no longer blare over the airwaves. AM radio's WLS no longer spaces those commercials apart with the same 10 rock 'n roll hits played over and over (and over) again. And Mr. Norm is no longer the Hi-Performance King.

With the downturn in factory performance in the '70s came a fast fade for Grand-Spaulding Dodge. Having relied almost entirely on supercar sales, and having done so with very little cooperation from Chrysler Corporation, Mr. Norm's dealership had nowhere to fall once Detroit pulled the chair out from under the musclecar in 1972. Grand-Spaulding closed its doors in 1975, with Gary Dyer going on to, among other things, successfully market his own street superchargers.

Norm Kraus tried various businesses; fleet leasing, customized vans, motorcycles, but it just wasn't the same. Although the building that for more than a dozen happy years was once home to Mr. Norm's Grand-Spaulding Dodge still stands, all it houses now is memories.

Last but certainly not least was Pontiac's superdealer. The home away from home for Poncho performance in the '60s was Royal Pontiac, located on North Main in Royal Oak, Michigan. Asa "Ace" Wilson, Jr., had established the franchise there in the late-'50s, and soon found himself closely allied with Pontiac as *the* hot dealership in the network.

As usual, the idea once again came from the high-revving mind of PMD adman Jim Wangers, who incidentally didn't live far from Wilson's business in Royal Oak. Early in 1960, Wangers proposed a series of dealer-attended seminars intended to promote performance sales. Pontiac's Sales Manager Frank Bridge shot down the idea, allowing only a test of the plan using a single dealership. Conveniently close, Wilson was recruited as the guinea pig.

Royal's first performance involvement came at the track as the dealership successfully campaigned a '59 Catalina in NHRA drag racing. Then came "Super Duty Monday," Labor Day in 1960, when Super Duty Pontiacs won three major competition events in three

Mr. Norm tried to keep the fires burning even as the musclecar era was dying out. In 1972, Grand-Spaulding Dodge offered a specially prepared supercharged Demon GSS, one of various dealership-modified models created over the years. Sadly, the Demon GSS would be the last.

different locations; NASCAR's Darlington 500 in South Carolina, Colorado's Pikes Peak Hill Climb, and the NHRA Nationals in Detroit. At the latter venue, Royal Pontiac's "Hot Chief" Catalina, driven by Wangers himself, claimed two stock-class championships, helping vault Wilson's firm into the national limelight.

Things quickly escalated from there. Wilson hired Dick Jesse to run his performance program. Other important players included John Martin, parts manager Sam Frontera, and performance service technicians Milt Schornack and Charley Brumfield. Frank Rediker, who didn't actually work for Royal, built the dealership's drag cars.

Hot parts sales were Royal's early priority; in 1961 and 1962, optional power equipment made up 15 per-cent of the dealership's parts business, and that per-centage rapidly rose from there. A few years later, a mail-order parts service identified under the Royal Racing Team banner was created, and by the late-'60s Royal was getting some 300 pieces of mail a day requesting performance kits or tuning tips. Car sales also benefited. By 1965, Wilson's men were moving an average of seven cars a day out the door; total sales hit 2,507, 834 of those GTOs. Two years later, the Royal Racing Team was corresponding with about 55,000 members.

Some of what Royal mechanics learned by playing with Pontiac parts ended up in the regular-production mainstream. In 1965, Royal men began developing the idea of sealing the Tri-Power's three air cleaners in a "pan" that sandwiched a large foam gasket against the underside of an opened-up hood scoop. This package became an over-the-counter dealer option from Pontiac in August 1965. PMD's full-force Ram Air engine option then debuted in February 1966.

Along with parts, Royal Pontiac also marketed more than one "conversion kit." Early examples in 1962 included a Paxton-supercharged "Royal Grand Prix" (one built) and a hopped-up four-cylinder "Tempest Tiger." Then came the first "Royal Bobcat," a big Catalina with all Pontiac's hottest parts, including a Tri-Power 421, and various tuning tricks and tweaks—recurved distributor, rejetted carbs, mechanical linkage instead of vacuum, to name a few. Distinctive paint and Bobcat identifica-tion—created by robbing the "CAT" block letters from Pontiac's Catalina emblem and combining them with two "Bs" and an "O" copped from Bonneville—were also added. A big, bellowing brute, that first Royal Bobcat Pontiac was just the beginning.

The work of Dick Jesse, the Royal Bobcat GTO simply was the right thing to do in 1964. One of these cars was used by Wangers as part of Car and Driver's famous "GTO vs. GTO" road test that year. And Wangers continued turning to Wilson for the Royal treatment any time in the future when he needed to deliver road test Pontiacs to the press. As it was, the automotive press was always interested in what was going on at Royal Pontiac, home to one of the fastest reputations in the country.

In its heyday during the '60s, Royal Pontiac was sell-ing a thousand Bobcat conversions a year, including GTOs, big 2+2s, Bonnevilles, Grand Prixs, and Firebirds. In 1968, Royal started dropping the 428 V-8 beneath GTO and Firebird hoods, a taboo practice (from GM's perspective) similar to the Chevrolet shenanigans performed by Don Yenko and the others.

Then in 1969, Ace Wilson simply decided he'd had enough. He sold his Royal Racing Team to Leader Automotive, run by John DeLorean's brother George. Perhaps coincidentally, perhaps not, Wilson made his decision to get out of the performance parts business about the same time Jim Wangers was leaving MacManus, John and Adams. The Royal Pontiac chapter itself came to a close in 1974 when Wilson also sold his dealership to pursue a land-development project. By then, the entire Pontiac performance story had all but closed anyway.

As had the era of the high-performance dealership.

Royal Pontiac's Royal Racing Team was less of a club and more of a mail-order parts business.

Opposite: Royal Pontiac, in Royal Oak, Michigan, was the leading Poncho performance dealer in the '60s. Along with building a series of "Royal Bobcat" models, the dealership also sponsored more than one drag race campaign. Here, Pontiac adman Jim Wangers pilots a Royal Pontiac "Hot Chief" Catalina in 1962. *Paul Zazarine collection*

Chapter Seven

1970
A Season for Horsepower

The baby boomer generation was zooming past 20 by 1970, a year that kicked open a new decade with enough force to let all America know the times never stop a-changin'. One year before, man had first walked on the moon, music fans by the hundreds of thousands had flocked to Woodstock, and baseball's "Amazin' Mets" had shocked everyone, including the Baltimore Orioles.

By the end of 1970, the death toll in Southeast Asia had surpassed 44,000, Janis Joplin and Jimi Hendrix had killed themselves, and we had killed our own at Kent State. Former St. Louis Cardinal outfielder Curt Flood—"a well-paid slave, but a slave nevertheless"—took major league baseball's long-standing reserve clause to court, opening the door for today's wide-open free-agent market. On April 13, a liquid oxygen tank aboard moonbound Apollo 13 exploded two days into space, and out of NASA's potentially greatest tragedy came one of its supreme triumph as astronauts Jim Lovell, Jack Swigert, Jr., and Fred Haise miraculously made it back to earth through no shortage of courage and will.

The Beatles had all but broken up by April when Paul McCartney announced he was leaving the Fab Four to produce a solo album. Americans were reading Dr. David Reuben's "Everything You Always Wanted To Know About Sex," movie-goers were watching *Midnight Cowboy* and *True Grit*, and pop music devotees were tuning in to Lennon and McCartney's *Let It Be*, or *I'll Be There* by the Jackson 5.

Richard Nixon in 1970 was two years into a tumultuous presidency unmatched in American history for its vast contrasts of achievement and failure. Recession became an economic reality as the Nixon administration tried to bring down an inflationary spiral that had begun

three years earlier. But unemployment and buying power here at home remained secondary issues behind the ongoing military conflict half way around the world.

On April 20, Nixon announced plans to cut America's troop strength in Vietnam by 150,000 personnel by early 1971. Then 10 days later, he told a national television audience of a joint U.S.-South Vietnamese invasion of Cambodia, escalation that incited violent demonstrations at colleges and universities across the country. The results were tragic. National Guardsmen on May 4 fired on 600 student protesters at Kent State University, killing four.

Air pollution had also become a prime public concern by 1970. During his State of the Union address in January, Nixon emphasized environmental protection as a major priority. Established on paper in July, the Environmental Protection Agency (EPA) was officially formed in December, with William Ruckelshaus confirmed as director. Then on December 31, the president signed the National Air Quality Control Act, which among other things mandated a 90 percent reduction in automotive exhaust emissions by 1975.

On the four-wheeled news front, Gary Gabelich established a new land speed record of 622.407 miles per hour on October 23 at Bonneville. Back east in Detroit, a United Auto Workers strike completely shut down General Motors, idling about 400,000 workers for an unprecedented 70 days beginning in September just as the new 1971 models were announced—this coming after production delays had already limited the

Opposite: Chrysler's exciting E-body debuted in 1970 as a new home for Plymouth's Barracuda. The platform also served Dodge well as the base for its first Challenger, a slightly longer rendition of the Mopar ponycar theme. The look was certainly hot, especially when fitted with options like the R/T package and a decklid spoiler. This particular Plum Crazy '70 Challenger R/T backs up its looks with a 375-horsepower 440 big-block.

Perhaps best representative of just how wild things had become on the American performance front by 1970 was Plymouth's Superbird, created with NASCAR superspeedways in mind. This Superbird is one of 716 built with the 440 Six Barrel V-8; another 1,084 came with the 440 four-barrel, and 135 used the 426 hemi.

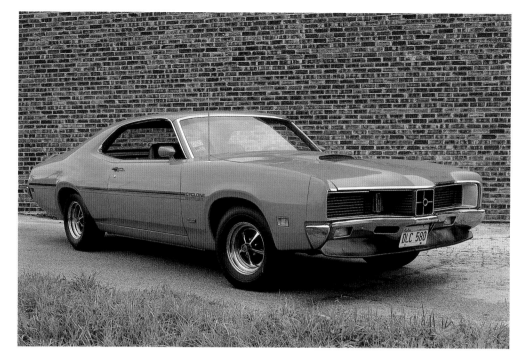

1970 run for Chevrolet and Pontiac's redesigned F-body pony cars.

Such troubles, however, didn't slow GM's divisions down at all as far as performance was concerned in 1970. Nor did heavy price tags, made even heavier by increasingly intimidating insurance rates. Those growing emissions concerns were also apparently of little concern then, at Ford, Chrysler, American Motors, as well as GM. The American supercar remained running strong in 1970, easily as strong as it ever had. And certainly stronger than it ever would again. It was almost as if Detroit's freethinkers were well aware they'd better get it while the gettin' was good. Even with so many detractors readying to bring this country's horsepower race to a close, automakers chose to soar to all-new heights one last time.

Arguably, 1970 was the pinnacle year for American muscle.

It was a year for the biggest, the best, and the brightest. Seemingly going against the anti-performance grain that had run constant at GM since 1963, Detroit's leading automaker dropped its 400-cubic inch displacement limit for its divisions' mid-sized models in 1970, allowing some of the biggest big-blocks of all time to snuggle beneath the hoods of GTOs, 4-4-2s, Gran Sports, and SS Chevelles; the 454 V-8 for the latter, a 455 for Pontiac, Olds, and Buick. Chevrolet even unleashed 450 horses in 1970, the most ever advertised for any street-going supercar powerplant. Meanwhile, Chrysler was busy painting its muscle machines in a groovy array of mind-blowing shades, most appearing every bit as hot as the cars they went on.

Mercury's hottest mid-sized muscle machine in 1970 was the Cyclone Spoiler, powered by the 429 Cobra Jet big-block.

Along with the high amounts of horsepower, high-profile, high-performance imagery was combined with full functionality many times over in 1970. Chin spoilers and rear wings were everywhere. Ford, Chrysler, and Pontiac all used through-the-hood "shaker" scoops that did just that whenever the pedal went to the metal. Chevrolet invented "Cowl Induction," which used a ceremonial flap at the rear of the Super Sport Chevelle's bulging hood to let everyone know when the Mk IV big-block below was sucking in huge gulps of cooler, denser outside air.

The Chevelle SS by that time had taken over as Detroit's best-selling supercar, having leap-frogged the GTO in 1969. "The Chevelle SS 396 has been a very fine seller and it is not difficult to see why," explained a 1970 *Road Test* review. "It has strong youth appeal but Chevrolet management feels that it is beginning to be noticed by a much older segment of the buying public. It is a car that can put a little excitement into the life of a jaded motorist without making him look a total hot rodder."

Getting behind an SS 396's wheel made anyone a believer. This supercar was the real deal, a complete package that offered all the right stuff in standard form, as well as a decent dose of style and roomy comfort. Continued *Road Test*, "you cannot buy the hottest engine without also buying the suspension, tires and brakes that

The Mopar performance lineup may well have represented the widest selection of Detroit muscle in 1970, including everything from Hemi 'Cudas, to Superbirds, to Road Runners, to Duster 340s. Appearing for the final time that year was Dodge's Coronet R/T, the car that had helped first pump up Chrysler's performance image in 1967. Per R/T base specifications, this Go Mango '70 Coronet relies on a 440 big-block for motivation.

General Motors let it all hang out in 1970, dropping its 400-cubic-inch displacement limit for its mid-sized cars. That year, the SS 454 Chevelle joined the SS 396, which itself was by then actually using a 402-cube big-block. King of the hill was the LS6 SS 454, shown here. A small number of LS6 convertibles were also built.

engineers have learned work best. Some manufacturers sell supercar with minimal suspension and brakes, assuming customers plan to go drag racing where such items matter little or will be altered. It's not such a hot idea to trust a customer that far. At Chevrolet they assume the customer can remove what he doesn't want for racing."

Still wearing its well-known badges even though engineers in late 1969 had bored the Mk IV V-8 to 402 cubes, the SS 396 in 1970 was joined by its limit-busting SS 454 running mate. Two versions were offered, beginning with the relatively tame LS5, rated at 360 horsepower. Top dog was the LS6, one of Detroit's meanest muscle mills. *Car Life* called it "the best supercar engine ever released by General Motors." Wearing state-of-the-art cylinder heads with huge ports and valves, the solid-lifter LS6 454 produced 450 real horses. What those ponies did on the street was downright scary.

"Driving a 450-horsepower Chevelle is like being the guy who's in charge of triggering atom bomb tests," claimed *Super Stock*. "You have the power, you know you have the power, and you know if you use the power, bad things may happen. Things like arrest, prosecution, loss of license, broken pieces, shredded tires, etc." Your grandmother could've driven this car down the quarter-mile in a click more than 13 seconds, and getting into the 12s was only a matter of letting her slap on some slicks

and bolt up a pair of headers while her cookies were cooling on the ledge. Either way, the LS6 Chevelle was all but unbeatable on the street. "That's LS as in Land Speed Record," concluded *Motor Trend*'s A. B. Shuman.

This kind of performance from a car gramma might've also been almost willing to drive to the store for a half-gallon of milk helped rank the LS6 SS 454 right up at the top of the heap—for the entire supercar species, '60s, '70s, or otherwise. Evidence of just how well this wild animal could survive in domestication came in production figures. Its additional $1,000 price tag notwithstanding, the slightly cranky LS6 Chevelle actually outsold its more affordable, less disagreeable LS5 brother, 4,475 to 4,298. No other supreme-performance machine of the '60s or '70s came anywhere close to the LS6's uncommonly high sales success.

But others did, in 1970, run right along with the 450-horsepower Chevelle when the light turned green. Although they didn't carry the same "advertised" oomph that year, corporate cousins from Buick, Olds, and Pontiac were still no strangers to the 13-second class. All three were exposed to a similar displacement explosion, in this case from 400 to 455 cubic inches. Both Buick's second-edition Stage 1 big-block and Oldsmobile's established W-30 motor were upgraded to the SS 454's stratosphere.

The B-O-P 455, however, was handicapped slightly by its longer stroke compared to Chevy's 454, a situation that, while it promised increased durability and helped churn out loads of torque, inhibited its high-revving capabilities. In Pontiac's case, the 360-horsepower 455 introduced as a '70 GTO option was not much more than a torque churn created more with station wagons in mind. "For street-prowling youths whose social standing depends upon having the meanest tire burner on The Avenue, the GTO may have lost its luster," explained a January 1970 *Car and Driver* review of the new 455 Goat. Luckily, tire-toasting tykes still could turn to the Ram Air IV 400, the 370-horse powerplant that again shown brightest as the division's top performance star.

Oldsmobile dropped its 400 big-block completely from its 4-4-2 line-up for 1970, opting solely for the 455 V-8 as a standard power source. Adding the W-30 option with its new fiberglass ram-air hood added only 5 more horses to the base 455's 365-horsepower advertised rating. At least on paper. Most knew actual power at the pedal probably went beyond the published 370 figure. Once again, the right rubber, a few underhood and chassis tweaks, and open exhausts could put the '70 W-30 Olds down into the high 12s.

The same could be said for Buick's GS 455 Stage 1, probably one of the greatest street sleepers ever to leave a

Even though most felt it was understated, the LS6 454's advertised 450hp rating was still the strongest figure ever printed on an air cleaner decal. The ram-air "Cowl Induction" hood shown here was optional.

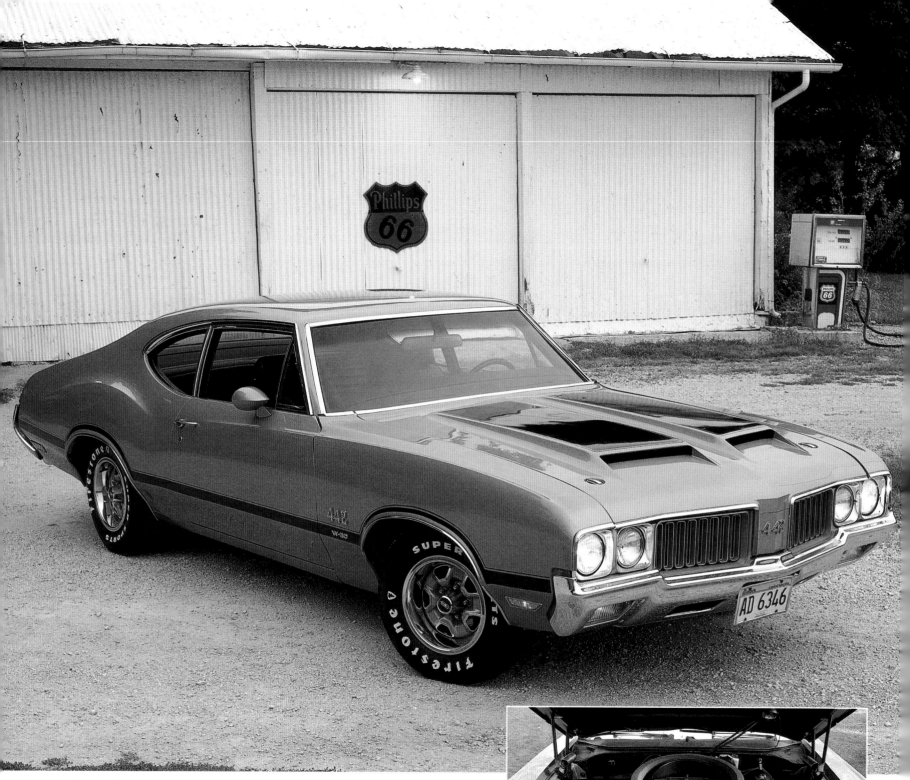

With no holds now barred, Oldsmobile in 1970 made its 455-cubic-inch big-block the main power source for the 4-4-2. Also new was the W-25 fiberglass hood for the top-performing W-30. This '70 W-30 has incorrectly painted wheels—color-keyed versions didn't appear until 1971.

The ram-air equipment and red plastic inner fenders quickly give away the identity of Oldsmobile's W-30 455. Output for the W-30 V-8 in 1970 was a healthy 370 horses.

foolish stoplight challenger sniffing exhaust. Flint had been building the Skylark-based Gran Sport since 1965 with little more attention than an occasional tip of the hat from those who could appreciate a gentlemanly approach to the supercar field. More muscle men began to take notice in 1969 when the first Stage 1 package was offered for the 400 V-8. Then came a very exciting new Skylark body in 1970, joined by the bigger 455 big-block.

"Buick, long known for sedate 'old people' cars has altered its image {with trendy styling}," announced a March 1970 *Road Test* report. "Now it shakes the very foundations of the 'Establishment' with the GS 455 Stage 1, a production car assault on the nation's drag strips." After watching with amazement as a supposedly stock '70 GS Stage 1 roared down the quarter-mile in only 13.38 seconds, *Motor Trend*'s Bill Sanders called this ground-shaking Buick an "old man's car inbred with a going street bomb." "It may be some vague sort of incest," he continued, "but the results are pretty exciting. It's not temperamental; you can drive though city traffic, then run at the strip and get those fantastic e.t.'s, then head right back to the old slow grind with no protest."

Hiding beneath twin functional hood scoops, the Stage 1 was laughingly rated at only 360 horsepower, a mere 10 more than the GS 455's base big-block. In Sanders' opinion, that advertised figure "must be some kind of understatement record." He doubted 360 horses could pull like the Stage 1 did. "Performance verges on a precipitous mechanical hysteria," continued the *Motor Trend* scribe. "The first time you put your foot to the boards a premonition of impending whiplash emanates from the base of the Achilles tendon."

As much as they loved to hear Sanders' raves concerning Stage 1 performance, Buick's image-makers must've failed to appreciate a reference he made labeling the car "the "sleeper of the year." On February 9, 1970, the division introduced its wide-awake GSX at the Chicago Auto Show. Along with a hot suspension, 15x7 sport wheels wearing fat G60 rubber, and power front discs, Buick's new A9 options package included what easily ranks among the supercar era's greatest image treatments. Spoilers were added front and rear, as was a hood tach and bold striping. Two special finishes were included, glowing Glacier White and radioactive Saturn Yellow. Either 455 could be fitted beneath the GSX's hood.

As if to not upstage the image, 360-horsepower GSX models did not receive those red-accented "Stage 1" badges worn by their GS 455 counterparts. Or perhaps Buick really did want Stage 1 performance to remain a surprise.

Perhaps 1970's biggest surprise awaited pony car buyers hoping to buy new Camaros and Firebirds early in the model year. GM designers had begun working on a

Of the 678 GSXs built in 1970, 400 were equipped with the 360-horsepower Stage 1 455 V-8, 118 backed by four-speeds, 282 with automatics. The remaining 278 models came with the 350-horsepower 455 big-block.

Able to easily run with the LS6 Chevelle—and blow it away in the flashy image department—Buick's GSX appeared in 1970 with as much pizzazz as the Detroit muscle crowd had ever seen. Two glowing paint schemes were offered, Apollo White and Saturn Yellow.

GM's restyled F-body shell fit the Z/28 Camaro like a glove in 1970, as did front and rear spoilers and new 15-inch wheels.

Chevy engineers in 1970 traded the Z/28's 302 small-block, used exclusively from 1967–69, for the Corvette's LT-1 350. Beneath a Camaro hood, the LT-1 was downrated 10 horses to 360.

Even more dramatic than the Camaro's 1970 transformation was that of its F-body running mate, Pontiac's Firebird Trans Am. But if all that macho, muscle-bound imagery was too much for your tastes, there was also the new Firebird Formula with its twin-scooped hood hiding every bit as much Ram Air V-8 performance potential as the Trans Am.

much-improved second-generation F-body image not long after the ink had dried on the first-edition's plans in 1966. Or at least Hank Haga's Chevrolet styling studio had. Jack Humbert's Pontiac stylists were first kept busy revamping their Firebird for 1969; they didn't start dreaming of a completely new 'Bird until the summer of 1967.

Both projects promised real excitement ahead, hopefully to arrive in the fall of 1969. But when the two divisions' new models for 1970 were announced in September, neither pony car was present. Various glitches, combined with designers' desires to do their thing as right as they could before unveiling the results to the public, forced Chevrolet and Pontiac to delay those introductions. Customers looking for the next greatest Camaro and Firebird in late 1969 and early 1970 were told to take leftovers and like it. Some didn't—like it, that is. Some sued.

All the confusion, however, was wiped away come February 1970 when the two totally fresh F-bodies finally emerged. Low, long, and wide, both sleek machines were commonly praised for the way their expensive-looking facades masked their affordable compact natures. Warmly welcomed updates beneath their sexy skins included front disc brakes as standard equipment.

Chevy's hottest Camaro, the Z/28, fit into its new sheet metal like Marilyn Monroe in a strapless evening gown. "It's quiet, quick, beautiful and all the parts look and act as though they belong together," claimed *Sports Car Graphic's* Paul Van Valkenburgh, who needed seven pages to explain that, for all intents and purposes, the next-generation Z/28 was every bit the sports car the '70 Corvette was. The only major difference was the price—the Corvette cost $2,000 more. "If you choose the Vette," wrote Van Valkenburgh, "you're spending [that two grand] on something that doesn't even exist—your image."

The two even shared engines; the Corvette's optional 350-cubic-inch LT-1 V-8 was standard for the '70-1/2 Z/28. The only difference here came on paper, where the Corvette's LT-1 was rated at 370 horsepower; the Camaro's, 360. Either way, most critics agreed Chevy's LT-1 was probably the greatest small-block V-8 to yet scream down the pike. And they were probably right. With a much wider, more usable power band than its 302 forerunner, the 360-horsepower 350 offered instant throttle response earlier Z/28 drivers could only dream about. "The ['70-1/2] Z/28 is as close to a mild-mannered racing car as the industry has come," concluded a *Car Life* report. " Despite the added weight and tougher emissions controls, it's faster than ever, and in a way that makes the car driveable by anybody."

Pontiac pony car buyers didn't get a new engine for 1970, but Trans Am fans were greeted with an excitingly

fresh face that was just as worthy of headlines as the LT-1 V-8. Among Detroit's more creative meldings of form and function, the '70-1/2 Trans Am not only looked the part of a certified street racer, it backed up that image in spades thanks to an excellent chassis, scads of big-block power beneath that trademark rear-facing scoop, and a distinctive body that at the same time would've made Racquel Welch and George Foreman (the younger, hungrier Foreman; not the older, well-fed Foreman) proud.

Functionality was key. Air extractors up front, airflow deflectors at the corners, a ducktail in back—it all worked. So did the chin spoiler, equipment most critics agreed was sorely needed in 1969 to defeat the first Trans Am's inherent tendency to lift its nose at speed. All told, the sum of the parts equaled, in *Car and Driver's* words, "a hard-muscled, lightning-reflexed commando of a car, the likes of which doesn't exist anywhere in the world, even for twice the price." Not everyone felt the same way, however. Ron Wakefield of *Road & Track* called the 70-1/2 Trans Am a "super-gook version of [the] Firebird, undoubtedly setting [a] new record in [the] number of unnecessary add-on put-ons."

As in 1969, standard muscle for the second-edition Trans Am came from a Ram Air III 400, upgraded 10 horsepower to 345 horsepower. Also returning for an optional encore was the Ram Air IV, now rated like its GTO counterpart at 370 horsepower. Only 88 370-

Easily ranking among the greatest musclecars of all-time was the Hemi 'Cuda, offered in both 1970 and '71. This '70 model was one of only 652 built. Beneath that purposefully prominent Shaker scoop are at least 425 horses—many believe quite a few more were hiding behind that advertised figure.

horsepower Trans Ams were built in 1970. Considering that the RA III T/A was commonly clocked through the lights in right around 14 seconds, it is easy enough to assume that the RA IV rendition would've put this muscled-up Firebird right up there with the best of the best in Detroit's best year for factory performance.

Even quicker in the 1970 pony car field than the new Trans Am and Z/28 were two equally fresh offerings from Chrysler, both based on the new E-body platform. E-body development dated back to 1967 when Cliff Voss's Advanced Styling Studio began considering an all-new Barracuda. With room for the most Mopar muscle available being a main priority, the design crew began by constructing the engine bay around a cowl layout borrowed from the bigger B-body (Road Runner, etc.) line. From there grew a truly spunky little car conveying a rakish image accentuated by its abbreviated tail perched high above the road. John Herlitz deserved the bulk of the credit for the E-body Barracuda's exterior.

Dodge designers were also given the E-body to use as they saw fit. In their case, they managed to create a very different slant on the same idea, a slightly longer, more angular pony car based on a 110-inch wheelbase, compared to the Barracuda's 108-inch stretch. Dodge's chief designer Bill Brownlie made it all work on the outside, and thus the Challenger was born.

In 1970, the sky was basically the limit for both the all-new Challenger and redesigned Barracuda. A 335-horsepower 383 four-barrel big-block was the base power source for the Challenger's R/T package and Plymouth's top-performance 'Cuda line-up. Options included everything from the hot, little 340 small-block, to the 440 big-block, all the way up to "King Kong," the 426 hemi. The tri-carb 440 was frightening enough beneath an E-body's long hood; those 425 hemi horses only promised even more shocks for the competition. Undoubtedly the strongest of the performance pony cars, the '70 Hemi 'Cuda damn near busted into the 12s in street trim, grounds enough to also consider it as one of the all-time greats among the entire supercar species.

Not too far off that mark was a 1970 offering from Ford. Dearborn's line-up was as strong as it had ever been, with the Boss 302 Mustang back for a second year, joined by the more marketable Mach 1, still featuring the 428 Cobra Jet big-block V-8 as its top optional power source. Back as well for another bow was the nasty Boss 429, another pony car capable of running well down into the 13s in the quarter.

King of the Mustang corral in 1970 was again the Boss 429 with its 375-horsepower "Shotgun motor." Only 499 were built before production was shut down early in the year.

Ford's Cobra officially became an upscale Torino in 1970, after debuting in "econo-racer" form the year before as a Fairlane-based model. Pricey options appearing here include those Magnum 500 wheels and ram-air Shaker hood.

In 1970, Ford traded the 428 Cobra Jet for a new and improved CJ big-block based on the clean-running 385-series 429-cubic-inch V-8—at least in the Torino Cobra. The proven 428 CJ remained a Mustang option. The Cobra's 429 SCJ was rated at 370 horsepower. Optional ram air did not change that advertised figure.

One more Blue Oval product was nearly capable of such numbers in 1970, the Torino Cobra. This venomous machine wore what the Better Idea guys preferred to call a "SportsRoof" body, a fastback to you. In 1969, Dearborn had first offered the Cobra as an options package on its mid-sized Fairlane, either as fastback or a notchback coupe. For 1970, the Cobra was elevated to the top as an upscale Torino.

It was also fitted with a new standard V-8, as the 428 CJ was superseded by Ford's new cleaner-running 385-series big-block. A clear concession to changing attitudes, the Cobra's latest base engine, the 360-horsepower 429 Thunder Jet, was only a shadow of its FE-series Cobra Jet forerunner. But if sharper fangs were required, the 370-horse 429 Cobra Jet was able to put the bite on any supercar rival that dared venture too close. Adding the Drag Pack equipment and its underrated 5-horse improvement

helped propel a Super Cobra Jet Torino to a 13.63-second burst in a *Super Stock* quarter-mile test—and this from a car that was big enough to bring your mother-in-law along for the ride. In that spacious trunk. At least in Ford terms, it just didn't get any better than this.

Performance didn't get much better in anyone's terms than it did during 1970. Everyone was in the ballgame that year, and everyone was running balls-out. Last only by size, American Motors wasn't left out of the mad rush toward supreme performance; AMX—in its final year as a two-seat, individual model—and Javelin both also had their moments in 1970 as there was more than enough horsepower to go around. Enough,

even, to make the Rebel Machine a real hauler, too.

The list went on and on. And on. SS 396 Novas and Camaros from Chevy. Six Pack Super Bees from Dodge. Hemi Road Runners from Plymouth. Cobra Jet Eliminators and Spoilers from Mercury. Ram Air IV Judges from Pontiac. W-31 small-block Oldsmobiles. GTX. Cyclone GT. Formula 400 Firebird. Coronet R/T. The line-up was as plentiful as it was powerful.

And it was also short-lived, for just as quickly as the supercar reached its zenith, it began a rapid fall from grace in 1971. Everyone in Detroit saw it coming. Maybe that's why they chose to make 1970 such a great year for performance—a fast farewell, if you will.

The American way was always on a different track from the rest of the world, especially when AMC jumped into the musclecar race. Following hot on the wheels of the Hurst SC/Rambler, the Rebel Machine rolled out in red, white, and blue regalia in 1970. It, too, was a Hurst/American Motors creation. Rebel Machines also appeared in solid colors.

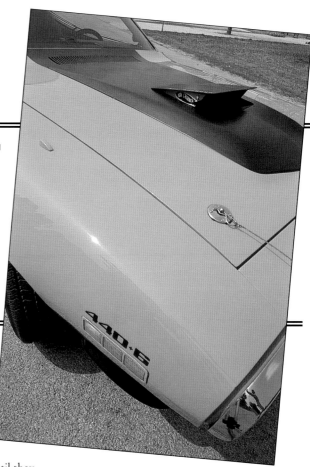

Chapter Eight

THE SIGNPOST UP AHEAD
American Performance Enters the Twilight Zone

For many musclecar maniacs, the end of the road finally came on Saturday, December 2, 1973. It was a bleak day indeed, even though it was sunny Southern California. Those who loved speed-shifting a hot car, who rarely missed a drag race, who followed NASCAR competition religiously, never thought they'd see this moment arrive. But it did. And the world would never be the same again.

On that winter day in Newport Beach, Linda Vaughn tied the knot, saying "I do" to drag-racing businessman Bill Tidwell.

"Linda Vaughn getting married?" asked *Motor Trend's* Steve Spence. "That's like Joe Namath getting married." Of course Namath's nuptials wouldn't have broken near as many hearts among red-blooded American male-dom. How many of these men had bought Hurst shifters or Schiefer clutches after falling victim to Linda's bountiful sex appeal is anyone's guess.

Linda Vaughn was *the* "Miss Hurst Golden Shifter" girl, the musclecar era's ever-present spokesmodel. Anyone who didn't believe there was a connection between Detroit's supercars and our sexuality needed only to open their eyes. There at races, at promotional events, in advertisements was lovely Linda—there, except for that weekend in 1973. Instead of appearing before a crowd of race fans saying then farewell to Long Beach's legendary Lion's Drag Strip as it closed down, Linda stood up before about 275 well-wishers and made it official.

With Linda Vaughn out of the running, what was left? By 1973, the supercar performance she had earlier helped promote was all but dead, done-in, in many critics' opinion, by an army of Washington bureaucrats and Detroit killjoys Ralph Nader, the Environmental Protection Agency, and Allstate finally had all gotten their wish. After reaching its zenith in 1970, the musclecar quickly nose-dived the following year, leaving only a few proud stragglers to carry on until they too were snuffed out after 1974.

One of the earliest major signs that Detroit would soon be shifting gears away from performance production came on November 20, 1970, when Ford Motor Company Sales Group Vice President Matthew McLaughlin announced his corporation's pull-out from all motorsport activities save for some limited support for drag racing and off-road competition. "The greatest peacetime non-governmental competitive effort to occur in this century has quietly drawn to a close—the victim of progress," wrote *Motor Trend's* Jim Brokaw.

Henry Ford II, the same man who had denounced the AMA factory racing ban in 1962 and then poured tens of millions of dollars into what seemed like his own personal vendetta with Enzo Ferrari in the international racing arena, had suddenly changed his mind as the '60s came to a close. Much inspiration for this change came from Washington's strongest demands yet on Detroit to build safer cars. Even more influential were governmental mandates to clean up the air. "In 1969, Henry II pledged the assets of the company to help whip the pollution problem," continued Brokaw's report. "He wasn't fooling. Shortly after his speech, Ford announced the allocation of $18 million for the installation of anti-smoke equipment on the factories' smoke stacks. Two

Chrysler Corporation probably deserves credit for creating the greatest gimmicks of the supercar era. But don't let the zaniness of Plymouth's flip-up Air Grabber scoop on this 1971 GTX fool you. It served a purpose, namely delivering denser, cooler air to the 440+6 big-block's three hungry Holley two-barrel carbs below.

Opposite: The last great American musclecar? Pontiac's 455 Super Duty Trans Am could have held its own in 1970, even with its emissions controls/low-compression handicap. But the 455 SD was introduced in 1973, a time when horsepower was on its way out in Detroit. Pontiac's excitement builders let the biggest of the big-block Super Duty's loose again in 1974 before surrendering to the realities of a radically changing automotive world. This '74 455 SD Trans Am is one of 943 built. Another 57 Super Duty Firebirds were also produced that year.

In this unaccustomed view, Linda Vaughn, Hurst's Golden Shifter Girl, shows off two other major attributes, one on top, the other at the opposite end. *Roger Huntington Archives, courtesy Dobbs Publishing*

Superbly flowing cylinder heads were the key to the 455 Super Duty's unbelievable smog-controlled performance. Even with only 8.4:1 compression, the 455 SD produced 290 net horses. A common trick to help the big Super Duty breathe even better involved unbolting the decorative plate in the back of the rearward-facing scoop, allowing the 455 to suck in cooler, denser air.

months later, the racing budget for 1970 was drastically reduced by about 75 percent."

In late 1969, Henry II also fired his president, Bunkie Knudsen, whose career had always seemed tied by an umbilical cord to the musclecar. The former GM exec had never been shy about promoting horsepower, dating back to his first top position as Pontiac's general manager beginning in 1956. "Knudsen likes performance and dabbles in it, some say, more than he should," said former California Ford dealer Chuck Foulger not long after Bunkie's jump to Ford in February 1968. "But he knows what the market wants and he knows how to accomplish his goals. I think Bunkie's dynamic thinking is just what Ford needs." In 1968, maybe.

By 1969, however, Ford was ready to start playing a whole new game. But Bunkie simply wouldn't give up the ball. "He was a racing nut, but he failed to understand that the heyday of racing had passed," explained Iacocca in his autobiography. "It's no secret that Iacocca questions the value returned for each racing dollar

[spent]," added a January 1971 *Motor Trend* report. "It's also no secret that deposed former president Bunkie Knudsen was a staunch supporter of racing, and anything that was in to Bunkie is currently out."

In September 1969, only 19 months after his headline-making hiring, Knudsen was dropped like a hot potato at Ford. Two weeks later, designer Larry Shinoda, another GM defector, was also let go. Iacocca's explanation for the purge? "I wish I could say Bunkie got fired because his ideas were all wrong. But the actual reason was because he used to walk into Henry's office without knocking. That's right—without knocking!"

Once Knudsen was knocked out, Iacocca temporarily took his place with two other men in a "troika" management arrangement. Then on December 19, 1970, the father of the Mustang became sole president. Needless to say, he had not been sorry to see the ex-GM exec fail in Dearborn. "The day Bunkie was fired there was great rejoicing and much drinking of champagne," Iacocca recalled. "Over in public relations, one of our people coined a phrase that soon became famous throughout the company: 'Henry Ford once said that history is bunk. But today, Bunkie is history.'"

With boss Bunkie out the door, and his ace designer with him, Ford's Boss Mustangs and all they stood for were sure to follow. The Boss 429 assembly line came to an abrupt halt in January 1970, and Boss 302 production also didn't survive the year. Neither did the home of the Boss 429, the Kar Kraft shop in Brighton, Michigan, which, ironically, after closing became home to Rectrans, Inc., a mobile home manufacturer run by Knudsen, with Shinoda again his designer. Ford's Special Vehicles director, Jacque Passino, resigned the day before Thanksgiving in 1970.

Meanwhile, Iacocca and his team were hard at work on yet another better idea. The new president knew the youthful market he had captured with his pony car in 1964 was growing older and wiser. He also knew their

dollars weren't stretching nearly as far as they had just a few years before. In response, Dearborn had introduced its economical Maverick midyear in 1969, followed by the truly affordable Pinto in 1971. Iacocca's second greatest mass-market marvel, his "little jewel," the radically reduced Mustang II, then debuted to high praise for 1974.

Yet even with all the trauma created late in 1970 by Ford's withdrawal from racing, Dearborn was not entirely through playing out its performance string. Reportedly, design improvements mandated by Washington's smog and safety crusaders had added as much as $360 to the price of every Ford for 1971, making an already expensive proposition in the case of the musclecar even more costly. Nevertheless, Ford engineers

still managed to keep the hot 429 Cobra Jet big-block around for one last performance as the top muscle-bound option for Mach 1 Mustangs and Torino Cobras.

Dearborn's speed kings in 1971 also built one of the quickest Mustangs ever, the Boss 351, with its 330-horsepower "HO" Cleveland-family small-block. In *Car and Driver's* words the Boss 351 "offers drag strip performance that most cars with 100 cubic inches more displacement will envy." While the 351 Cleveland V-8 did survive in less potent form as a still-potent Mustang power source up through 1973, the Boss 351 was a one-hit wonder, as well as a suitably strong send-off for the Blue-Oval breed of musclecar.

"This is probably the last chance you'll have to buy a machine of this kind," predicted *Sports Car Graphic's*

Ford had given up on racing the year before and stood poised to put its chips into the downsized Mustang II's basket, but Dearborn engineers in 1971 still managed to put together one of the best Blue Oval musclecars ever, the Boss 351 Mustang. Power came from a 330-horsepower 351 HO small-block V-8.

Even with the end of the musclecar's road in sight, Oldsmobile's W-30 4-4-2 continued running strong in 1971, the year mandated compression cuts began leading many performance engines down the off-ramp to oblivion.

Previously limited only to cars sold in California, smog equipment became a requirement on all American automobiles in 1968. Most common was the "air pump," which injected oxygen into the exhaust port area to help burn hydrocarbons. Ford's Thermactor and Chevrolet's Air Injection Reactor were both of this design.

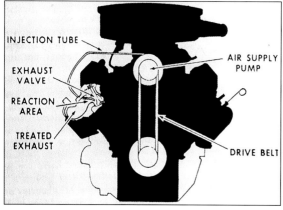

road test of the Boss 351. "Ford is now diverting racing dollars into solving safety and pollution problems. We have heard that all ['72] Fords will be detuned to run on regular fuel. That means lower compression. The current exhaust-popping 11:1 [ratios] will probably be lowered 15 to 20 percent, and the only way to regain the lost power is through expensive modifications—which will probably become illegal. Perhaps we'll just learn to live with the situation, like war and taxes. But we have a few years left. We might as well live it up while we can."

Prophecies like this were running rampant among the press by 1971. But such comments were nothing new, and in fact could be traced back as early as 1965, the year Washington began taking Detroit to task over the way its cars both purportedly threatened drivers and fouled the air. The earliest, loudest warnings of things to come showed up in 1967 on the pages of *Car Life*, courtesy of veteran performance reporter Roger Huntington.

"Black clouds are on the horizon," began Huntington's piece entitled, appropriately enough, "Super Trouble for Supercars." "Powerful forces are at work today in this country that will tend to downgrade performance in the future, not ten years from now, but within two or three years." Of course, Huntington was referring to the three horsemen: toughening auto safety legislation, tightening federal emissions standards, and rising insurance rates.

The last of those "powerful forces" had been gaining strength since 1964 as insurance men quickly made a connection between high accident rates and high-horsepower, high-profile supercars like Pontiac's new GTO. Before then, buyers could order big, brawny V-8s in their cars with relatively little worry over what their insurance man might say since most of these non-descript performance machines drew minimal attention to themselves, as did the high-horsepower market as a whole. Not so once Detroit's image-makers began slapping bawdy badges all over their new supercars and began playing up go-fast images in maximum-attention-grabbing advertisements.

By creating a distinct, definitely noticeable new category for its performance machines in 1964, Detroit managed to readily attract even more ire from the conservative crowd who always saw excessive horsepower as being inherently unsafe—with stronger engines going into smaller cars, that safety question began begging itself ever louder. The new supercar also caught the eye of those who saw the chance to profit off that purported inherent nature. As the August 1964 issue of *Car Life* reported, "the National Automobile Underwriters Association has finally gotten around to taking a long look at [high-performance] cars and it apparently is not too keen about what it sees. The

Association is researching methods to more properly reflect in the premium the hazard of higher-than-ordinary powered vehicles. However, the group faces a problem in defining how high is high-powered, and at what point horsepower becomes hazardous."

That latter mention represented the rub. In 1964, insurance executives proposed placing as much as a 25-percent surcharge on premiums for cars with higher-than-normal horsepower-to-weight ratios. All such cars, with little or no regard for the driver's age or record. Forget that such a sweeping, all-inclusive proposal was patently unfair. Many critics of this plan felt such charges were nothing more than greedy exploitation, a profit-gouging ploy based solely on perception, not fact. "Have any major underwriters been forced to abandon construction on their latest multi-million-dollar office monuments that often rival the Hanging Gardens of Babylon in grandeur because supercars have become open sewers for their capital?" asked Eric Dahlquist in a March 1970 *Motor Trend* editorial.

No sound statistics existed, at least not in the early '60s, that clearly demonstrated a profound link between performance cars and higher accident rates. Obviously, the potential was there, that couldn't be denied. And certainly many drivers put behind the wheel of a performance car were high insurance risks. But at what percentage did these high-risk drivers in supposedly high-risk automobiles exist?

"Undeniably there are a certain number of muscle car buyers who indulge in reckless driving on the street," explained Ford's Jacque Passino in a 1970 *Motor Trend* guest editorial. "And as is the case in so many areas today, these relatively few bad drivers give a bad name to everyone who purchases a high performance car. Perhaps even more repugnant to most citizens are the professional street racers. All of this has helped to create an image in the public's mind of a multitude of fire-breathing cars on the road with black-jacketed young hoodlums at the wheel ready to race at the drop of the hat, and heaven help one in the way."

However, as Passino and others in the industry tried to point out, such perceptions were the product of the actions of a distinct minority. Not all musclecar owners were "young hoodlums." In 1970, the average age of a performance-oriented Mach 1 buyer was only four years less than the typical Mustang customer; the average age of a Torino Cobra buyer was 28. Cost was a prevailing factor in keeping young riff-raff out of the supercar country club. Performance has never been cheap; not then, not now. Few "kids" could afford the '60s supercars, and most that could were well aware of how much cash they were risking by driving foolishly.

"But images are hard to dispel," said Passino, "and street racing and irresponsible behavior behind the wheel are stigmas draped like a millstone around the neck of the muscle car." Such stigmas made it all too easy for the insurance industry to do as it damn well pleased.

By 1965, some insurers were simply refusing to cover certain cars with certain horsepower levels; say, compacts with more than 300 horses, full-sized models with 400-plus. Corvettes quickly became kings of the taboo class, a group of uninsurable untouchables that varied widely by insurance company. One firm in 1965 had a list of 21 cars it wouldn't issue policies for under any circumstances.

Additional lists were created for the cars that qualified for the new sky-high premium rates. Such groupings were often as unfair as the all-encompassing rate hikes themselves since defining what was or wasn't a supercar continually seemed too tough a job for decision-makers who basically knew very little about the technical specifics of the products they were dealing with. While GTOs, 4-4-2s, and the like were generally recognized by everyone in the industry, other cars were either incorrectly included or inexplicably overlooked. By 1967, some companies were targeting anything with a four-speed. Others considered any fastback model fair game for a higher premium. At the same time, Buick's Gran Sports—performance cars the last time anyone checked—were commonly not saddled with an extra surcharge.

Most firms simply followed similar basic formulas using power-to-weight or displacement-to-weight ratios. A 1967 car carrying 10 pounds for every advertised horsepower was a shoe-in for the high-premium class. Amazingly enough, so were some four-door sedans and larger-displacement automobiles with little or no go-fast potential. Many mild-mannered machines were caught up in the net right alongside their supercar brethren, with the end result being yet another shooting-fish-in-a-barrel windfall for the insurance industry.

Customers couldn't believe their checkbooks. In 1967, when an unmarried man under 25 spent about $3,500 on a performance car, he might've faced doling out nearly half that much more to insure his pride and joy over the next two years—and this even with a good driving record. A previous accident or a ticket or two promised a completely unaffordable situation. And it only got worse. Insurance companies three years later began instituting surcharges as high as 50 percent on performance car premiums. In some cases, musclecar owners who might have financed their new machines for three years could've ended up paying half again as much more in insurance premiums over that same span. Even if emissions controls hadn't strangled the life out the American musclecar, the breed would've never survived long into the '70s under such economic restraints.

Detroit's automakers weren't blind, they knew they couldn't continue offering youth-oriented automobiles to young drivers who couldn't afford to drive them. According to Lee Iacocca late in 1967, unfairly high

Buick tried that GSX thing a second time in 1971 before ending the short string. Again, Apollo White and Saturn Yellow were the only "official" colors, but additional paint schemes were available by special order. Red and black GSX Buicks are known.

insurance rates for young Americans represented the auto industry's biggest problem at the time—and that was saying a lot considering how much safety legislation and emissions mandates would soon be costing Detroit. One solution involved offering less-powerful performance cars—Ford's decision to trade the '66 Fairlane GT's standard 390 big-block V-8 for a 289 two-barrel small-block in 1967 was one small example of this kind of thinking.

Another answer came in the form of a quieter approach. Many performance engines in the late-'60s were grossly underrated on paper, as was the case with the 275-horse 340 Mopar small-block V-8 and 335-horsepower 428 Cobra Jet big-block from Ford. In 1968, Oldsmobile engineers put together their impressive W-31 350 small-block and dropped it into their

less-noticeable Cutlass, not their "hey-come-and-look-at-me" 4-4-2. The result was a polite, yet potent street machine able to run with its big-block brothers at a much lower cost. Sometimes approaches like these worked, sometimes they didn't.

Meanwhile, automakers continued claiming unfair treatment. "Cars don't cause accidents," went the typical defense, "car owners do." Insurance industry officials undoubtedly couldn't have cared less since cars don't pay the premiums, either. But while Detroit's protests continually fell on deaf ears, consumer complaints were not overlooked. In 1968 came talk of a congressional investigation of the insurance business, and people at Ford and GM were also examining the possibilities of providing some type of insurance themselves to customers in the 17-25 age group.

In 1970, Senator Phillip Hart's Antitrust and Monopoly Subcommittee did finally begin looking into both the automotive parts business and the insurance industry. Senator Hart—from Michigan, of course—couldn't understand how the latter group could get away so easily with throwing the baby out with the bath water. "One of the hardest things for me to swallow is the idea that any individual must pay the price for the sins of his peers," he told *Motor Trend*. "That's why I get upset when I hear how insurance companies take whole groups—ranging from bartenders to clergymen—and label all members of the group 'bad risks.'"

That insurance companies still discriminate against under-25, unmarried males in the same fashion is indicative of just how strong the industry's lobby is in Washington. As it was, even if Senator Hart's committee had changed things, the American musclecar wouldn't have been around to reap the benefits anyway.

Closely tied to the insurance issue in the '60s was Washington's sudden concern over automotive safety. Not that insuring safe travel on American roads and highways wasn't important and hadn't been addressed before. But previous congressional efforts to investigate just how much of a risk our daily driving represented were kept low key. As it was, public perceptions of the issue were almost non-existent, as were motives in Detroit to address such a problem, if indeed there was one.

In 1948, when independent automaker Preston Tucker had tried to do Detroit one better in every way with his innovative, rear-engined, aerodynamic automobile, he had refused to include ground-breaking standard seatbelts in the equation because he didn't want to imply any inherent lack of safety in the basic platform. Nearly 10 years later, Ford ended up with egg all over its face after foolishly trying to turn customers' heads by promoting its cars' added safety features. Were Dearborn's automobiles such threats to begin with that they needed all these new upgrades to protect passengers from some then-unknown dangers?

In July 1956, Alabama Representative Kenneth Roberts first brought to order the House's subcommittee on traffic safety, with his initial focus involving possible automotive design defects. His small committee's investigative efforts immediately met stiff resistance, not the least of which came from Detroit lobbies by way of the Department of Commerce. Expected opposition also appeared from the Automobile Manufacturers Association. The end result of Roberts' work was a watered-down set of safety-conscious design standards finally announced in June 1965 by, of all groups, the General Services Administration.

It was then that the Senate took over. In July, Senator Abraham Ribicoff opened his committee's hearings on American automotive safety. This time, any and all stumbling blocks were rudely kicked out of the way as a witch hunt of sorts developed. And, as is typically the case in Washington, it soon became difficult to sort out those with honest concerns for the issues and others interested primarily in their own personal political agendas.

Outspoken consumer advocate Ralph Nader quickly became one of the main stars of Ribicoff's show, as did Senator Robert Kennedy, never one to shirk from a public confrontation. The crusading Kennedy's jousts with GM's soon-to-retire chairman, Frederic Donner, not only highlighted the hearings, they also demonstrated to the automakers' ruling elite that Washington wasn't only paying lip service now. Nor would it tolerate any extra-curricular activity. Donner's replacement, James Roche, was forced to make a public apology to Nader in front of the Ribicoff committee after it was disclosed that GM had hired private detectives to hopefully uncover a skeleton or two in Nader's closet. Such a foolish move only helped support government claims that the biggest of the Big Three operated in arrogant disregard of fair practices, as well as customer safety.

Before the Kennedy-Ribicoff hearings, the tail had basically wagged the dog concerning the way government agencies had held automakers accountable for their products. By the end of the summer of 1965, however, it was Detroit that was on the defensive. Once Nader's *Unsafe At Any Speed* hit the shelves, the American public began believing they too were smelling a rat. Or a lemon. And with public opinion then involved, it was like spilling blood in a sea full of sharks, with legislators being the Great Whites. Detroit executives could point their fingers all they wanted at bad drivers or claim that 50,000 highway fatalities a year were not all that alarming considering the trillions of miles traveled. There was then no stopping the federal government from mandating the redesign and production of safer automobiles.

Such legislation had become Roger Huntington's top concern in 1967 when he wrote about trouble ahead for performance. Even though automotive safety was a three-pronged issue involving drivers and roads along with the automobiles themselves, "it appears that cars will receive a major portion of lawmakers' attention in the near future," he reported. "As long as drivers can vote, and must pay the taxes that build better highways, Detroit will remain a more convenient whipping boy."

Hot on the heels of the Ribicoff hearings came the Traffic Safety and Highway Safety Acts in 1966. To administer these, Washington created the National Highway Safety Agency, with Dr. William Haddon, Jr., assigned to run it as this country's first "traffic safety boss." Or "federal safety czar," as *Motor Trend* called him. Like Nader, Haddon was especially incensed over what he deemed to be too much horsepower coming out

of Detroit. "The way the auto industry's pushing muscle cars borders on criminal irresponsibility," said Haddon. "The image that is being sold at great expense to the American public is that you don't have safe transportation, you have thrills on the highway. Automakers are going to face condemnation by society and probably restrictions by government or they will put curbs on horsepower themselves. It's long overdue."

Admen reportedly were as much to blame as the cars they were attempting to sell. "Inflammatory advertisements, directed toward teenagers and young men in their early 20s, goad and spur them to handle their vehicles as 'nuclear deterrents' or to become 'human cannonballs,'" chimed in Nader in 1970 before the National Violence Commission.

In 1966, among Haddon's first orders of business were various new safety standards, which all of Detroit's cars would have to meet beginning in 1968. Among these requirements were front and rear seatbelts, headrests to prevent whiplash, better exterior lighting and reflectors, tougher tires and rims, and strengthened fuel tanks.

The total list was quite extensive, and in part, according to a Ford official, was also "arbitrary, unreasonable and impractical." Many in Detroit claimed there just wasn't enough time to design in everything Haddon's office demanded within the specified deadline. Still others pointed out that many of the standards were superfluous or of little proven improvement. As Dearborn's Bunkie Knudsen later said in 1969, "we have the responsibility to listen to our critics and heed them when they make a good case." But, he continued, "we [also] have the responsibility to the public to contest and speak out against proposals that seem to us ill-considered."

Ill-considered or not, Haddon's 1966 proposals would become reality by 1968. In the meantime, the GSA's existing list of safety standards went from 17 to 26 for 1967 models. Among these were specifications calling for energy-absorbing steering columns and an overall "softening" of interior protrusions. The downside, from a consumer's perspective, was that these improvements tacked on about $50 to the typical price of a typical 1967 car. That added cost jumped to $150 the following year, a third of that credited to the new emissions controls also mandated for 1968. Detroit's total bill for its legislated design changes that year was reported at $1.1 billion.

Additional safety standards proposed for the years to follow promised even more costs passed on to the consumer. Of special interest to supercar buyers were proposals for both engine governors and limited horsepower outputs. Early in 1970, Transportation Secretary John Volpe also asked that driver's-side air bags be made mandatory equipment by 1972; for the passenger by

Mid-sized Mopars in 1971 received a truly attractive new body that enhanced the image of hot cars like Plymouth's GTX even further—a suitable send-off for legendary performance mills like the 440 Six Barrel V-8. Both this engine and the 426 hemi were cancelled after 1971.

1974. While speed controls never saw the light of day, and airbags came much later, other government-ordered improvements were added, with the result being new car price hikes in some cases of about $350 by 1971.

Additional repercussions included the way high horsepower was marketed. GM in 1967 began toning down its ad campaigns, and also deleted multi-carburetor intakes from all its divisions' cars except for the Corvette. The corporation additionally placed a limit on its '67 models (again excluding Corvette) of no more than one horsepower per 10 pounds of weight. Of course, this limitation came mostly on paper. Examples included the SS 396 Chevelle's optional L34 big-block, which went from 360 horsepower in 1966 to 350 the following year, only to appease the gods of advertised output. Chevrolet's potent L79 327 was also downrated for 1967, from 350 horses to 325, again basically in name alone. The L79 small-block was deleted entirely from the compact Nova's 1967 options sheet, although as many as six such cars did escape before the barn door was slammed shut.

Earlier in 1966, Zora Duntov's engineers had at first pegged the Corvette's top 427 big-block at 450 horses before word came from GM's upper office to tone that rating back down to 425. This action didn't stop Chevy from returning in 1970 with a 450-horsepower air cleaner decal atop the LS6 454. It was a short stay, however. The LS6's industry-leading output figure, still a conservative number, felt the axe in 1971, dropping to 425 horsepower as a result of lowered compression, itself a product of yet another ongoing attack on the musclecar's well-being.

Unlike safety concerns and insurance surcharges, this particular threat wasn't nearly as personal; it didn't pick out performance cars as being any more or less worthy of attention. Plain and simple, all automobiles since the beginning of time have spewed atmospheric contaminates out their tailpipes. Forget all the arguments that automotive exhausts have never been any more of a threat to the air we breathe than forests full of trees or neighborhoods full of bathroom vent flues. Or whatever. What the internal combustion process leaves behind isn't

good for anyone, especially so when it's allowed to accumulate in massive concentrations in massive metropolitan areas. Like Los Angeles.

West Coasters had become well aware of the potential problems presented by too many cars in too small an area in the early '50s. Crop damage in Southern California due to "smog" had been detected as early as 1944. By the end of the '50s, state legislators were already calling for new ways to control smog, the product of automotive hydrocarbon emissions plus prolonged exposure to sunlight. One of the earliest, partial cures was the positive crankcase ventilation system, developed by GM's AC Division in September 1961. After that date, all cars sold in California were required to be equipped with PCV valves, which allowed internal engine fumes to be rerouted back into the carburetor to be burned, as opposed to previous designs that simply let these gases escape directly into the atmosphere. PCV valves then became a federal requirement for all American cars two years later.

California legislators next began work to stamp out the real root of the smog problem: unburned hydrocarbons and carbon-monoxide emissions. By 1964, West Coast lawmakers had established new emissions standards to be met by California cars beginning with the 1966 model year. These standards required exhaust emissions to not exceed 275 parts per million of unburned hydrocarbons and 1.5 percent carbon monoxide. Such measurements were believed to be about one half the emissions of a totally uncontrolled engine.

Automakers responded to these standards in various fashions. Ford's answer was the "Thermactor" system, an "air pump" design that injected oxygen through a plumbing maze into the exhaust flow directly outside the exhaust port to aid in the additional burning of escaping hydrocarbons. GM also chose the air pump route, using an "Air Injector Reactor" (A.I.R.). Chrysler's approach differed completely in that it went about reducing emissions by maximizing combustion within the cylinders. The "Cleaner Air Package" (CAP) consisted of a leaner-jetted carburetor and a special distributor that automatically advanced the spark on deceleration to better burn the wasteful flood of

In a world dominated by Detroit's Big Three, American Motors men had to try harder. "Different" was only the beginning when it came time to describe most of AMC's muscular offerings. Such was certainly the case concerning the '71 Hornet SC/360, a real sleeper that fooled many a stoplight challenger—as well those darned insurance agents. Standard power came from a 245-horsepower 360 V-8. Quarter-mile performance was quoted by *Motor Trend* testers as 15 seconds flat.

Introducing a sensible alternative to the money-squeezing, insurance-strangling muscle cars of America. The Hornet SC/360.

The Hornet SC/360 lists for only $2,663'. Which is surprising when you consider what the September issue of Motor Trend had to say about it:
The SC/360 is just a plain gas to drive. It has lightning quick performance...It handles like a dream, especially on the TransAm road course at Michigan International Speedway where we had an opportunity to test it.
A 360 CID V-8 engine with 245-horsepower is standard.
So is a 3-on-the-floor, all synchromesh transmission. A heavy-duty clutch. D70 x 14 Polyglas™ tires. 14 x 6 mag style wheels. Space saver spare. Rally stripe. And individual reclining seats.
To make it even gutsier, the SC/360 also comes with a long list of options.

Among which you'll find a 4-barrel 360 V-8 that develops 285 horsepower. An all synchro 4-on-the-floor with Hurst shifter. Ram air induction with hood scoop. 3.54 or 3.91 rear axle with Twin-Grip. Dual exhausts. White letter tires. Heavy-duty suspension. And a big tach.
But even with the added cost of these options, the SC/360 ends up with a lower list price than most of its bigger, muscle-bound competitors.
And because of its standard 12.5:1 weight-to-power ratio, insurance on the SC/360 ends up lower, too.
As a leading car magazine has said, "The day of the heavy 400-cube, 400-horsepower supercar may be just about over."

Manufacturer's suggested retail price. Federal taxes included. State and local taxes, if any, distribution charges excluded.

If you had to compete with GM, Ford and Chrysler what would you do? ⚡ **American Motors**

Ford's last big-block 429 Mustang appeared in 1971. From there, the top performance model was still the Mach 1, with the hottest engine option being the 351 Cleveland small-block. This '72 Mach 1 is fitted with a Cleveland V-8, as well as the optional ram-air hood.

fuel entering the combustion chamber upon throttle-down. Yet another development was Oldsmobile's "Climatic Combustion Control," which pre-heated incoming air by way of a duct system that routed warming airflow from around the exhaust manifold to an "oven box" on the air cleaner's snorkel. With incoming air then heated to 100 degrees, leaner jets could be used in the carburetor, meaning the spark had less fuel components to burn off.

While all these designs did help cars sold in California in 1966 meet the state's tough emissions requirements, they also created various other headaches. Warm-up operation became more of a hassle, and throttle response was lessened. Both fuel economy and performance suffered as efficiency was hindered noticeably. Using Ford as an example, *Car Life* reported in 1966 that there was "something amiss in Thermactor-equipped models." Dearborn's "California-equipped" high-performance V-8s tended "to 'run out of breath' some 1000-1500 rpm before they should," continued the report. "It would seem the adoption of the Thermactor system may have been done in too great a rush. As usual, the customer gets the ultimately frayed end of the stick—this time in a loss of performance."

Although California customers were the first to feel that loss, they weren't alone for long. Washington's first Clean Air Act was signed in 1963, then amended two

years later, and yet again in 1966 and 1967. That first amendment in 1965 inspired an initial rush of federal laws aimed at, among other things, cleaning up Detroit's act. One of the earliest mandates required all American cars to also meet, by 1968, the same emissions standards earlier set down by California law. Already under heavy attack by Nader's safety crusaders, Detroit suddenly found itself again labeled the bad guy, unfairly so in the opinion of many inside and out of the industry.

"The automobile engine may be legislated out of existence in one of history's worst miscarriages of justice," wrote engineering editor Joseph Callahan in his six-month long 1966 *Automotive News* series, "The Billion-Dollar Smog Hoax." "Without fair, conclusive evidence, [the] engine already as been found guilty of being the major cause of air pollution."

In defense of Detroit, Callahan and others claimed the automobile's role in the air pollution problem wasn't as great as environmentalists and lawmakers made out. Sure, the pollution issue needed to be addressed, and automotive exhaust emissions did require some serious cleansing. But many industry watchers felt that clean-up could come at a slower pace, with the goal being to do a better job of creating more efficient, less costly systems. In their minds, Washington was typically demanding way

CONTINUED ON PAGE 176

The Envelope, Please...

Considering that competition was what the supercar genre was all about, it's only right to argue that one particular model was more super than all the rest. But should raw speed and power be the only determining factor? Granted, getting from point A to B in the shortest order was the main priority here. However, weren't supercars still cars? Didn't they also have to perform various other tasks in addition to melting tires and tripping the lights in fantastic fashion at the far end of a quarter-mile?

Not all performance-minded customers three decades ago wanted to go racing. Most simply wanted to look the part while driving to work. Or cruising the Dog 'n Suds. Or running to the store for a jar of Tang. Or picking up the kids from John F. Kennedy Elementary.

Pontiac didn't sell a few hundred thousand GTOs because all of those few hundred thousand were the fastest cars on the road. Mass marketing performance in 1964 meant offering a new breed of horsepower, a potent package made up of many different things for many different people. Some buyers liked go-fast imagery, many also preferred reasonably roomy comfort, all wanted just enough muscle to make them feel like they were kings of the street even if they really weren't. In an ideal world, a supreme supercar would've hopefully stopped as well as it started; handled the road with relative ease without jouncing your eyeballs out of their sockets; looked bitchin', groovy, or sano; and done all this while also serving practical everyday duties like hauling the Samsonites in the trunk and the mother-in-law in the back seat. Or vice versa.

To fairly honor all of what the supercar represented, the job of judging which example really was king of the street should take into account what automotive muscle meant to most people, not just what many saw it as meaning on drag strips and speedways. Image, general popularity, overall abilities, practical applications—all this and more worked in concert along with horsepower under the hood to make the musclecar what it was in the '60s and early '70s.

If elapsed times alone are used as measuring sticks, the factory racers will get the nod as Detroit's greatest musclecars every time. Super stockers like Super Duty Pontiacs and Max Wedge Mopars were potential 12-second screamers. At the strip. They were never meant for the street, although a few brave souls did try to domesticate some of these wild beasts, they with their surly natures and bad attitudes—the cars, not the brave souls. In the civilized world, all of these cantankerous machines were nothing more than warranty work waiting to happen.

Then again, so were many of the supposedly mass-marketed supercars to follow. Living with a fully armed musclecar in the '60s was never easy, even more so when things like solid lifters, metallic brake linings, heavy-duty clutches, locking differentials, and long-duration cams were included in the deal. More muscle generally meant more potential headaches. No pain, no gain.

Cars like the tri-carb 440 Road Runners and Super Bees of 1969, COPO Camaros, 427 Fairlanes, and Boss 429 Mustangs were outrageously fast machines. But they were also a bitch to handle in extended use, or lacked many of the basic creature comforts most drivers commonly take for granted. Again, daily transportation wasn't the goal, racing was. Thus there was often no need for things like radios or heaters. And even hood hinges in some cases.

Similar conclusions could be made concerning the Trans-Am pony cars, which weren't as narrowly focused as other factory racers, but were still obviously built with one thing in mind. While their overall performance was better balanced, these road rockets did tend to be rough as cobs on the street. And Trans-Am small-blocks like the Boss 302 and Chevy's 302 could be every bit as disagreeable in everyday use as some of Detroit's meanest big-block bullies.

As a whole, Pontiac's Trans Am lineage probably stands out as the leader of the pony car pack, if only because of its longevity and long-running popularity. Outstanding in this group was the rare Ram Air IV Trans Am of 1970, which, although it did probably fall into the gnarly-natured class, ranked well up there with the greatest all-around muscle machines of all-time.

Perhaps a better Pontiac pony car candidate for the best-of-the-best list would be the Super Duty T/As of 1973 and 1974. Being Trans Ams, these road-roasting Ponchos

The image was certainly there, as was the chassis and horsepower. So did the '69 Ram Air IV Trans Am qualify as the winner of the musclecar race?

Chevrolet's LS6 454 did claim the top prize in Detroit's advertised output sweepstakes—450 horsepower was the highest number ever published. But did that automatically rank the LS6 SS 454 Chevelle as the greatest of the great?

could handle, stop, and ride with the hottest performance machines ever built to that point. Image was a given. And beneath its signature shaker scoop was 455 cubic inches of state-of-the-art Super Duty muscle, an amazing compromise of government-mandated low compression and free-breathing excitement only PMD engineers knew how to build. That the 13-second 455 SD Trans Am was able to offer pre-smog performance—legally, to boot—at a time when horsepower had been all but choked out represented suitable support for this supercar's claim to fame.

From a popularity perspective, if any one supercar breed deserves credit as the industry's best it was Chevrolet's Super Sport Chevelles, the SS 396 and SS 454. Counting the small-block models built in 1971 and 1972, SS production for 1966-72 was 390,981, second only to the GTO's total of 395,127. However, in the "big years" for factory performance, 1969 to 1971, Super Sports outsold Goats by 37 percent, 167,972 to 122,968.

From its beginnings as a mass-market musclecar in 1966 (this considering the '65 Z16 SS 396 was basically a limited-edition "prototype") the SS 396 offered decent performance at a decent price in base form. While most were mildly muscular—turning the quarter in the 15-second range—many were true street killers in fully loaded 375-horse L78 form. "Although [the SS 396] is not the fastest machine right off the showroom floor," wrote *Popular Hot Rodding*'s Lee Kelley in 1968, "it does possess much more potential than any other car in its field."

The basic package grew more attractive as the years progressed. Front disc brakes and spiffy five-spoke sport wheels joined the standard equipment list in 1969, followed by Chevy's excellent F41 heavy-duty suspension the following year. Add to all this the car's well-known image and proven practicality as a daily driver and you get the picture. "The best-selling Supercar isn't the quickest," commented a 1970 *Car Life* review. "But it looks tough. And it's kind to women and children. Adults can ride in the rear seat, as they should be able to in a car this size. With the handling package, brakes, etc., the SS 396 makes a fine family car."

As the '60s wound down, the SS 396 legacy had grown so respected that Chevy image-makers didn't dare play with the numbers after the Turbo-Jet block was bored to 402 cubic inches late in 1969. "Ess-Ess-four-oh-two?" No way, no how. It was "Ess-Ess-three-ninety-six" or nothing at all. Unless, of course, it was the new SS 454, the supreme evolvement of the A-body Super Sport species.

Already born of that great bloodline, the feared and revered LS6 SS 454 simply couldn't lose, not with 450 horses coupled with Chevy's willingness to build these beastly babies by the relative boat load. While a few rivals could stay with the LS6, not one could match its "market saturation." Total 450-horsepower SS 454 production was 4,475: not a lot in relation to the industry as a whole, but a major pile from a musclecar's point of view.

LS6 rivals included two other GM products. Oldsmobile put one of Detroit's finest supercar chassis beneath its 4-4-2s, cars that offered every bit as much spacious comfort and muscular imagery as their A-body cousins from Chevrolet. Adding the W-30 "fresh-air" option beneath the hood only made this machine run every bit as strong as it looked. By 1970, the 455 W-30 Olds was cavorting with the Motor City's biggest dogs. As was Buick's Stage 1 Gran Sport. Perhaps Detroit's classiest musclecar, the GS was also every bit as nasty as the LS6 when the 455 Stage 1 V-8 was added to the equation in 1970. Choosing the GSX Stage 1 insured an image worthy of all that power.

Rivals to the throne outside GM included Chrysler's 426 hemi. Any of the 11,000 hemi Dodges and Plymouths built from 1966 to 1971 rate among the greatest supercars. With little fuss or muss, all were capable of running in the 13-second bracket, especially so once the 425-horsepower 426 found its most prominent home beneath E-body 'Cuda and Challenger hoods in 1970. The downside to the hemi/E-body hook-up was the extra weight piled on at the nose. Hemi pony cars were suited for little more than eating up a straight line in a hurry. Anything else could've become a real adventure.

Slightly slower, yet every bit as impressive in all facets were Ford's Cobra Jet Mach 1 and Boss 351 Mustangs. Both featured loads of power—the first with a big-block, the second with a small-block—an excellent chassis, and a sporty image able to turn heads with the best of them. Dearborn's top Torino Cobra in 1970 was no slouch, either.

All these machines had the right stuff. And all also could be picked on from a negative perspective. So which one was the king of the musclecars?

You mean you don't know?

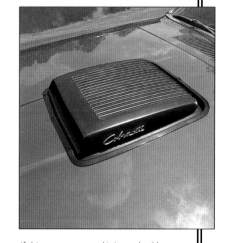

One word says it all here. Chrysler's hemi was always a pain in the butt to any stoplight challenger, be it Chevy, Ford, Pontiac, or whatever. Imagine what performance levels might've been reached had the 426 hemi not been such a lard-ass. Excessive underhood weight was probably the Elephant motor's lone downside.

If this scoop was rockin', you had better not come a knockin'—that is unless you were packin' one of the other engines mentioned here. If Ford's FE-series 428 Cobra Jet (shown in 1969 Mustang trim) wasn't big and bad enough, the Better Idea guys in 1970 unleashed a more potent 429 CJ. What might've happened with this equipment had Bunkie not been fired in 1969?

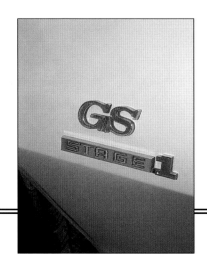

Even Buick fans will tell you the 455 Stage 1 ran better than it should have, what with its detrimental long stroke and all. Yet run it did, probably right up with anything ever offered in the performance ranks. When the best musclecars were being built, did Buick build them?

With its exceptional canted-valve heads, the 351 Cleveland small-block was an able performer, even when fed by a two-barrel carburetor and saddled with all that early-'70s smog equipment and low compression. Net horsepower rating for the 351-2V V-8 was 177 horses. Optional ram-air equipment was only available with the two-barrel 351. The air cleaner's fastening nut is an aftermarket dress-up piece.

CONTINUED FROM PAGE 173

too much way too fast. "Technology is not yet up to [controlling emissions] without considerable expense, reduced performance and lower gas mileage," added Callahan.

Others from the performance press even considered a different agenda behind some lawmaker's insistence that Detroit radically reduce exhaust contaminates. "Is [smog equipment] a legislative 'lever' by which political gains can be made through a 'let's clean up our air and young delinquents at the same time' measure?" asked *Hot Rod's* Jim McFarland in 1968.

By then, Detroit's automakers had spent $500 million to meet Washington's 1965 requirements. Of course, that cost was passed right on to the consumer, adding up to about $50 more atop the average car's bottom line. What buyers got for their extra fifty bucks was a reported 80 percent reduction in hydrocarbon emissions, another 70 percent drop in carbon monoxide. But that wasn't enough.

Federal lawmakers in 1968 also proposed that hydrocarbon emissions be reduced another 30 percent by 1970. And early in 1969, California legislators began pursuing nitrogen oxides (NOx), with the goal being to add further controls for these emissions by 1971. Automakers balked, claiming both that two years was not enough time and NOx

emissions did not represent anywhere near the problem then made out. As usual, their complaints were ignored and emissions standards continued growing tighter in rapid fashion.

In 1968, legislators also changed the way emissions were measured. Previously, pollutant levels were rated by percentage. Even though large engines produced more contaminates by volume, they were considered "cleaner" than small engines, which released greater concentrations of carbon monoxide and hydrocarbons relative to total exhaust flow. Beginning in 1970, a new measuring stick was used to quantify emissions in terms of pollution-weight-per-mile, rather than as a parts-per-million concentration

"This is an important change," explained a May 1968 *Car Life* report. "For the past few years, manufacturers have moved [toward] large-displacement, mildly turned engines to satisfy existing emissions laws more easily. New regulations place a premium on efficient, smaller engines. This could start a new breed of domestic powerplant."

One of the best examples of this new breed was Ford's 351 Cleveland small-block V-8, introduced in 1970. Dearborn had invested $100 million in an addition to the Cleveland engine plant to build this nicely efficient, exceptionally clean-running performance powerplant. Manufacturing Vice President Bill Innes claimed the 351 Cleveland ran 80 percent "cleaner" than engines built 10 years before. And, according to *Motor Trend*, "with some modifications, the [Cleveland V-8] will meet the 1971 California standards for reducing oxides of nitrogen."

At the same time, the 351 Cleveland offered real performance, ranking it right up with the strongest runners of the low-compression smog-era V-8s, big-blocks included. Perhaps the best among the emissions-controlled small-blocks, the Cleveland V-8 wasn't just Ford's only performance option for post-1971 Mustangs and Gran Torinos, it was also a fine choice for anyone looking to travel from point A to B in fast fashion without fouling the air we breathe.

By 1970, that air had been cleaned up considerably in comparison to what Americans had been breathing in 1965. Additional changes to come promised an even brighter sky. That fall, automakers announced compression cuts across the board for nearly all their new 1971 models. Ratios of 11:1, 10:1, even 9:1 overnight became things of the past as engineers began building powerplants using 8.5:1 compression. Why the drop? Less compression was required to allow Detroit's latest breed of cleaner-running engines to operate on low-octane, supposedly cleaner unleaded fuel.

Discovered in 1923 by GM researchers Charles "Boss" Kettering and Thomas Midgley, Jr., tetraethyl lead had been the key to Detroit's horsepower race. This new additive instantly upgraded the 55-octane gasoline of the day by 15 octane points, which in turn meant engineers could raise compression ratios beyond the then-unheard of 6:1 threshold. Once compression began rising, engines began producing serious horsepower. Without high-octane "ethyl" gas, true high performance would've never been born.

Nearly a half century later, most of Detroit's top-performance high-compression engines needed octane ratings in triple digits to run as designed without knocking or pinging. Predetonation is the result when high-compression temperatures ignite low-octane gasoline before its time—those knocking and pinging noises are the sounds of premature explosions occurring while the intake valves are still open. Octane ratings for unleaded fuels, however, measured in the high 80s, perhaps the low 90s—surefire invitations for predetonation. At least in the case of engines with compression ratios in excess of 9:1 or so.

But if unleaded fuel created such havoc in higher-compression engines, why was Detroit forced to use it? Most early explanations relied solely on claims that burning unleaded gasoline would not only get rid of those nasty lead particulates, it would in itself also reduce emissions of both unburned hydrocarbons and oxides of nitrogen. Many oil company ads even led consumers to believe that by spending those extra couple cents per gallon for unleaded gas, they were instantly helping clean up the air. Not entirely so, at least not to any greater degree than what had already been designed into the engines in question.

The real reason behind the appearance of unleaded fuels in 1971 was to begin paving the way for the introduction of catalytic converter exhaust systems, additional emissions controls included as part of Washington's latest cleaner air requirements, these to be met by 1975. Catalytic converters and leaded gasoline didn't mix; thus came the final nail in the musclecar's coffin. Low-lead gasoline came first in limited supplies in 1971. By July 1, 1974, every retail outlet across the country "at which 200,000 or more gallons of gasoline was sold during any calendar year beginning with 1971" was required by law to offer unleaded gasoline of at least 91 octane.

In late 1970, GM announced that 90 percent of its early 1971 models would be able to run on 91-octane low-lead gasoline; 100 percent by the end of the year. Chrysler reported 93 percent of its 1971 products would do the same, with that extra 7 percent made up of Dodges and Plymouths equipped with the 426 hemi and tri-carb 440 V-8s, two of Detroit's few remaining high-compression survivors.

Even with compression ratios dropping all around them, many industry-watchers in 1971 still believed reporting the musclecar's death would be premature. "Our luck is holding," explained Steve Kelly in *Hot Rod*. "When it looked like the next few years would bring an end to super performers, Detroit found a way to keep the breed alive."

Indeed, Detroit's hottest cars were still hot as hell in 1971. "Of immediate concern to motorists used to the power of high compression engines is the type of performance that can be expected from the low compression '71s," wrote *Motor Trend's* A. B. Shuman. "Reports so far indicate that the average driver won't notice any difference." The list of supercars still out there kicking tail and taking names in 1971 remained long. Super Cobra Jet Fords. Hemi Mopars. 455 HO GTOs. Olds W-30s. Stage 1 Buicks. If any name was notably absent it was Chevrolet's Super Sport Chevelle, the industry's best-selling performance machine.

In 1970, Chevy's LS6 SS 454 had stood atop the supercar heap. "The past is gone," claimed Kelly about the dominating '70 LS6. "The future may never see a car like this." It didn't. After initially promising a lower-compression, 425-horsepower LS6 SS 454 for 1971, Chevrolet officials recognized it just wasn't worth the effort. A 425-horse '71 SS 454 was road tested by the press but never made it into customers' hands. And the much more tame LS5 SS 454 was nowhere near capable of even carrying the LS6's treads in 1971. Making the LS6's loss appear even greater that year was the arrival of a mild 350-powered Chevelle SS, the first small-block A-body Super Sport since 1965.

Just as the LS6 had done, another tried-and-true GM performance product also appeared late in 1970 for test drives then was unceremoniously canceled before 1971 regular production could begin. Oldsmobile's hot, little W-31 small-block Cutlass might've fooled the insurance man, but it couldn't get by the exhaust sniffer.

Many other high-powered haulers hit the end of the road by 1972, the year Detroit began using less impressive, much more realistic net horsepower ratings in place of the previously used gross numbers, which sometimes were seemingly drawn out of a hat. Along with being the only year for the Boss 351, 1971 was the last for Ford's Cobra Jet 429, as well as the vaunted 426 hemi and triple-carb 440 from Dodge and Plymouth.

Supercars were dropping like flies, but once again some onlookers remained relatively unconcerned. "Despite compression ratio drops, low-lead fuels, insurance premiums, and public scorn, there's still a lot of smoke and fury waiting at the rear wheels in Detroit," began an October 1971 *Motor Trend* review entitled "Where There's Smoke, There's Hope." "We went looking for it to settle in our minds whether the fun has left Detroit. The fun is still there. Perhaps the problem isn't one of performance being destroyed; perhaps we've just been spoiled."

Others weren't quite so optimistic. Rumors circulating in the summer of 1971 claimed Detroit would soon stop building "sporty cars" entirely, with GM reportedly readying to delete its F-body Camaro/Firebird platform after 1972 due to declining sales. While the F-body did

survive, one of its high-performance derivatives didn't. With the catalytic converter age coming the next year, Chevrolet dropped the Z/28 Camaro in 1974. Chevy's last Chevelle SS had appeared the year before, itself only a faint shadow of its former industry-leading self.

Both Ford and Chrysler rolled on after 1971 with small-blocks only; the aforementioned 351 Cleveland for the former, the still-hot 340 V-8 for 'Cudas and Challengers. The last lukewarm Ford stragglers disappeared along with the original Mustang in 1973; Chrysler's E-bodies forged ahead through one more year.

Interestingly, General Motors was home to the musclecar's last great gasps. "Interestingly" because so much had been said and done over the years to make sure GM divisions didn't dabble in performance. Cease and desist memos. Anti-racing policies. Displacement and horsepower limits. Orders to tone down publicity. Through all this, Pontiac, Chevrolet, Oldsmobile, and Buick managed to built most of Detroit's fastest cars in the '60s and '70s. And the "B-O-P" trio was still running strong even as Chevrolet was rapidly fading away.

Buick continued offering its Gran Sport Stage 1 455 in reasonably proud fashion up through 1974. Although the small-block 350 was made part of Oldsmobile's 4-4-2 package in 1972, the big W-30 455 remained on the options list that year for one last high-powered performance. The W-30 455s used under Hurst/Olds hoods in 1974 and 1975 were warmly welcomed, but didn't quite compare to their more-free-breathing forerunners. And when the W-30 designation returned on Hurst/Olds fenders in 1979, it referred to a truly mild 350 V-8. Oldsmobile also tried to play off its once-proud performance legacy in 1980, labeling its last 4-4-2 with a W-30 decal. No one was fooled. By then most didn't even care.

If any one automobile qualified as the last great musclecar, it was Pontiac's Super Duty Firebird, offered against all odds in 1973 and '74. PMD's Special Products Group, led by Herb Adams, simply didn't want to give up the ghost, even with increasingly tougher emissions standards making their job more difficult by the day. "In spite of the Feds, Pontiac is still building exciting cars," claimed *Motor Trend's* Chuck Kock late in 1971. That the Trans Am itself managed to struggle on through the lean years of the '70s and early '80s still with a modicum of excitement was achievement enough. What its top-performance edition managed to do in 1973 bordered on miraculous.

"How it ever got past the preview audience in GM's board room is a mystery, but here it is—the car that couldn't happen," announced *Car and Driver* in a review

of a pre-production 455 Super Duty Trans Am. Amazingly able to meet EPA requirements while also offering every bit as much performance potential as the strongest supercars of the '60s, the 455 SD was introduced to the press by Herb Adams on June 28, 1972, at GM's Milford Proving Grounds. Key to this low-compression (8.4:1), high-output big-block were its excellent cylinder heads, according to engineers, the best-flowing heads ever designed by Pontiac. Ever.

Adams promised availability of the 310-horsepower 455 SD, optional for the Grand Am, Grand Prix, LeMans, Trans Am, and Formula Firebird, by the fall. Deliveries, however, didn't begin until April 1973, and only then for the two Firebird models. No other 455 SD installations ever reached private hands. Additionally, the Super Duty V-8 by then had been downrated to 290 horses after EPA officials forced Pontiac engineers back to the drawing board following the discovery of a little emissions testing hocus-pocus. Road tests of the early 310-horsepower '73 Super Duty Trans Am shocked everyone as the car ran well into the 13s. With an automatic transmission. And full exhausts. And street tires. "The Last of the Fast Cars comes standard with the sort of acceleration that hasn't been seen in years," claimed *Car and Driver*.

After building 300 455 SD Firebirds for 1973 (252 Trans Ams, 48 Formulas), Pontiac sold only 1,000 more (943 Trans Ams, 57 Formulas) in 1974 before finally giving in to reality. A beast like the 455 Super Duty V-8 would've never gotten along with catalytic converters. And so closed the door on Pontiac's legendary supercar performance legacy. The Trans Am continued to be recognized as one of Detroit's "hot cars," but by the '80s that label was purely relative.

What had looked so strong in 1970 had been beaten down into oblivion in only a few short years. Even with Pontiac's 455 Super Duty on the scene, optimism among performance fans in 1973 stood as nothing more than denial. All the hopes for new and better technology qualified as false, all the promises from industry executives didn't mean spit. GM President Ed Cole had stated in 1970 that his corporation would continue offering performance cars for as long as demand was there. Although strongly inhibited by what Washington had wrought, that demand did carry on into the '70s. It was the cars that didn't show up.

"A lot of people think the demise of the musclecar is at hand," said Ford General Manager John Naughton late in 1970 in a *Motor Trend* interview. "I don't believe that because I don't think the American male will all of a sudden turn off his love for performance." Maybe so. But by 1975, there was nothing left to love.

By 1973, GM all but owned the streets with Pontiac's Trans Am, Oldsmobile's 4-4-2, and Buick's Gran Sport still running strong and kicking a little butt. GS buyers that year could still even order a 455 Stage 1 big-block for their Buicks. This very rare '73 Stage 1 also features a four-speed manual transmission.

Chapter Nine

REVIVAL & REBIRTH
American Muscle Returns

Z28
The Camaro's Camaro

You remember this car. Low and lean. Born to run. It's back. The Z28. Take one Camaro and add the blackened grille • Body-colored bumpers • Extra-wide body-colored 15 x 7 wheels • White-lettered GR70 steel-belted radial tires • High performance dual exhausts • Double sport mirrors • Tachometer • Power disc brakes • Spoilers, front and rear • "Z28" spelled out loud and clear, front, sides and back • F-41 sport suspension • Stowaway spare • 350 4-barrel V8 connected to a performance axle • Heavy duty Borg-Warner 4-speed manual transmission*. And there's more.

Z28. We won't build many. So, if you want to move "Z" style, you better get moving.

Turbo Hydra-matic required in California.

Chevrolet

Time does so many different things. It waits for no one. It marches on. It flies while you're having fun. It heals all wounds. Perhaps above all, time lets us discover the future, whether we want to or not. Time also allows us to understand the history left behind, even if we didn't have a clue while the past was still in the present. Such was typically the case a quarter century ago. Just when we thought we might've figured out the '60s, along came the '70s.

We could call it progress, we could call it evolution; whatever else that might be said about the '70s is purely your call. Consider, for a moment, history's offerings. The '60s gave us so many great things. The GTO. The Beatles. The no-bra look. Brash Broadway Joe and his Super Bowl-champion Jets. A man on the moon. Friday night movies on the tube. Did we say the no-bra look?

What did the '70s bring? The Vega. The solo career of Ringo Starr. The leisure suit. Bad-knees Joe and his equally bad Jets. Tricky Dick's fall from the free world's highest post. Cable television.

At least the '70s was a time for learning. We learned all about inflation. We learned how gasoline could be turned into gold. We learned what it's like to finally lose a war. We learned what disco could do to our souls. Funny thing, though; we never did learn what the hell fine Corinthian leather was. On the other hand, we did learn to live without high-performance automobiles.

Industry critics could no longer complain about brakes once the American musclecar began screeching to a halt in the early '70s. One year after horsepower had hit its peak in 1970, tightening emissions standards forced a drop in engine compression, meaning power cutbacks were sure to follow. Pure performance powerplants like Chrysler's

426 hemi, Ford's 429 Cobra Jet, and Chevy's LS6 454 were dead by 1972, the year Detroit began using those wimpy net horsepower ratings. A hemi tagged at anything less than 425-horsepower? Blasphemy!

Low-lead fuels made the scene along with low compression in 1971, followed by catalytic converters in 1975. Low performance was the instant byproduct. By 1978, one of Detroit's hottest musclecars was a truck, Dodge's Li'l Red Express. As the decade wound down, *Hot Rod, Car Craft,* and the rest were letting us discover everything we always wanted to know about custom vans. Whether we wanted to or not.

Marketing men all around the Motor City were kept busy in the early '70s trying to hitch their bandwagons to horses of another color. It was Chevrolet that somewhat amazingly turned perhaps the industry's most abrupt about-face, an even greater reversal than Ford's considering how much of the performance market had been wearing Bow-Ties for so long.

Chevrolet had begun redirecting its approach in 1970, introducing the upscale Monte Carlo as a personal luxury A-body alternative to the Chevelle Malibu. In 1973—the year *Motor Trend* editors made the Monte Carlo their "Car of the Year"—an all-new Chevelle appeared with more of the Monte Carlo's status-conscious flair and less of the Malibu's previous performance potential. Far less. An SS package was offered one last time that year, then completely replaced by the lukewarm Laguna S3 in 1974. It wasn't the same. Chevrolet in 1974 also closed the door on the Z28 Camaro and the 454 Corvette.

The late '70s were a bleak time indeed for performance buyers. But a ray of hope did shine down onto the faithful midyear in 1977 when Chevrolet revived the Z28, which had been cancelled after 1974.

Opposite: This baby has certainly come a long way. When introduced in 1967, Chevrolet's first Z/28 Camaro was an unruly beast quick to demonstrate its uncivilized, race-ready nature. Every bit as hot as its forefathers, the LT1-powered latter-day Z28 (a '94 convertible is shown here) is as docile as a kitten in everyday operation.

While all these muscle-bound legends were falling by the wayside, Chevrolet's prime movers were hard at work promoting a new breed, the Vega, introduced in 1971 to compete with Ford's Pinto and AMC's Gremlin. These trend-setting, truly small compacts were rolling proof that the times were once again changing, to the dismay of car lovers everywhere.

Attitudes toward all automobiles, not just performance machines, were almost reformed overnight in the '70s. By then, most Americans were convinced the internal combustion engine was the main culprit behind our air pollution problem. But more important to nearly all drivers was the impact made on their pocketbooks by both politics and environmentalist pressures. Gasoline prices began steadily rising in the early '70s, thanks first to the extra cost passed on to consumers beginning in 1971 for the mandated distillation of low-lead fuels, the first step toward meeting Washington's tougher emissions standards established for 1975.

Additional proposals to clear future skies of even more smog were even more drastic. Environmental Protection Agency officials in late 1972 began considering a strict gas rationing program, a move that would obviously mean

Twelve years after Chevrolet's SS 454 Monte Carlo faded from the scene, a new Monte Carlo SS was introduced in 1983, just in time to begin a long reign as NASCAR's winningest competitor. On the street, the Monte Carlo SS was among the hottest things running in the mid-'80s. This '85 SS is powered by the 190-horsepower high-output 305-cubic-inch small-block V-8.

Ford's Special Vehicles Operation unleashed its SVO Mustang in 1984. A scooped hood, aero nose, four-wheel discs, 16-inch wheels and a 175-horsepower turbocharged 2.3-liter four-cylinder were the main players. The SVO Mustang was discontinued after 1986. *Ford Motor Company*

fewer miles on the road for the infernal internal combustion machine, thus fewer pollutants spewed into the air. Two years later, suggestions were made in Congress to raise gasoline taxes. Per these requests, an extra 15 cent per gallon tax would by 1990 reduce automobile running time by 12 to 15 percent. A 30-cent raise could perhaps mean a 25-percent drop in auto usage. Thankfully, neither of these "tailpipe approaches," rationing or heavy taxation, became reality, at least not as an intended part of a plan to control pollution.

As fate would have it, the winter of 1972-73 was an especially cold one, leading energy producers to concentrate on the distillation of heating oils. This was done at the expense of gasoline and diesel fuel production, resulting in shortages at station pumps come the warmer days of 1973, a reality some Americans believed was more contrived than market-created. Either way, these events did represent a handful of the many dominoes in a long line then falling down.

By the early '70s, increasingly powerful environmentalist factions had already begun inhibiting the exploration and development of domestic energy sources, creating a situation where the United States was growing more and more dependent on overseas oil imports—a potentially volatile mix that presented foreign powers with a political apple ripe for the picking. All arguments on these shores concerning whether or not the fuel crisis of the previous winter was fact or fiction were rendered moot on October 17, 1973, when 11 Middle Eastern nations placed an embargo on crude oil shipped to all countries supporting Israel. A thoroughly real crisis resulted. So did long lines at many filling stations and the dreaded gas rationing in some areas. In 1974, the federal government also instituted the national 55-miles per hour speed limit to help conserve every precious ounce of gasoline.

In the meantime, our fossil fuels became even more precious as prices began to soar, from an average of 38.8 cents a gallon for leaded regular in 1973 to 53.2 cents in 1974. Thanks to Secretary of State Henry Kissinger's diplomatic efforts mediating the Egypt-Israel mess, the Arab oil embargo was lifted on March 18 that year, but gasoline continued gaining value. The average gallon of leaded fuel cost 62.2 cents in 1977, 85.7 in 1979, 119.1 in 1980, and a whopping 131.1 in 1981. Unleaded was averaging 137.8 cents a gallon by 1981.

Drivers in the '60s rarely blinked an eye while watching their supercar travel less than 10 miles on a gallon of high-test. But that kind of performance was soon unaffordable for Average Joe in the '70s. And "gas hogs" quickly became targets of derision by those who were sure the world's oil supply was being fully depleted right before their eyes on American roads.

Chevrolet had first turned to modern fuel-injection in 1982, offering its Cross-Fire injection for both the Corvette and Camaro small blocks. A more serious effort to jump on the EFI bandwagon came in 1985 (shown here) with the debut of Tuned-Port Injection. TPI small-blocks have since helped put Chevrolet (and Pontiac) at the modern performance forefront. *Chevrolet Division*

The Gremlin, Vega, and Pinto represented the beginning of Detroit's latest—and greatest—downsizing trend, this one aimed at making everyday transportation more fuel efficient. Along with the cars themselves, engines also began shrinking, taking power outputs with them. By mid-decade, "mpg" would take full precedent over "mph" as far as the vast majority of this country's cost-conscious car buyers were concerned. We were then left with car lot after car lot full of underpowered, marginally efficient, totally boring automobiles.

Nothing was sacred, not even Ford's old horse, the Mustang. In 1974, Lee Iacocca's attempt to recapture the magic of April 1964 culminated in the Mustang II, a little pony that at first appeared to be the right car for hard times. Initial sales were swift, and the popular '74 Mustang II followed Chevy's Monte Carlo as *Motor Trend's* "Car of the Year." A few years down the road, however, the too-small, too-weak Mustang II was doomed, and not even the '78 King Cobra—a car any John Travolta wannabe would've been proud to park out in front of Studio 54—could save it from extinction.

With its gaudy decals and spats, slats, and spoilers, the King Cobra was an obvious knock-off of the one surviving musclecar that did manage to keep a high-performance image alive in the '70s. Markedly "detuned" yet still relatively strong, the Trans Am continued rolling on

American turbo performance probably reached its peak in 1987, with contributions to that claim supplied by the Shelby Charger GLH-S. Powered by a 175-horsepower 2.2-liter intercooled turbocharged four-cylinder, the GLH-S could reportedly run from rest to 60 mph in less than seven seconds. *Shelby Automobiles*

Another hot turbo machine introduced in 1987, Buick's limited-edition GNX ranks right up with some of the greatest musclecars of all time. *Buick Division, General Motors Corporation*

Ford grabbed the best bang for the buck lead in the late-'80s with its EFI 5.0-liter HO V-8. Introduced in 1987, the 225-horse "five-oh" small-block put Dearborn at the head of the pack. Shown here is the '88 Mustang GT's standard 5.0-liter.

towards the '80s, with Pontiac slapping its "screamin' chicken" decals on Firebirds just as fast as Burt Reynolds could wrap them around bridges and other immovable objects. And what "the Bandit" did for new Trans Ams on the wide screen, the Duke boys of Hazzard County mimicked in more proliferous fashion behind the wheels of countless classic Dodge Chargers on the boob tube. Yes sir, those cars sure could fly.

Everything else in the late '70s could barely leave the gate. Nearly everything else. A warmly welcomed consolation did come midyear in 1977 when Chevrolet brought back its hot-to-trot pony car, the Z28, to "an unsuspecting industry and a delighted public," according to *Car and Driver*. "Gasoline certainly won't be getting cheaper in the months and years ahead," wrote *Road Test's* Bob Hall, "and the '77 emission standards are the toughest to date, so why bother with a performance car like the Z28?" Simple. If Pontiac could still move Trans Ams like hot cakes, Chevy could do the same with its F-body legend. More an aggressive road handler than a high-output hauler, the '77-1/2 Z28 nonetheless signified that Chevrolet engineers did indeed have a trick or two left up their sleeves. The musclecar story wasn't over yet. In fact, it was just beginning to turn a page.

Yet another new decade represented a time of catch-up for Detroit's engineering fraternity. Remember, as cynics often say, these guys only do that voodoo that they do so well when they're forced to. Whether that's true or not, engineers in the '80s did suddenly rise up to meet the challenges weighed down upon them in the '70s.

Before emissions controls and sky-high gas prices entered the equation, more performance had always been the product of more cam, more compression, and more carburetor. And in most cases, more cubes. In the supercar's heyday, fuel-efficient operation and maximum performance had been polar opposites. Concentrating on the former in the mid-'70s meant losing the latter. At first.

Performance-minded designers in the '80s at least had one physical law in their favor: most available platforms then were lighter than their forerunners, some much more than others. Added into this mix was a technology that, although it wasn't new at all, did appear excitedly fresh in the minds of most Americans. Forced induction—more specifically, turbocharging—became all the rage in the early '80s. Initially emerging in the late '70s as a quick, easy way to squeeze more horses out of smaller-displacement engines, most turbos served only to barely bridge the gap between efficiency and performance in econo-buggies that couldn't get out of their own way. A turbo badge by no means meant the machine beneath was a hot car.

But sometimes it did.

One of the more notable early applications of turbo power came from Ford in 1983 when Dearborn's Special Vehicle Operations justified its existence by actually producing a special vehicle, the SVO Mustang. A certified road rocket, the Euro-style SVO Mustang relied on an intercooled, turbocharged four-cylinder that amazingly produced 175 horsepower from only 2.3 liters. Two years later, an improved SVO turbo four was pumping out an even more impressive 205 horses.

Chrysler Corporation was probably the biggest promoter of turbo cars in the '80s, although nearly all were

far more bark than bite. Exceptions to this rule were supplied by Carroll Shelby, who joined the Mopar camp in 1982 on invitation from former Ford boss Lee Iacocca, himself having taken on the task of saving Chrysler from itself in November 1978. As he had done 13 years earlier, Iacocca turned to Shelby to again heat up his company's image, this time resulting in a wide array of small cars and trucks with hot attitudes. Hottest were the GLHS Omnis and Chargers offered in 1986 and 1987 as the supreme rendition of Shelby's GLH theme. "GLH," appropriately enough, stood for "Goes Like Hell," which the GLHS certainly did. Power came from an intercooled turbo four rated at 175 horsepower, enough muscle to propel a lightweight Shelby Dodge into the high 14-second range for the quarter-mile.

Buick was also a big player in the turbo game, with its bad, black Grand Nationals running the streets like they owned them from 1984 to 1987. Output for the Grand National's intercooled 3.8-liter turbo V-6 ranged from 200 to 245 horsepower. Published performance figures ran as low as 14.2 seconds for the quarter-mile run. If that wasn't enough, Buick in 1987 also built the fabled GNX with the help of McLaren Engines and the American Sunroof Company (ASC). This limited-edition black beauty featured 276 turbo horses beneath its bulging hood. On the strip, the '87 GNX reportedly could trip the lights in a sizzling 13.4 seconds—all those musclecar fans who thought high-performance had died in the early '70s needed to think again.

Helping Buick's exceptionally strong V-6 bulk up was another bit of high-tech induction technology only then making a widespread impact on the American automotive scene. Along with being turbocharged, the Grand National's 3.8-liter powerplant was also fitted with sequential fuel injection, an advancement that helped Buick's V-6 operate efficiently *and* perform like a champ, while at the same time staying comfortably emissions-legal.

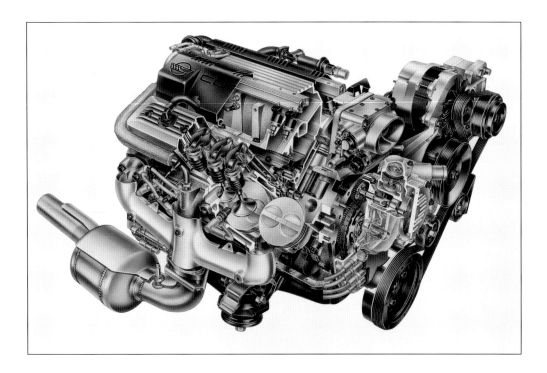

Like turbocharging, electronically controlled fuel injection was by that time old news, as was mechanical fuel injection itself. Chevrolet first began offering its Ramjet "fuelie" setup in 1957, and FI equipment remained the top Corvette option up through 1965. As early as 1970, Pontiac was testing a Bendix-built EFI V-8 with wonderfully clean-running results, inspiring *Motor Trend's* Karl Ludvigsen to then conclude that electronic fuel injection "could be the vital link in enabling the internal combustion engine to meet stringent emission standards." Germany's Bosch company pioneered regular-production EFI usage in America, creating its Jetronic system for Volkswagen's 1600 engine in 1968 to help VWs imported into this country comply with the new emissions standards established that year. Various other European makes, including Saab, Volvo, and Mercedes, quickly jumped onboard the EFI bandwagon.

Trading carburetors for computer-controlled fuel injection was much slower in coming on the domestic market. Smaller turbocharged engines began losing favor among the performance crowd in the late '80s once electronic fuel injection technology began appearing full-force

Chevrolet engineers blew everyone away in 1992 with their second-generation LT1 small-block V-8, a TPI pushrod motor offered first as the 300-horse heart of the Corvette. Within two years, the LT1 was powering everything from fiberglass two-seaters, to Camaro Z28s, to the big-boy Impala SS. The Z28's 275-horsepower LT1 was also borrowed by Pontiac for its Firebirds. In 1996, LT1 output in non-Corvette applications jumped to 285 horses. *Chevrolet Division*

Street Legal Performance Engineering first teamed up with Pontiac in 1993 to produce the 300-horsepower ram-air equipped Firehawk Firebird. In 1994, top SLP Firehawk power increased to 315 horses. And in 1995, a one-year-only convertible joined the SLP lineup. Only 92 were built. Trying to compare these droptop Firebirds (the other is a '69 400) from two different eras would be like putting a Korean War F-86 Sabrejet up against a Desert Storm F-15. The 17-inch wheels on this '95 Firehawk convertible are owner-installed items—only the Firehawk coupes used these wheels. The "Ram Air" hood decals were also added by the owner.

atop various formerly carbureted American V-8s. In 1982, Chevrolet introduced its "Cross-Fire" injection for Corvette and Camaro small-blocks. Three years later, a much-improved tuned-port injection setup appeared, and TPI-equipped Camaros then jumped well out in front of the meat-and-potatoes performance pack, which was once again rumbling almost as loudly as it had 15 years before.

Ford's street fighters dropped their gloves, as well as their turbocharged SVO Mustang, in 1986 when they fitted the already proven "five-oh" small-block V-8 with EFI induction. In 1987, the 5-liter Mustang was running on 225 horses, enough power to catapult it ahead of the Camaro in Detroit's latest "best bang for the bucks" race. But push translated into shove, and Chevrolet retaliated in 1992 with its second-generation LT1 V-8. First offered that year as the Corvette's exclusive 300-horsepower motivator, the LT1 350 was soon passed down into the Camaro ranks as a 275-horsepower powerhouse. It also became the Firebird's top performance option, and in 1994 was used to get the reborn Impala SS rolling, in this case with 260 horses.

Dearborn's Mustang corral in 1995 included these three winners; (right to left) the 5.0-liter GT, 351-powered SVT Cobra R, and rarely seen GTS. The latter model was introduced with next to no notice as a "poorman's GT"—like the earlier 5.0-liter LX, the GTS offered all the GT's performance at a lesser cost thanks to various deleted baubles, most notably the rear wing and foglamps.

Clearly, technology has more than made up the difference between federally mandated restrictions and performance potential. Modern musclecars are every bit as tough as their '60s forerunners, maybe more so when you consider the bigger picture. Some cars available today can turn the quarter in the 14-second neighborhood and still get more than 20 miles out of a buck-and-half gallon of Amoco Ultimate. All present-day American performance machines start easy, purr like a kitten at idle, and deal with everyday traffic conditions with no sweat. But drop the hammer and these docile creatures turn into wild animals in a hurry. Fuel efficient, easy to handle, kind to the environment, and mean as hell, all at the same time? Who'd-a thunk it?

American performance machines of the '90s also stop better than ever and handle the road with ample forgiveness for even the meekest drivers. Stronger brakes; bigger, better tires; huge wheels; hundreds of totally tractable, fully functioning horses—all this and more combine with the latest gonzo CD stereo and convenience gizmos and all that leather-covered comfort to help make some aging baby boomers almost forget the original musclecar ever died.

But it did. And other long-time car crazies aren't so easily convinced it has been resurrected. Without a doubt, 1996's hottest machines—Viper, Camaro SS, Ram Air Trans Am, SVT Mustang Cobra, LT4 Corvette—each represents more than enough mechanized muscle to overheat the blood of any born-again Speed Racer. All of these automobiles can run circles

Thirty years of Camaros were commemorated in 1997 by a special-edition ponycar mimicking the orange-on-white Indy Pace Car replicas of 1967 and '69, shown here at the upper left. Camaros also paced the Indianapolis 500 in 1982 (second from right) and 1993. Chevy's ponycar performance legacy is still running strong today— perhaps even stronger than it did three decades ago. *Chevrolet Division*

Pontiac performance became the stuff of legend in the '60s thanks to the series of so-called Ram Air 400 V-8s. PMD engineers again turned to ram-air technology in 1996, boosting the Firebird's LT1 small-block from 285 horsepower to 305 with the WS6 options package, offered for both the Formula and Trans Am. The WS6's scooped hood alone looked mean, even while standing still. Also included in the $2,995 WS6 deal in 1996 was a hot suspension with 17-inch wheels.

Ford's Special Vehicle Team always seems to be ready with something drastically new each year. In 1996, it was the Mustang Cobra's Mystic Clearcoat Metallic paint, an $815 option. Featuring a specially created "prismatic" clearcoat, the Mystic paint actually changed colors through refraction. Four basic metallic shades could be seen: green, amber, gold, and purple. These hues also blended together depending on light angle and intensity to create various combinations, including burgundy, emerald green, amber-gold, and root-beer brown—the latter demonstrated here just before sunset.

around the majority of their ancestors from the classic musclecar era. That can't be denied.

Yet there does appear, in some minds, to be something missing. Could it be that simply running fast and handling the curves with no fear alone isn't enough to earn the time-honored title of "musclecar?" Has Detroit revived the body but lost the soul? Or do such minority complaints only come from a nostalgia-bent group of 40- and 50-something drivers who refuse to separate this special breed of car from the times in which it was born? To that latter line, someone must point out that we can resuscitate the heart of the beast, but we can't go back and relive its former glory. We enjoyed that then, let's enjoy this now.

Though if there is one tangible hang-up, one obvious missing link between then and now, it typically involves money. On a relative scale, top performance today costs a helluva lot more than it did in the '60s. The average '90s young-

blood can't even come close to affording the automotive muscle his more carefree counterpart could've back then. This financial reality serves as a cold slap in the face, an often painful reminder that cars aren't playthings anymore, they're major investments. Horribly bad investments at that.

The realities of musclecar ownership three decades ago were far less harsh, as was reality in general. These cars *were* toys—that, along with being young, was allowed then. They were also mood machines. Get behind the wheel, turn the key, click on the AM radio, and everything was cool. And so were you. No one then, at least not early on, felt guilty or ashamed of the fact that they were openly admitting to using a macho machine as an extension of their personality—or the personality they wished they had.

Part of the deal along with the car was the attitude, a far out, groovy feeling of self-gratification and individual freedom enhanced even further by appropriate musical

accompaniment and the female companionship commonly included as optional equipment. Warm women and hot cars still go together today, as do hot cars and cool tunes—the latter probably to a greater degree now that most of us drive around with much more high fidelity than we have at home. It still isn't quite the same.

America these days again has musclecars. For that, performance buyers must be thankful. Thirty years ago, this country had musclecars, too. But we also had Hurst shifters, Cragar wheels, and Hooker Headers—and were proud of it, enough to plaster decals all over our wing windows saying so. We knew exactly how a Holley double-pumper worked and could tweak out a little more muscle with a simple spark advance. We looked up to Dyno Don Nicholson, Big Daddy Don Garlits, Grumpy Jenkins, and Gas Ronda. We adored Linda Vaughn. We believed in Dr. Oldsmobile. We bought performance from Bob Tasca, Mr. Norm, and a former Texas chicken rancher named Shelby. We never once considered giggling when someone talked of having a hemi. We were well-versed in the clan's codes—LS6, W-30, SCJ—and nodded in honor and respect when they were mentioned.

We also, of course, knew all the nameplates; R/T and Super Sport, 4-4-2 and GT, Cobra and 2+2, Cyclone and Road Runner. The musclecar era may have involved, encompassed, or encased much more than just nuts and bolts, but the cars were still kings. As were we when we drove them.

Americans will never see such days again, if only because the art of being young itself has been all but lost.

Iacocca, Pete Estes, Bunkie Knudsen—these men knew what being young was about, and they used that knowledge to build time machines for everyone. Time, however, then took over, bringing change after change along with it. Sure, technology did adapt, as it always will. And demand may inspire supply for as long customers continue remembering what excitement on wheels is all about. But the attitude, the spirit in the machine, will remain forever lost.

History, nonetheless, will repeat itself. Not too many years from now, when we're driving electric cars and looking at LT1 Camaros and 305-horsepower SVT Mustangs in museums, we'll be yearning again for fast times gone by.

Long live the kings.

Chevrolet joined Pontiac as an SLP Engineering client in 1996, resulting in the Z28 SS, a Camaro done up in similar fashion to the Firehawk Firebirds. Beneath that '70s-retro hood scoop was a ram-air LT1 producing 305 horsepower, enough muscle to put this modern mauler well into the 13-second bracket down the quarter-mile.

Ford in 1996 dropped its long-respected 5.0-liter pushrod V-8 as the Mustang's main muscle in favor of a 4.6-liter overhead-cam small-block. As an SVT Cobra power source, the DOHC 4.6 produced 305 horsepower. *Ford Special Vehicle Team*

Far Left: At a different angle in varying light, the '96 Mystic Cobra shows off its true colors—yes, this is the same car shown on page 190. Mystic Cobras would appear to radiate different shades simultaneously depending on position and time of day. Production was 1,999, all coupes.

INDEX